Blackfreyars

The Glo

The Third Globe

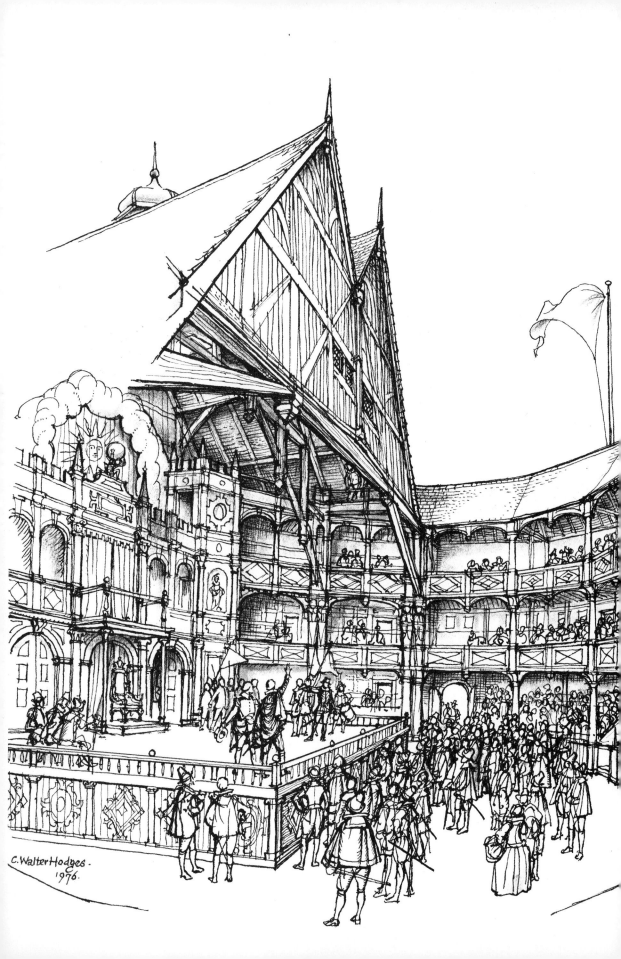

C. Walter Hodges.
1976.

The Third Globe

Symposium for the Reconstruction
of the Globe Playhouse,
Wayne State University, 1979

Edited by C. Walter Hodges, S. Schoenbaum, and Leonard Leone

Wayne State University Press / Detroit, 1981

Library of Congress Cataloging in Publication Data

Symposium for the Reconstruction of the Globe Playhouse (1979 : Wayne State University)
The third Globe.

  Includes bibliographical references and index.

  Contents: Modern uses for a Globe Theatre / John Russell Brown—The Globe: documents and ownership / Herbert Berry—The value and feasibility of reconstruction / C. Walter Hodges—{etc.}

  1. Globe Theatre (Southwark, London, England)—Congresses. 2. Theater—England—London—History—17th century—Congresses. 3. Shakespeare, William, 1564–1616—Stage history—Congresses. I. Hodges, C. Walter (Cyril Walter), 1909–   . II. Schoenbaum, S. (Samuel), 1927–   . III. Leone, Leonard, 1914–   . IV. Wayne State University. V. Title.
PR2920.S97 1979   792'.09421'64   81-3362
ISBN 0-8143-1680-8   AACR2

Publication of this volume has been made possible in part by a grant from the Michigan Council for the Arts.

Jacket illustration by C. Walter Hodges

Endpapers illustration, Long View of London, *by Wenceslaus Hollar*

Contents

*T*he essential facts regarding the two historic Globe playhouses, while well enough known to all serious students, had best be briefly summarized here. The first Globe, built in the Bankside district of Southwark with timbers salvaged from the company's earlier playhouse in Shoreditch, was open by the early autumn of 1599. On September 21 of that year a visitor from Basel, Thomas Platter, crossed the Thames with a party of playgoing friends at around two in the afternoon and reported: "In the straw-thatched house we saw the tragedy of the first Emperor Julius Caesar, very pleasantly performed, with approximately fifteen characters; at the end of the play they danced together admirably and exceedingly gracefully, according to their custom, two in each group dressed in men's and two in women's apparel."

Fourteen years later, on June 29, 1613, during the performance of a new play, *All Is True* (almost certainly Shakespeare's *Henry VIII*), a spark from one of the pieces of ordnance used for the stage spectacle landed on the thatch of the roof. A certain Sir Henry Wotton, writing from London, related how the flame "kindled inwardly, and ran round like a train, consuming within less than an hour the whole house to the ground." A Puritan commentator discerned with satisfaction the hand of God in "the sudden fearful burning, even to the ground, both of the Globe and Fortune playhouses, no man perceiving how these fires came." However that may be, within a year a new and more splendid Globe had risen from the ashes of the old, on land owned by the Brend family. This time the roof was tiled rather than thatched. The second Globe remained a Bankside fixture for three decades; it was pulled down by Sir Matthew Brend in April, 1644, so that he could erect "tenements" on the site.

Theatre historians, patiently assembling and evaluating often fragmentary and inconclusive evidence, have long attempted to reconstruct Shakespeare's Globe, both the original and its second incarnation, in their

7

minds' eye. More recently, attempts at an actual physical reconstruction have been considered. Such plans have so far come to nothing, but there is now reason to believe that a third Globe, on the banks of the Detroit River, may become a reality. At the first World Shakespeare Congress, held in Vancouver in the autumn of 1971, a proposal to build a full-scale reconstruction of the second Globe Theatre was endorsed. The resolution added: "The Congress considers that such a reconstruction would be of the greatest value to Shakespearean scholarship and to the history of the theatre, as well as of widespread interest to people and to education everywhere in the world." Accordingly, in the spring of 1979 a group of Shakespearean theatre scholars met at Wayne State University in Detroit to explore possible ways of putting the proposal into practice.

In the ordinary way, an academic conference need not be oriented toward any particular outcome, but the participants whose papers are collected here worked from the beginning on the assumption that the goal of their discussions was the erection of an actual building. There was also a hope, which happily was confirmed, that the chief participants in the Detroit meetings might continue to advise on planning as the reconstruction project took shape. Thus, at the end of its allotted three days, the symposium could be considered as adjourned rather than concluded: the conclusion would be the building itself.

For good and obvious reasons, the study of Elizabethan drama usually proceeds through its dramatic literature, which we can see in print, rather than its physical tricks of the trade, our knowledge of which is and must always be to some extent conjectural. Nevertheless, speculative or not, with an actual building in view such technical matters could hardly be left out of account. For this reason the conference program was designed to bring in specialists from fields not usually included in studies of Elizabethan drama. For instance, we felt it important to include an authority, Stuart Rigold, on the carpentry and building crafts of Tudor and Jacobean London. It was also very much to the purpose to find a specialist, John Ronayne, who understood the technical aspects of the painted decoration and modeling and the artificial and mechanical effects available to the operators of playhouses of Shakespeare's day. Glynne Wickham's cautionary advice to keep certain parts of the stage, such as the tiring-house wall, flexible and movable in order to test pertinent theories and incorporate any relevant physical discoveries was most useful in our discussions.

One may, however, ask why, if room could be found in the program for any sort of speculation, it should be limited to these topics. Are there not many differing theories about the uses of the Elizabethan stage, theories that depend upon many different assumptions about its structure? Such matters were not forgotten, but we wished to avoid opening up a free-for-all of heresies and orthodoxies which in the end would probably not advance any particular view and would only divert attention from the conference's main purpose—the planning of the building of a third Globe. The organizers decided that such contentions could be fought out later, if necessary, upon the stage of the building itself. A starting point was therefore fixed: the Globe as it is reliably shown in Hollar's well-known contemporary picture. The attention of the participants was therefore directed toward examining *that* Globe.

One particularly significant outcome of the third Globe discussions calls for notice here. The data upon which, until recently, almost all speculations about the size and structure of the London playhouses have been based—the dimensions given in the Fortune contract in the Henslowe papers—no longer appear as essential as they once did. The contract is the best single piece of evidence we have for building detail, but it describes the detail of one playhouse among many. Too often in the past, as is now clear, the dimensions of the Fortune playhouse have been used like a corset to hold in the different compasses of others. The findings of this symposium, as seen in the papers of Richard Hosley and John Orrell, have confirmed a different standard of measurement as well as a good foundation for the new building.

At the adjournment of the symposium, a joint announcement by the mayor of Detroit, Coleman Young, and the president of Wayne State University, Thomas N. Bonner, endorsed the work of the panelists and declared a civic commitment to reconstruct the Globe as part of the new landscape along the riverfront. The joint effort will have value for both the city and the university. The Globe will provide a center for world study and research for Wayne State. The theatre will stand as a demonstration piece in its own right—the only example of the great Elizabethan and Jacobean stage in existence. It will also be a living laboratory for continuing research into the dramatic methods of Shakespeare's time, a place where his own plays and those of his contemporaries can be presented under conditions similar to those in which they were originally seen. It will be a natural center for the study of the performing arts of the Renaissance and will provide a new theatrical space for experimentation in the writing and composition of contemporary drama, opera, dance, and music. For all of this, the academic and research opportunities provided by Wayne State University will give the greatest possible advantage. The house will be available for performances by a fully professional resident company, and visiting Shakespearean companies from all over the world will find it an ideal setting. For the citizens of Detroit and visitors alike, it will stand as a museum of remarkable historic interest, with exhibitions for scholars and the general public. The building can also function as an exhibition space, as a facility for music and dance, both classical and modern, and as a lecture-seminar and reception hall for civic use.

Thus there is every hope that, as a result of the initiative of

Wayne State University and the city of Detroit, leading to the Globe symposium and the proceedings published here, a restored Elizabethan playhouse, the third Globe, will at long last open its doors to enhance the lives of multitudes.

The symposium upon which this book is based was made possible by the generosity of the Ford Motor Company Fund, Leonard Kasle, Mrs. Robert G. Hartwick, the Michigan Council for the Arts, and the Wayne State Fund. The editors would like to express their appreciation to all those who made these meetings possible.

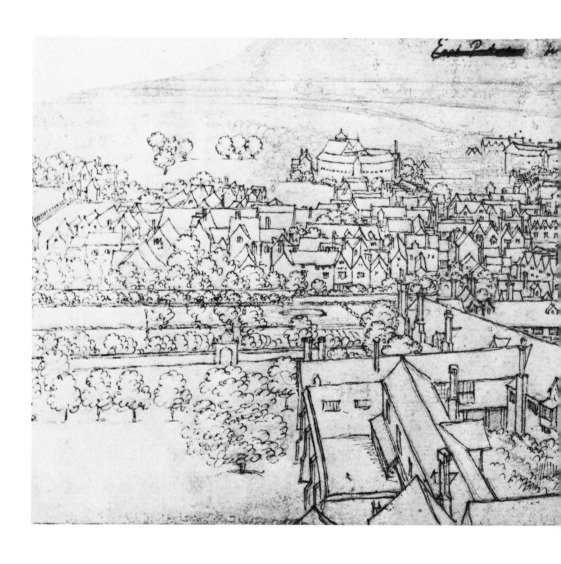

Wenceslaus Hollar, drawing of Bankside, showing the playhouses. (Courtesy Mr. and Mrs. Paul Mellon.)

I. *Modern Uses for a Globe Theatre*

*W*e have come here to see whether the Globe can be built again. My task is to start the debate by considering what hopes we can have for this project and the uses to which the building might be put.

The first reason for such an enterprise is that we want to know more about Shakespeare's Globe Theatre, and to build it is to take the next step toward that end—an essential step that has been long awaited. If we are to know more about the Globe, the time has come when we need more than scholarly papers and plans and models; that is self-evident, I think, as soon as we begin to evaluate our own experiences when moving into theatres, working in theatres, taking over new theatre buildings; when we stop reading books and look and listen; when we visit Epidaurus and climb for the first time to get a convenient seat, wait for the performance, and notice that great Mediterranean sky, which acts upon our senses, over and above the actors, throughout the performance. For too long, we have been reading and talking about Shakespeare's Globe with only learned articles, plans, drawings, and various sets of dimensions to help us. That is quite insufficient if we are to understand the home where Shakespeare's great plays were brought to life.

When I first joined the National Theatre in London,[1] in 1973, I saw a huge mass of drawings and plans for the new Olivier Theatre, with all the relevant facts, figures, schedules, and costs. We were shown a wonderful model that was two meters square and could be taken apart section by section and then reassembled. It could be observed from different directions and levels, and we spent a lot of time on hands and knees, peering about as if moving inside this model. A little camera on tiny wheels could record the effect of the stage from this angle and that. Moreover, since the National Theatre took years to build, we had the shell of the building in which we could sit and talk, discussing our future plans and future repertoire. Then, back in the wooden huts in a yard behind Aquinas Street, we started to draw up our strategy, taking into account every conceivable consideration.

At that time we had a very good idea about the Olivier Theatre and the basis for our plans, but now, six years later, we realize that we are only just beginning to understand that theatre, its capabilites, and the ways to use it to best advantage. It is now completely furnished, and it is so substantial that only a bomb could get rid of it; more than a dozen new productions have been performed in it. We have had a few local difficul- ties, like building delays of about three years, budgets half what they should be, and equipment that does not function; we have faced alarming inflation rates and had a series of strikes. We have had to tear up many plans and our job has not been easy, but in one very important sense we feel now that our feet are on firm ground. We are much more sure of the theatre now that it has been built and now that it has been used. We know the horse we are sitting on; we know it is a horse and not a donkey. Nothing but the existing building and our first attempts to make it work could have told us all these things. In vital ways, possession of the theatre and the experience of working in it—sometimes very successfully and sometimes less so—is the only absolutely firm basis of knowledge and efficient forward planning.

Here are a few examples of how the fact that there was a building, and not just plans, descriptions, figures, and bright ideas, has altered our thinking. Anyone who has been to the National Theatre would immediately recognize the first. When we started work we believed what we had been told, that every seat in the Olivier would be as good as any other; it had been part of the architect's brief to make it so. We had, therefore, a single price for all seats—it was just two pounds fifty—and for that sum you could sit anywhere in the theatre except the first two rows, where there was less leg space, and the two rows at the back of the circle. (We wanted to make sure that some seats cost only seventy-five pence, in order to keep faith with the young theatre audience that used to fill the galleries in the Old Vic and sometimes saw a play six times a week.) All seats, we believed, were good seats, and we could quote specifications to prove it. They had looked equally good as the little camera had moved around inside the model. But now, of course, we know the facts. The upper level is about half as good as the lower, and seats at the center of the main stalls are much better than those in the raised areas at the sides of the stalls. So now the Olivier has a conventional price structure, with center stalls more than twice as expensive as side seats at the back of the circle.

An example of National Theatre directors learning from the experi- ence of working in the Olivier is seen in the contrast between the two Restoration comedies so far produced there. We had thought that the open stage would allow asides and short soliloquies to be played out to the audience, but, in my view, we miscalculated the effect of the larger scale of the Olivier Theatre in comparison with those theatres for which the plays were written. *The Country Wife* in 1977 seemed a slow and comparatively heavy production, too deliberate for the quick and multiple ironies of the writing. For *The Double Dealer,* a year later, the chosen pace was basically slower, but asides were handled in a lighter manner and were not persistently addressed to the audience. Asides were opportunities for the audience to overhear something inward instead of being given a deliberate message. The set was far more complicated, helping to keep the actors' consciousness within its world, rather than encouraging outward contact with the audience. Paradoxically, the production seemed much livelier, and I believe closer to the effect of the original conditions of performance, while being further from them in method. It is as if we had turned our production style for the Restoration theatre inside out. I do not think we have got it quite right yet at the Olivier, and it may be that Restoration plays will always work better in a smaller house, like our Cottesloe Theatre, which seats only 400. But we have found one good way, and we have discovered something about the dramatic qualities of a certain kind of text.

If I were asked pointedly, and looked closely in the eyes, I would have to say that we have not yet found a way of doing Shakespeare in the Olivier Theatre. We have tried two different ways and we are about to try a third; a fourth is up our sleeve. We may yet retreat into the little Cottesloe, lick our wounds, and try again there. Marlowe, on the other hand, seemed to me to work the very first time, in 1977. *Tamburlaine* lived with the full stream of Marlowe's poetry, without cutting the long speeches or the slow elaboration of the longer scenes and without added business devitalizing the excitement, bravery, daring, and irony of that play. We got the pace, length, and breadth of Marlowe's two-part play right at first throw. And we learned that not by taking thought, but by having a theatre to try it in.

At first we did not think the Olivier Theatre would be a stage for new writing. I can remember taking various young playwrights around the theatre, when it had a roof and began to have some seats, and sensing their apprehensiveness. I recall conducting Tom Stoppard on a tour when we kept getting lost, finding workmen in odd places on the stage and under the stage and above the stage, and all the pleasure we took in that empty building seemed unrealizable in modern dramatic terms. I felt that the scale of the Olivier, the open space of its auditorium, the strong and intense focus on the center of the stage, were all wrong for the plays that most dramatists were writing at that time. Edward Bond, however, was taken round the half-finished theatre, and I am happy to say that he has proved me wrong. The first new play presented at the Olivier, *The Woman,* was Bond's, and he started to write it at the time he saw the theatre. We now have a modern play that could fill Stratford, Ontario, the Guthrie in Minnesota, or a Globe rebuilt in Detroit.

The Woman certainly came fully alive in the Olivier. It shocked or worried most critics, and we had some bad notices. For the first month or

16

two attendance was poor, but the last performances of that play were some of the most exciting events the Olivier has yet witnessed: a modern writer had used the new space and stage in ways not like Shakespeare's at all, but in his own ways. In the beginning we dared not hope for this; the theatre seemed wrong for a generation of dramatists trained by working for small fringe theatres in cellars and attics or for peripatetic theatre companies thriving on one-night fit-ups; and wrong for those dramatists trained by producing thirty-five-minute or, if they were lucky, fifty-five-minute shows for the little box, where their vision had to accommodate the domestic convenience of millions of viewers or the long serial with characters inherited from somebody else. The Olivier also seemed wrong for writers inspired by the excitements of film, who wanted to open up their writings to contain mountains, crowds, political effects, and newsreels. The most we had planned for newer plays in the Olivier was to do Beckett's *Happy Days,* hoping that its precise, sensitive strength could be maintained and perhaps extended in this great playing space we were about to take over. Now the National Theatre Company has got in and all this is changed; I am happy to say that there is a queue of new plays awaiting their premieres in the Olivier Theatre.

The fact is, one can know the plan of a theatre but not know what that theatre is good for. One can know its dimensions and see the cunningly contrived model, but still be ignorant. A theatre is like a wife; until one has lived, worked, and learned with her, until pleasure and adventure and disappointment have been shared, there is no true knowledge. No matter how skilled one is at prognostication, no matter how experienced in producing plays under varying conditions, how visually imaginative, how clever at calculations, prognostications, forecasts, imaginary reconstructions—all very fascinating, but also very misleading—one can be wrong about a theatre. Facts, plans, and models all lie. They cannot help it, because of the scale-effect and because true experience is so complex. Even standing in the empty shell of a building is inadequate preparation, because there is no audience, no true acoustic, no indication of what it is like to step out from behind stage to onstage—to be there, to confront an audience, to create something out of the bare words of the text, which are the beginning of the performance, but only its beginning.

When we consider rebuilding the Globe, we are trying to create a globe, a world in which at least thirty-seven plays can come to life—thirty-seven plays on which we have spent a lot of time, getting to know them in other, unnatural conditions. We have seen only a zoo with the animals in cages or wide-ranging open spaces, neither of which are their natural habitat. If we can get closer to the habitat of Shakespeare's plays, we will add to our experience of the plays and will fuel our imaginative exploration. We will move from theory and guesswork to a new experience. We have waited a very long time to do this.

All these things must be said at the outset. We are unnecessarily ignorant about the Globe Theatre. And we will remain ignorant until we can enter and use a theatre as close as possible to that developed form of theatre which was the second Globe, rebuilt by the King's Men on the foundations of the first.

If we could wave a magic wand, however, and those wharves and areas of concrete could disappear and the Globe rise on the banks of the Detroit River tomorrow, I do not believe that enlightenment would come then, at a stroke. We would have the Globe, but we would still have to learn to use it; we would have to explore, experiment, and create. Enlightenment may sometimes arrive in a blinding flash, suddenly, but the more valuable part of our experience will come when we have overcome our surprise and developed a considered view of the new possibilities. After six years in the Olivier, we are beginning to think we know.

If the theatrical parallel of the Olivier Theatre on the South Bank in London does not persuade you, take a parallel nearer home; I believe it is equally valid. Remember how much is learned about a new house *after* the family has moved in and got used to living and working with it and in it. There is enormous fun—the sort of fun that Shakespearean scholars have been living on for years—in going through books and plans, until one begins to get desperate or one's pocket begins to feel more than usually empty. There is even fun in looking through newspaper advertisements and imagining what all those other houses might be like. But each house is different. Each has its own secret, even if it is one house among several all looking very much alike. Besides, every family is different, and makes its own demands. We can learn only from our own experience. We must think long and hard about the house we want to buy and the kind of family we are going to put into it, and we must still be prepared for an adventure. If we are to have a new Globe and use it well, we shall have to exchange views, share previous experience, research, projections, calculations; once the new Globe is there, we shall have to collaborate in many kinds of practical work. It will have to be a center for continuing research, experimentation, and exploration, and, allowing for some disasters, a source of enjoyment.

The first use for the new Globe, therefore, will be to gain new knowledge about the theatre developed by the King's Men, who premiered all Shakespeare's plays and supported Shakespeare in his astonishingly sustained and varied career. General scholarly agreement will not follow—there are plenty of theatre directors, and still more critics, who believe that they could manage the Olivier Theatre very much better than the present incumbents. But the argument will move into a new, third dimension. Our debate will be an interchange in which the human factor and the complications of possession will never be forgotten, and in which reference to the theatrical experiences of actors, audiences, and dramatists will never again be left out of account.

New opportunities will arise on all sides. Not only could we study plays as well as theatres—how Marlowe is different from Shakespeare, and Webster from Shakespeare and Marlowe, and so on—but we could also learn about the continued and habitual use of the theatre by a particular group of players. I suspect that what the building will teach a group of actors in some kind of permanent possession will be one of its most important achievements. The establishment of a company of actors modeled in some ways on the King's Men may sound a dry and impracticable subject, but organization is one of the most difficult and fascinating elements of theatrical work, and close to the heart of any play in performance. As actors react individually and together, interchanging with the characters they play; interchanging in confidence, excitement, and inspiration one with another; interchanging their momentary stage-life with their continual life in the world outside the theatre, the deep-set power of drama is released. We have to know how such a theatre as the Globe would influence actors in these intimate and infinitely varied ways.

Of course, we already have many theatres that are in some sense like the Globe—"based on" the Globe, "adaptations of" the Globe, "developments of" the Globe. Existing buildings, round or rectangular, have been made to look like the Globe or to reproduce some of its characteristics. We have new thrust stages in buildings with wide, large, and saucer-shaped auditoria. We have several small-scale replicas. We have various toys and compromises, and none of them is good enough. Dimensions and scale must be as accurate as possible. (These things are vital in a house, as everyone learns after having taken up residence.) The dimensions of a theatre are of the utmost importance not only onstage, but behind stage as well, and around, beneath, and under the stage. Building materials and the means of furnishing, decorating, and fitting out should also be close to those of the original. We should be able to reproduce not only the building but also the conditions for performance. If a larger tiring-house is required for some of the new purposes to which the theatre might he put, then the original tiring-house should be able to be blocked off from the extension necessary for visiting companies, for the occasional use of scenery, for the occasional accommodation of orchestras.

We must know what it is like for a group of sixteen actors to run a theatre, together with some hired men and stage doorkeepers. An extraordinarily active life must have gone on behind those tiring-house facades in order to keep thirty plays in repertoire and, on any one day, to bring the chosen play into performance within two-and-a-half or three hours. The nature of the human contact among actors, and among tire-men, book-keepers, prop-keepers, and whoever it was who was free to set off the gunpowder, must have drawn together a very special kind of organism. That closeness of work—with, I suspect, its constant exchange of responsibility—is worth reconstructing, because as one works with different the-

19

atre companies and sees the same plays mounted by different companies, one begins to understand that theatrical organization is one of the crucial elements of any theatrical experience. The life of a company always inspires, infiltrates, and sometimes defeats what is attempted onstage.

So the close backstage quarters of the Globe is one of the many elements that should be reproduced in order that we may know what it is like for an actor to step out of that busy, thriving, darkened world onto the empty platform with the crowded audience twenty feet away all around him. What sort of moment of truth was that? Surely what has happened behind stage is as important as what happens onstage.

Still more difficult to reproduce, but just as important, is the nature of the Globe audience. A true Elizabethan audience is, needless to say, unobtainable. But we could take steps to give prominence to what might be called its economy-class element. The young and the poor—and also the addicted and the fearless—should be able to behave as they did in the Globe Theatre, to stand and move about, to talk, eat, and drink, even if on many other occasions seats are put into the yard and silence carefully induced. A standing audience paying minimal entrance fees is a vital constituent in the reconstruction of the Globe, and it should be free there, awash in the bilbos of the theatre, ready for whatever reaction takes its mind. Our actors will need such an audience to sustain them, not only with active support and applause but also with competition, even enmity. Such immediate confrontations will keep the play open to the world in which it is being performed—a condition of performance which is all too rare today.

With whatever safety precautions must be added to placate the guardians of fire and building regulations, this lively audience must be allowed to enter within those tall walls, through a narrow doorway, and then stand in an open yard having around them the protection of three galleries of carved pillars, ornately painted and gilded as we know they were. Each member will thereby be cut off for the equivalent of a penny from the world of ordinary fare.

That kind of expectant, waiting audience—to get a good place in the Globe Theatre you had to come early—is something we must give the actors when they open in a play by an Elizabethan or Jacobean dramatist in the new Globe Theatre. Originally, these plays were performed not very far from a brewhouse, and that condition or some close equivalent should also be reproduced, so that the audience is encouraged to drink and eat and enjoy a casual freedom for talk and movement and competition between themselves, before, during, and after a performance. It should be possible, at least on some occasions, to have no reserved seats so that all members of the audience must arrive early, pay for the better galleries at each separate entrance, and, before the play begins, make themselves individually at home as well as they can. Various subtle or perhaps unsubtle modifications to their original dispositions would be made as the play proceeds to take them deeper into Arden, or further onto the Heath, or into the darkness of *Macbeth*.

The steep angle of view from the upper galleries should be retained with no cheating and no compromise. The audience should be able to be in the same daylight as the actors. Some plays could start in the middle of the working day and finish as daylight disappears. The reconstructed Globe need not always keep to these Elizabethan ways of handling an audience or lighting a stage, but if they are not practicable the exploratory use of the new building will be greatly diminished.

Materials used in the building should be as close to the original as possible. Because I live in a large sixteenth-century house, full of timber beams up to thirty feet long, I know the special acoustics of a building like the Globe and how it responds to love and care and all sorts of misuse. Movement, sudden action, noise, and quietness seem to have special force or magnification. The house opens itself to its inhabitants, almost insensibly, but physically and unmistakably. If one knows the house, one is aware of how it receives, quite literally, a crowded Christmas party of fifty or a hundred people. A timber building has means of reacting to whatever is done within it—the rumbling of stage thunder, the shot of an explosion, the reverberations of a standing crowd applauding with a great roar. The actor in a wooden theatre might actually hear his "stretched footing" on a wooden scaffold at certain moments, as he was said to do. All these are real experiences, far beyond modern, familiar experiences in nice, neat boxes of plastic, brick, and concrete.

Building a replica of the Globe will give us a real and a fuller knowledge of the original building as well as an opportunity to experiment in the staging of Shakespeare's plays and so, perhaps, to discover more about those plays—which are, after all, the deepest reason for our interest in the Globe. We cannot reproduce exactly the living organism of the King's Men or conjure up Shakespeare's audience to fill the new theatre. We cannot bring back Shakespeare's London, which is the only fit environment for such a playhouse. But we can get close to some of the original conditions and so learn more about the plays themselves.

Even a few steps closer to original conditions of performance can greatly modify our response to the plays. When William Poel re-created an Elizabethan-type stage in St. George's Hall, London, in 1881, and so performed Shakespeare's plays at very quick speed, without any stops for scene changing, he started a minor revolution in our understanding of how Shakespeare's plays were constructed. Early critics believed that at the end of *Antony and Cleopatra* Shakespeare had thrown up his hands, unable to cope with thirteen or fifteen scenes all within a single act; after all, they argued, the other tragedies make us suppose he wanted to concentrate attention on the figures of the protagonists. But Granville-Barker's preface to *Antony and Cleopatra* (1930) shows what an experience of continuous performance could do to the critical assessment of Shakespeare's grasp of his material and the uses he made of it.

William Poel's very limited and clumsy reconstruction of Elizabethan conditions also guided him and others toward a new liveliness of speech and action, a simplicity and forthrightness in the engagement of Shakespeare's characters one with another. Granville-Barker's productions at the Savoy and Kingsway theatres in 1912 and 1914, stemming out of Poel's experiments, established the new tempo. Earlier recordings of Barrymore or Irving show how a portentous Shakespearean style was exchanged for one of excitement. The audience had to follow as best it could a drama that never settled down to allow the actor to build simple overwhelming "points" and histrionic effects or to imprint on its memory a single, carefully studied gesture. The plays now had continuous action and excitement.

Since the Second World War the early experiments with Elizabethan-type staging have had further influence on our understanding and staging of Shakespeare, although our theatres are still nowhere near Elizabethan in design or theatre practice. For example, Tyrone Guthrie's production of *Henry VIII* at Stratford-upon-Avon in 1949 had what was then believed to be an Elizabethan background to the action, with an inner stage, an upper stage, and a couple of doors. Steps had been added to vary the acting levels, but, basically, Guthrie and his designer, Tanya Moiseiwitsch, were trying to use the facade of an Elizabethan tiring-house to give the play continuous life. Free from the elegant refinement of Granville-Barker and the fussy archaism of Poel, they discovered how to use certain fundamental symbolic properties and to rely on them as structural devices of the dramaturgy, thus ensuring clear exposition and establishing ironic constrasts. Thrones, crowns, gates, and doorways were seen to give repeated patterns of action that draw the play together, relating apparently discordant episodes, not by what the characters say, but by echoes of the action and stage pictures of previous scenes. In the first volume of *Themes in Drama* (1979), edited by James Redmond, there is a long and hyperbolic account of a recent production of the *Henry VI* plays by the Royal Shakespeare Company which relied still more heavily on stage properties, in Elizabethan style:

> Henry V's coffin, draped with his colours, and helmeted, is spotlit amid the black drapes. A harsh brass Dead March brings on the six lords in slow file out of the darkness, in rich black hoods and cloaks, black and gold shields at their shoulders. They turn and swing in single file down-stage. . . . The coffin remains centre-stage for the entire scene . . . while messengers cause the groupings to break and re-form down-stage. The scrambling chaos at the death of Henry V has begun. . . .
>
> To a great deal of music, light, noise and smoke, four enormous

cannon are rolled forward, with the young French lords, swaggering before them, parodying the slow down-stage swing of the ancient English lords. . . . Joan la Pucelle is the first distinctive figure . . . in an open white calico tunic; hers is the first body not smothered in cloaks, armour, insignia or all three (p. 253).

There is much further to go along the road of rediscovery. A third Globe in Detroit, with new staging, organization, rehearsals, and sound effects, a new style of performance, and a new relationship to the audience, will be the means for achieving this. There is much to be learned about Shakespeare's art of exposition, how he takes over and develops the consciousness of an audience and sometimes invites participation. We may discover why "a well-graced actor" left the stage of the Globe followed by applause.

At this point, in considering the modern usage of a reconstructed second Globe, my mind stops functioning properly. I have very little experience that is at all close to this kind of theatrical adventure. I have been to theatres in the round and directed plays in them. I have worked on thrust stages for audiences surrounding them on one, two, and even three levels. The best of these theatres have been those in which the audience sat in the same light that shone on the actors. I have been in cabaret theatres, most recently in the Public Theatre of New York; but, while I drank and ate and talked and was conscious of the presence of my friends, the performance was pushed out at me with amplified sound and the precision of well-drilled choruses so that the freedom given by the space and the occasion was taken away by the method of production. From time to time I have found a way for audiences to share the actors' exploration and committal to a Shakespearean text, in workshops with actors from the National Theatre and, more recently, in the great hall of the Folger Library with actors from Washington's Arena Stage; but always these open explorations, shared between actors and audiences, have been for brief occasions and for small audiences. I have gone away from such experiences clutching, as if it were the grail, a memory of shared experience and the excitement of some unexpected revelation that had been realized by myself, the actors, and the audience. Conventional performances of Shakespeare's plays in most present-day theatres produce quite other reactions.

At Peter Brook's theatre in Paris, Les Bouffes du Nord, I have watched the actors take fluent possession of the space previously occupied by the orchestra stalls. Members of that audience are not very comfortably seated but know each other quite well, having met in the street or the café next door and having entered together through a crowded vestibule and spent some time waiting to get seats—which are lit by the same eight quartz lights that cover the acting area of this almost empty theatre. I have sat in Peter Brook's theatre and felt a strong interaction between actors and audience, but I have gone away feeling that I did not discover this for myself; I have submitted to the wand of a magician who has rehearsed and practiced for that performance for at least six months. I have been at a celebration or a preordained game, something that has been rigged in order to provide the kind of shared experience that can happen, I know, in much less deliberate and much less expensive ways.

Perhaps seeing Arsenal Football Club play Southampton on their home ground at Islington, among a crowd cheering, silent, and cursing by turns, is the nearest thing I have experienced to the sort of performance that will be possible in a rebuilt Globe. At Islington the players were very small figures, hundreds of feet away from me, and of course, they had no script to speak or to try to live up to; nor did they consciously have to hold the whole auditorium silent for the next most difficult moment of the game. But there was a shared tension that would be very appropriate for Shakespeare's plays in performance. We know Macbeth will die and what he will say immediately before he dies, but we do not know how he will die; in that sense the play should be at risk and partly in our hands.

If we can rebuild the second Globe so that the audience is not cut off from the action of a play by darkness; so that the action is not carefully displayed across the whole width of a picture or dominated by a set or by lighting; so that the actors are in our world—our size, almost within touch, certainly within easy speaking distance—where they encounter one another with Shakespeare's text as their guide and as their deep and endlessly suggestive inspiration; if we can do all this, we shall be on the threshold of a rediscovery of Shakespeare centered in the actors, their relationship to the audience, and their imaginative realization of Shakespeare's plays.

"If we can rebuild the second Globe": how easily those words trip off the tongue. Why has it not been done before? Are we the first to have the idea? Obviously not. There have been many half-hearted attempts and, like anything half-hearted, they have come to almost nothing. It is a bold thing to try to set the clock back. It is a very bold thing in the theatre, where each new success lasts only for each new moment. Besides, we have been unsure how to do the job; our enthusiasm has been quenched by "if" and "but" and "perhaps," and "Won't that go against that new fact that will be discovered next month by X, who has been sitting on documents in the Public Records Office for at least twenty years?"

But now we have a new strategy, for which we must thank Walter Hodges. He has taught us to say, "Let us start with the second Globe, not the first: let us build on the reliability of Wenceslaus Hollar as a witness, and start with those dimensions." Here is a firm basis for our cogitations and for a brief to an architect and to craftsmen to build a Globe again. We are, thanks to Hodges, in a new position academically and architecturally: rebuilding the *second* Globe is different from rebuilding *the* Globe. But still we have hesitated, at least since 1971, when the new strategy was propounded at the Vancouver Shakespeare Congress.

There should be enough facts to build on; yet we hesitate, for reasons that are more difficult to answer. We can rebuild the second Globe, but we cannot revive the Elizabethan actors, the world in which they lived, the financial and personal conditions under which they were organized, their audience, their times. We cannot reconstruct the form and pressure of the world that Shakespeare inhabited. Moreover, it is dangerous to make a theatre that looks like a museum, a theatre based on dead plans. Theatrical experience is like a waterfly—it lives and dies its own complicated life within a day, within a few hours of performance. If anyone seeks to reproduce a theatrical success, it starts to wither in the hand that plucks it from the past. But these general arguments can, I think, be answered. I do not want to follow an antique drum, and I find it stimulating, rather than daunting, to know that however thorough we are in approaching the second Globe in all aspects of its re-creation, not only of building materials and fittings but also of organization, performance, audience, and the interest of a community, there are bound to be times when we wish we could go further. What we do in Detroit, or in London or anywhere else, will be all that we can do; and that very limitation will ensure that our reconstruction is truly alive. When we realize that something is wrong, we may learn about ourselves. When we are baffled, we may not be faulted because of something we have got wrong about Shakespeare's plays or about Shakespeare's theatre, company, or audience; we will also have to question ourselves, our own ways of performing, our own ways of acting as audiences or theatre producers, our own response to the theatre we are trying to make for the here-and-now. A movement back to the Globe will set us up a glass in which we will be able to see more about our own theatre in its own very complicated—and very shaky—present state.

The Globe can never be as it was. Let us accept that, but not let it delay us. Let us take that as a primary fact and agree that we will adhere as closely as we can to Elizabethan precedent so that we achieve far more than we could have done ten years ago. Let us experiment as fully as we can and attempt organizational, fund-raising, and imaginative jobs that have not been attempted before, in quest of Shakespeare. Then let us examine both successes and failures so that we can learn about ourselves. Let the Globe be rebuilt for the sake of the theatre that we and others are making now, all over the world.

The Globe, when it was named—and I think that was one of the most cunning word usages that ever spun out of Shakespeare's mind—was given a new word for its name, a word that had been in the English language only since 1550. It spoke of Drake sailing around the world from west to east for the first time in 1577; it spoke of Hercules holding the world on his shoulders; it spoke, therefore, of human beings who were brave and vital, capable of performing unparalleled feats of strength and cunning. The Globe in our world today would be, as well as an old thing, a new thing. It will need strength and cunning to support it, but in actually trying to accomplish this feat we may learn more about the theatre and ourselves.

The more the new, third Globe, in its minutest detail, is like what we think the second Globe was, the more we will be able to use it to rediscover the Shakespearean past and to discover ourselves and what we can do today. The brave spirits who will live and work in this theatre might be compared to those human guinea pigs who were paid by a British television company to live in Stone Age conditions somewhere in the wilds of England. Of course these experimental groups were not Stone Age human beings. They remained modern people, but their lives were curiously and variously changed. The spectacle of twentieth-century people trying to live primitively, farming and killing pigs, sleeping in the rough, and doing without doctors, information, the ordinary comforts and pleasures was sometimes very funny when viewed on television. But that experiment has changed the lives of several of the people who took part in it, and it has brought genuine new experience to the study of the remote past. Something like this might happen in the Globe Theatre. Some of us are going to hate using the theatre, but even if that is all that happens, it will be worthwhile trying to live and work in the third Globe. Those who go away wishing never to return may well go on to do other things that would not have been thought about without work in the Globe Theatre.

The practical experience of this new-old theatre is something that scholarship and the continuing life of the stage everywhere cannot afford to ignore. Of course we cannot tell how it will be significant, but the minor and very limited experiments already undertaken have brought huge rewards, despite the ridicule that greeted many of them when they were first attempted.

This project could influence theatre in all its manifestations, beyond the specifically Shakespearean. There are very few good actors who have not fed upon the experience of acting in Shakespeare's plays. The continuing availability of these plays in the world's repertoire—however antique their language, however obscure some incidental references, however unscientific the understanding of character, however incomplete our realization of what they might have been in Shakespeare's day—has stretched, developed, and trained the imagination and talents of great actors, ever since the plays were first performed. Name the great contemporary actors who have not returned again and again to Shakespeare, and the list is small. But the list of those who have done so is long and impressive: Gielgud, Richardson, Olivier, Ashcroft, Guinness, Scofield, Hepburn, Tandy, Cronyn, Brando, Sindon, Finney, Plowright, Maggie Smith, Bedford, Keach, Plummer . . . the list goes on to the newest generation. A restored Globe would make possible an experience for developing actors that might well forward their ability to perform in many different kinds of plays. In *Empty Space* (1969), Peter Brook said that Shakespeare, even in the second half of the twentieth century, is "still our model," training ground, touchstone, teacher, and guide. Experiments that are as open as possible to the theatrical ways that Shakespeare used will help to keep his plays alive for future generations of actors. The effect could be far-reaching.

Today there are many kinds of theatre buildings. Bring architects and theatre specialists together and their discussions can be stopped only by some arbitrary intervention. The relation of stage to audience, theatre to environment, and of stage to backstage seems to offer so many possibilities to architects that the mere thought of designing a theatre can set their minds spinning so unrealistically that there is rarely enough money left to finish the backstage or build a car park or do various other necessary jobs. Let us attempt, whatever else we may do, a full and basic realignment of a theatre that has been so lost that its rebuilding will seem like a new opportunity to actors, directors, designers, craftsmen, stage managers, salesmen, musicians—everyone who works in our theatres.

Perhaps it is our playwrights who most need a restored Globe. We must find enough money to allow promising and already accomplished writers to be attached to the theatre and its company over a period of time, so that the third Globe and its new relationships between actor, stage, and audience can also be a challenge to writers. Today's plays often rely heavily on the mechanism of theatre, even when dramatists are trying to speak most directly about life as it is lived outside the theatre. Take, for example, David Hare's *Plenty* (1978), which tells the story of Britain after the Second World War and centers on a girl who had worked for the resistance in France during the war. Its last scene adds nothing to the story and is more cinematic than theatrical in its means and impact. Very complicated and careful stage directions indicate that an interior setting alters as different colors appear in certain sequences, and the kind of "reality" we have been led to know in the play dissolves in a gigantic, generalized impression of a sun-drenched countryside in which the heroine sheds twenty-five years and becomes nineteen years old again. She meets an unnamed French peasant and they agree to go home to his cottage for a meal of soup. The last line of the play is, "There will be days and days and days like this." The "like this" is not created by the actors so much as by a stage picture contrived by more than twenty stagehands and technicians, onstage, backstage, and in the light and sound boxes. A kind of miracle is achieved that allows the author to end his play on an upbeat, a manifestation of innocence, sentiment, and social challenge. But to my mind, a precise and witty play is spoiled at this moment by something spongy, an almost wordless ending of a guaranteed-beautiful stage effect that overwhelms our minds by technical cunning, and at considerable expense. It contains nothing equal to, or able to answer, the nervy, spiky, restless, dissatisfied, pushing drama with which David Hare had anatomized postwar Europe. The effect is technical: its resonance is limited by its means.

How would *Plenty* finish in a new Globe Theatre? The challenge, I think, would make the author imagine a different ending, one that gained its greatest effects from the acting. He might question the reality of his play's final statement, and not take us into a scenic and lightly lyrical world of once-upon-a-time. There is a human scale, a marvelous reality, tangibility, touchability, in Shakespeare's theatre, even at its most fantastic, that I long to see revived in new performances of his plays and in new plays, acting skills, and stage effects.

II. *The Globe: Documents and Ownership*

$\mathcal{M}$y task has been to review the most likely classes of primary evidence to see whether I might in a few months find new information about the Globe as a building and to estimate whether, given more time or luck, anyone is likely to do so hereafter. That meant, in effect, holding W. W. Braines' book *The Site of the Globe Playhouse Southwark* (London, 1924), the "second edition, revised and enlarged," against the documents he had used to see what, if anything, he had missed in those and similar documents. It also meant looking as he did at the maps and panoramic views of London to see whether the competitors of Hollar's *Long View of London* (1647) have much to tell us.

Braines strove mainly toward a limited and difficult conclusion. He was trying to prove that George Hubbard and C. W. Wallace, among others, were wrong to put the Globe on the north side of Maid Lane (or Park Street, as it now is), and he had to defy a crucial and palpably genuine document that places it there. He did deal with much else about the Globe, including its features as a building, but more or less in passing. He did not try seriously even to place the Globe precisely on modern maps. He searched through the main classes of primary documents diligently, however, and he used accurately those that concern the Globe. I have been able to find more information about the Globe in the same places, but nothing that contributes much either to his case or to ours. I take his conclusion to be brilliantly proved. I suspect that we shall not find substantial new information about the building by seeking answers to likely questions in the main kinds of documents. New information about the building probably exists somewhere in primary evidence, but in unexpected places or in answers to unusual questions. I am convinced, however, that an exacting study might well show more closely than Braines attempted to do where precisely on modern maps the Globe was—where, so to speak, one might dig for its potsherds.

I have not attempted that study, but even so, my journey through

29

primary evidence in Braines' rather intimidating shadow was not without rewards. I can add something to his remarks about how early cartographers and artists drew the Globe, and at much greater length I can introduce its landlords. They are the people who collected the payments of the rent, who, as I put it, owned the Globe, for its builders, unlike those of its predecessor, the Theatre, had no clause in their lease allowing them to remove the building. Neither Braines nor anybody else has considered them in more than the vaguest way. Yet they were interesting people who did interesting things, and if those things often seem peripheral to our concerns here, they are not always so, and, in any event, peripheries have their uses.

In the sixteenth and seventeenth centuries maps were of two kinds. There were flat maps like ordinary modern maps, developed toward the end of the period. There were picture maps, "map-views," in which buildings and other features are not two-dimensional outlines but three-dimensional pictures drawn from a vantage point in the sky which deliberately varies from section to section of the map so that the user sees many places clearly, however illogical it might be for him to see one from the vantage point of another. These maps are very common throughout the period. Darlington and Howgego treat both kinds in their splendid bibliography *Printed Maps of London* (London, 1978), the second edition, revised by Howgego alone (hereafter referred to as D&H). Allied to maps are "panoramas," or "panoramic views," in which the maker's vantage point purports to be constant so that the result is meant to lie somewhere between cartography and fine art. Some of these have been used in studies of the Globe for a long time, like the Hondius, Visscher, Merian, and Hollar (1647) views. The maker of these means at least partly to produce an attractive picture. Irene Scouloudi deals with those made from 1600 to 1660 and their derivatives in her *Panoramic Views of London, 1600–1660* (London, 1953).

I have not dealt extensively with these panoramic views because Braines (*Site of the Globe,* pp. 46–60) and I. A. Shapiro (*Shakespeare Survey I*) have dealt shrewdly with the early ones as they apply to the Globe, and others are now dealing with Hollar's view of 1647. Instead I have looked extensively at what others in pursuit of the Globe have usually ignored, the maps of London to the end of the seventeenth century. In doing so, I have found myself looking also at relatively unnoticed panoramic views, for almost from the beginning of the making of maps of London, publishers not infrequently included with their maps a "prospect" of the city which is simply a panoramic view. The idea, evidently, was to show in one part of a sheet of paper what the foot might travel and in another what the eye might see from a given vantage point. It occurred to me that where map and panoramic view appear together and have something to say about the Globe it might be worth comparing one kind of record with another. So in addition to looking for the Globe in maps, I look for it also in those panoramic views that accompany maps.

Anyone who looks at early maps of London must be struck by their crudities. The Norden map of 1593 (D&H, 5), for example, crudely shows the two entertainment places that stood south of the river when Norden drew it, the Beargarden and the Rose, labeled "The Beare howse" and "The Play howse." Worse was to follow, for the map was reissued without change in 1623 as "a guide for Cuntrey men," when, presumably, the rural user was to see the Beargarden as the Hope and the Rose as the Globe and not to miss the Swan or notice that the Globe was on the wrong side of Maid Lane. It was reissued again in 1653, when all the playhouses south of the river were gone and the printshop's only reaction was to add shading to the Beargarden and Rose to make them more realistic. Moreover, someone, apparently Norden, redrew the map to appear in John Speed's *The Theatre of the Empire of Great Britaine* of 1611 and 1614 (D&H, 7), leaving the theatrical scheme of things south of the river exactly as it was in 1593, despite the appearance in the meantime of the Swan and of the Globe and the disappearance of the Rose, but mercifully omitting the labels for the two theatrical buildings.

Was this the spirit of the map trade throughout the period? To find out, I applied later maps to the question of when the Globe disappeared. According to a famous document that is often suspected to be a forgery, the Globe was pulled down in 1644. According to an obviously genuine contract of 1655, which Braines found quoted in two Chancery lawsuits and I in three more, the Globe had by then been replaced by "tenements . . . erected and built where the late playhouse called the Globe stood and upon the ground thereunto belonging." A remark in the records of the sewer commission for the area makes the same point in 1653. Local folklore in the eighteenth century, however, persistently had it that the Globe remained standing for a very long time after it had ceased housing plays in 1642, and at least one writer now accepts that it did.[1]

Chambers remarked that "the old maps . . . do not give much help in a pinch," but he did not look systematically enough at them. The first relevant map here is the Dankerts (D&H, 9), which in its first edition (ca. 1633) shows not only the Globe and the Hope more or less where they should be, but the Fortune and the Curtain as well. In its second edition (ca. 1645), however, Southwark has been redrawn so as to remove the Globe and present a new picture of the Hope (the Fortune and the Curtain remain unchanged), and this arrangement is repeated in the editions of ca. 1675 and ca. 1710. If one disregards for a moment the maps with which Hollar had to do and the 1653 edition of Norden's map (which is obviously useless here), of all the maps of London printed from the 1640s to the end of the century only two show the Globe. This muster includes the three maps issued between then and the fire, two in the 1650s and one in 1661 (D&H, 11–13). It also includes the first map of that part of London which may reasonably be described as accurate by modern standards, Morgan's of 1681–82 (D&H, 33), and others like it that appeared later. It includes in all some forty-eight editions of twenty-four maps that deal with Bankside in a scale big enough to show playhouses.[2] Evidently the Globe really was pulled down in the 1640s or soon after. The Hope was pulled down in the same period and a new beargarden built to the south of it; this new beargarden continued to appear on maps until 1676 (D&H, 29), from which time an open space usually appears instead, sometimes labeled Beargarden.

According to Darlington and Howgego, Hollar made nine maps of London, which were published from 1655 to ca. 1675. Four include Bankside and are drawn to a scale big enough to show playhouses. The earliest of these four (1655) shows both Globe and Beargarden reasonably where they should be. The next (1666) shows neither. The next (1666) shows both, but the Globe is unlabeled and on the wrong side of Maid Lane (this map was reissued in 1673 and twice thereafter). The last (1667) shows the Globe where it should be and not the Beargarden (reissued in 1668).[3] Can one argue that Hollar is right and so many others wrong? Even if he were consistent about the Globe it might be a waste of ingenuity to try to do so. As it is, his inconsistency gives the game away and makes such argument impossible. One might better argue that on three occasions he drew the Globe not because he thought it was still standing but because he liked drawing it. Perhaps it is significant that he was one of the very few map-makers of the time who took such an attitude toward their work as it applied to the Globe.

Until 1700 or so, the Globe appears in seven printed maps: the Norden map of 1600, the Dankerts map, the three Hollar maps, and the Oliver(?) (D&H, 32, ca. 1680) and Aa (D&H, 51a, ca. 1700) maps. The Norden map perforce shows the first Globe, the others presumably the second. The Globe is on the south side of Maid Lane five times in these maps, on the north side twice (in the Aa map it is virtually on the river). It is polygonal in the Dankerts and Aa maps but round in the five others. It has a flag over it only in the Norden and Dankerts maps, and exterior staircases in none. It has a hut of a single gable in the Norden, Dankerts, and, probably, Aa maps. It has no hut in the so-called Oliver map, nor in the first two of Hollar's. In his third map, Hollar gave it a hut with the familiar double gable, but badly drawn so that the hut could be the tops of two houses standing in the yard and facing (as the true hut evidently did not) the southwest (D&H, 21). The Norden map correctly shows the first Globe covered with thatch, and all the other maps equally correctly show the second covered with something apparently more solid. The Hope and its successor appear much more often, sixteen times in fifteen maps (twice in the Dankerts) which ran to twenty-six editions. They are polygonal eleven times and round only five. They have a flag only in the Dankerts and Porter (D&H, 11) maps and external staircases not at all. They have a single-gable hut in the Dankerts and one other map (D&H, 50), and a kind of cowl in the Porter and Aa maps, which may be what Hollar shows in his view of 1647.[4]

Panoramas that show Bankside accompany the Norden map of 1600 and eight others dating from 1666 to the end of the century. All nine panoramas include the Globe, but only the Norden map does, and even here the map has a round Globe, the panorama a polygonal one. No map, that is, agrees with its panorama about the Globe. Moreover, all nine panoramas show what one might call the Beargarden-Hope, but only four of the accompanying maps show it, and in each case the building is round in one and polygonal in the other. No map, in short, agrees with its panorama in the most obvious ways about either the Globe or the Beargarden-Hope. The statistic is blatant: eighteen attempts at the same things, eighteen fundamental disagreements. One may look for significances.

Since eight of the panoramas were published when the Globe no longer stood, as all eight of the accompanying maps show, one significance seems clear. The maps and panoramas were the results of two different assumptions, the one pointing, however crudely at times, toward a record of the present and the other toward fancy, a pleasant picture, and the past. Shapiro argues that the same assumptions also lie behind the Norden map and panorama: the map is relatively accurate, much of the panorama "obviously purely conventional and 'artistic.' " Publishers and buyers, that is, expected the map and panorama to convey different kinds of intelligence about the same aspect of London. A glance at the Hondius, Visscher, and Merian views must suggest that what was true of the panoramas published with maps was equally true of many of those published on their own.

Five of the panoramas published with maps relate to Hollar's *Long View of London.* Four of these appeared within a year or so of the great fire of 1666 and are drawn from a vantage point in Southwark so as to show the buildings of Bankside standing starkly in the foreground while the city burns in the background. One of the four has the labels of the two playhouses reversed (D&H, 16), as does the *Long View,* and another, much in Hollar's style, appears with one of his maps (D&H, 14). The fifth and perhaps more interesting version of Hollar's view appears with his map of ca. 1675 (D&H, 26). Here the city is shown as in the view, before the fire, and here, too, the labels of the playhouses are reversed. In these five panoramas, the Globe is always round, the Beargarden-Hope polygonal once and round four times. The Globe has a double-gable hut four times, and once the sort of cowl which the Beargarden-Hope has in the *Long View.* The Beargarden-Hope has that cowl twice and no superstructure three times. The Globe has a flag only once, but the Beargarden-Hope has one four times. The Globe has external staircases four times, the Beargarden-Hope three. The three remaining panoramas published with maps all date from the very end of the century or just after, and all have as their models not Hollar's *Long View,* which treats Bankside

33

as it was in the early 1640s, but the Visscher and Merian views, which treat the place as of about 1600.[5]

What, then, may one say about Hollar's *Long View*, which has become so important in our calculations about the Globe? His Globe is conspicuously a more reasonable building than that in the Hondius, Visscher, and Merian views and their progeny. But it belongs to a convention the assumptions of which militate against accuracy, and Hollar was obviously no champion of accuracy as applied to playhouses in the maps that he also made. Did he defy convention and his own instincts as shown in his maps when he drew the view? Evidently not. Scouloudi warns us against taking the view literally and points out several respects in which Hollar preferred to ignore fact: he does not show St. Katherine's by the Tower; he shows eight bays on the south side of the choir of St. Paul's but eleven in his elaborate plan of the building drawn on another occasion; he has the New Exchange incorrectly located (pp. 61–62). He left out the thirty-odd tenements that stood around the Globe. To suppose, as we seem ready to do, that the Globe was polygonal rather than round as he has it, we must argue that he made it round not because he could not draw or take the time to draw a polygonal building, but because roundness, like the omission of the tenements, was right in the mind's if not the body's eye. The substitution of fancy for fact led Hollar to a more attractive picture. The many differences between his partly inked-over pencil sketch and the finished engraving show that the process went on richly, as do the differences between the pencil lines and the lines inked over them. It is not unreasonable, therefore, to expect that Hollar made other adjustments to the fact of the building with the same motive. Nor is it unreasonable to conclude that where the evidence of the Fortune contract is at odds with that of Hollar's view, the view may not always be right.

And now let me proceed to proprietary matters.

A family named Brend (as they came to spell their name) owned the Globe through its whole history. The first of them who is important in that history is Thomas Brende, who acquired the site and passed it to subsequent generations but did not own it while the Globe stood on it. He was born in 1516 or 1517, became a citizen and scrivener of London, and in 1548 or so was living in the house of William Cawkett, scrivener, perhaps as his journeyman. Like other scriveners, Brende devoted himself at least partly to dealings in the money market of London and eventually in real estate. The Close Rolls are littered with the bonds and mortgages with which he secured the borrowings of his clients, and only one with which someone else secured one of his borrowings. These bonds and mortgages begin in 1547 and diminish sharply after 1558; most belong to 1548 and 1555–56. From 1554 to 1591, mainly from 1562 to 1566, the same rolls preserve numerous contracts by which he acquired a good deal of property in London, the Home

Counties, and elsewhere. The first of these acquisitions, in October, 1554, was the site of the Globe in Southwark, which he bought for £240 from John Yong, a citizen and skinner of London who had inherited it from his wife, Christian, and she from her grandparents, Thomas and Christian Rede. Brende bought the place in his first wife's name as well as his own, so perhaps the money was at least partly hers. From 1583, finally, to the last year of his life, these rolls also preserve contracts by which he gave up six pieces of property, one in a legal wrangle, one as a gift to a relative, four as sales.[6]

An antagonist of Brende's said in 1578 that he "became" very "soone welthye" and that this sudden wealth was the result of "false or subtylle dealinge." A fellow lodger in Cawkett's house thirty years before, however, denied the assertion and offered a better reason for Brende's wealth: the "rich mariages he hath had." We may well believe the man, for in addition to having known Brende more than thirty years, he had been called as a witness to sustain, not deny, the assertion, no doubt because Brende had once sued him for defamation.[7]

Brende's first wife was Margerie, who died June 2, 1564, having borne him ten children, four sons and six daughters. His second wife was Mercy, daughter of Humphrey Collet, a bowyer, it seems, of Southwark, and widow of Francis Bodley of Streatham. She brought a son into Brende's family, John Bodley, who becomes important in the history of the Globe, as does her brother, John Collet.[8] She set about bearing Brende eight children, four sons and four daughters. Brende grew to be very old indeed. He outlived most of his children. His second wife died on April 13, 1597, and he drew up a new will two months later, on June 15. He then had one son living, Nicholas, born between September 22, 1560 and September 21, 1561, hence the child of the first wife, and five daughters: Anne, Judith, Mary (who had married a man named Maylard and was a widow in 1601), Katherine (who had married George Sayers, or Seares), and Mercy, born in 1572–73, hence the child of the second wife (she was to marry Peter Frobisher, son of Sir Martin Frobisher, the navigator).[9]

Among Brende's possessions were lands at West Molesey in Surrey (including the manor), the Star and other places in Bread Street, London, numerous properties grouped together in Southwark (including the site of the Globe), and a townhouse in St. Peter's Hill, London. Brende lived at his manor and in his townhouse.[10] He was sensitive about his progress from bourgeois to landed gentleman. From the 1540s to the 1570s he regularly described himself as citizen and scrivener of London, and he continued occasionally to describe himself so for the rest of his life. In one part (1578) of an extensive legal struggle, he is described as alive and "late Cytizen and scrivener of London," probably because he had by this time given up his shop. In another part, a deposition of his of 1582, the examiner wrote "gent" after his name; then, no doubt at Brende's insistence, crossed it out and wrote "esquyer" above the line; then, at Brende's further insistence, crossed that out, too, and wrote the unvarnished fact, "Exam[inan]t." He signed the deposition thus:

He gave himself as "gentleman" once, in 1583, but did not do so again. From 1580 he often preferred the splendid euphemism "citizen and writer of the court letter of London," suggesting not only that he had risen above plain scrivener but that he preferred to think of his scrivenership as having to do with calligraphy rather than the lending of money.[11]

Brende had one quite indirect brush with theatre, in 1581, and it cost him a great deal of money. He guaranteed a loan of £200 for that famous patron of a company of actors, the lord admiral. Brende had been led into the business by his neighbor in Surrey Richard Drake, who was one of the lord admiral's chief followers and equerry to the queen. When the lord admiral failed to repay the money, Brende had to do so. He had for his pains only a bond for £400 that Drake had given him as protection, which for some reason he did not pursue through the courts of law.[12] As his burial inscription in St. Peter's Church, West Molesey, reads, Thomas Brende "lived the age of fovrscore and one yeres And departed this worlde the xxi of September 1598."[13]

His son, Nicholas, married Margaret Strelley in 1595 or somewhat before, when Nicholas was about thirty-four years old. It was an unusual marriage and not merely because the groom was approaching middle age. He did not get his father's consent to the marriage or even tell him about it until some time after it had occurred. Neither did he give his wife a jointure, though she may well have brought him a portion (she could not have been a pauper, and eventually the Brends seem to have owed her something). They had their first child, Jane, in 1595 or 1596, another, Mercy (evidently they had taken his sister into their confidence), in 1597, and yet another, Frances, in 1598.[14] Nicholas' father, who was eighty at the time, had discovered these arrangements by June 15, 1597, and was not amused. He took "a very hard oppinion and conceit" of his daughter-in-law. He redrew his will on that day and added a distressed note to explain: "I haue stryken out my sonne to be one of my Executors in consideracion that he did marry without my knowledge or consent." He named his daughter Anne (presumably the eldest) instead.[15]

Margaret Strelley had trusted Nicholas Brend to deal fairly with her without carefully negotiated compulsion. It was a daring thing to do, whether she was young and merely enthusiastic, or of responsible years, perhaps even a widow, having herself and her money at her own disposal.[16] It is curious, to say the least, that a man of Nicholas Brend's years should have married in such a way. Whether the lady was of age in 1595 or so, she must have been many years younger than her husband, for she lived to have at least twelve children, perhaps more, and six years intervened between one group of children and a second. One can only guess at why Thomas Brende was hostile toward her, and at why Nicholas anticipated this hostility. She was not lacking in social pretensions; indeed, her background was probably superior to that of the Brends. She was cousin to Lady Jane Townsend and, more significant, to that lady's brother, John Stanhope, a gentleman of the privy chamber at court who, shortly after the marriage, was knighted and made treasurer of the chamber (July, 1596). As such, he was paymaster of, among others, the actors and musicians who performed for the queen. Eventually, Margaret Strelley's father may also have been knighted, and her cousin became vice chamberlain and Lord Stanhope (1605).[17] Perhaps her father-in-law was more impressed by financial pretensions, and hers were considerably less than he thought those two marriages of his and a long life of lending and buying should have yielded.

If Thomas Brende refused to make his son an executor, however, he did not disinherit him. In his redrawn will he did not mention either the properties in Southwark or some of his other principal possessions, nor did he say that his son should not have them. When Thomas Brende died, Nicholas was thirty-seven years old.[18] Nicholas seems to have had no trouble taking possession of his father's unmentioned properties. He had no ready cash, however, and he must have been several hundred pounds in debt. Yet, his first legal act was to buy up the properties that his father had left to his two sisters, Anne and Judith.[19] He paid, or rather promised to pay, £1,150 for them on November 17, thereby keeping his father's estate more or less together, but rendering his own financial state difficult. Thanks to his wife's connections at court, perhaps, his next legal act was to lease a part of his property in Southwark to the Burbages and their associates. The arrangement was substantially agreed before Christmas (it was to take effect at Christmas), but the contract was not signed until February 21 following, by which time the worthwhile pieces of the Old Theatre in Shoreditch had probably been lying about the place for some six weeks, ready for assembly.

Once the players had taken up their lease there, the Brends' property in Southwark seems to have been worth at least £90 a year clear, of which the players paid £14.10s.0d. (16 percent). Their leasehold comprised two pieces of land separated by a lane, four gardens and various structures on one piece and three gardens and various structures on the other. Adjoining these pieces of land on both east and west were the other parts of the Brends' property, on which there were numerous buildings during the whole history of the Globe. The whole property in 1601, two years after the Globe opened, comprised "small & ruinous howses" in thirty tenants' hands (two of whom represented the Globe), according to a

man in whose interest it was to disparage them.[20] In that year the whole
property was described twice in legal documents as "all those messuages
tenements howses edifices buildings chambers roomes playhowse gardens
orchards voidgrounds and other lands and heredytaments Whatsoever."
The tenants of these places were given as four gentlemen (including
Richard Burbage and Shakespeare), two tanners, two watermen, two beer-
brewers, and a dyer, armorer, baker, porter, draper, tailor, saddler, and
one person whose work was unidentified. Some of these people, like
Hendrik Sturman (later Henry Stearman), the armorer, held more than
one of the places. This description and these tenants were recited as
current in 1608 and in 1622, suggesting, perhaps, that the neighborhood
had not changed much in two decades. When the Globe was finally
separated contractually from its neighbors in 1624, it was described as
"all that the messuage or tenement and all that the Playhouse comonly
called or knowne by the name of the Globe with their & either of their
rights members & appurtenants set scituate lying & being in or neere
Mayden lane . . . together with all & singuler efifices buildings cellers
sollers chambers lights easemts orchards gardeines Courts backsides walles
inclosures waies pathes and all other profitts comodities & emolumts
whatsoeuer to the said messuage or tenement & Playhouse called the
Globe or either of them belonging." By that time, if not before, the
Globe was an extensive holding consisting of two main buildings and
numerous subsidiary matters. Its occupiers, "now or late," were John
Hemings, Cuthbert and Richard Burbage, and Shakespeare.[21]

Nicholas' two unmarried sisters, Anne and Judith, both died in
1599, so that he became his father's executor after all, on May 8. Judith
was living in John Collet's house when she drew her will on April 20.[22]
What the two of them did with their brother's bonds does not appear, but
his finances did not improve. He sold a small piece of property at West
Molesey for £340 to Dame Dorothy Edmunds, one of the ladies of the
queen's privy chamber,[23] and he borrowed £105 from his widowed sister,
Katherine Maylard. Meanwhile, his family continued to grow. His first
son, Matthew, was born February 6, 1600,[24] and another son, John, little
more than a year after, so that he now had five children. He owned a rich
estate, but when he grew mortally ill early in the autumn of 1601 in his
father's house in St. Peter's Hill, all he could contemplate were numerous
debts either due already or shortly coming due, three daughters without
portions, an heir who was less than two years old, and a second son who
had just been born. He thought that his debts amounted to £1,478, but
they proved eventually to amount to £1,715. Not only had he no ready
money with which to pay these debts, but he needed £250 to see him
through his present difficulties. Moreover, his properties around the Globe
and in Bread Street needed extensive repairs, so that his real indebtedness
was something like £2,150, about half again as much as he thought.[25]

Evidently he saw no chance that his wife might be able to make sense of all this, any more than he had. So in his last hours he summoned his step-brother, John Bodley of Streatham, now a cloth merchant, who quickly organized an elaborate scheme for rescue. Because Bodley could not finance his scheme himself, he summoned that other relative, John Collet, now a merchant tailor, and Sir Matthew Browne. Bodley would pay the debts and in return take a mortgage on the properties in Bread Street and Southwark, including, now, the Globe. Nicholas would provide other properties that Bodley would sell to raise portions for the daughters (£400 for Jane and £300 for each of the two others) and money to help maintain them while they were minors and provide for Nicholas's wife and second son, John.[26] Bodley, finally, would see to it that Nicholas had £250 in cash at once. Bodley agreed to do these things, and Collet and Browne to finance him, because, despite Nicholas's apparent difficulties, his estate was worth a good deal.

So on October 7, Bodley, Collet, and Browne agreed in writing to pay the debts and Collet to give Nicholas £250 in cash. In return, Nicholas mortgaged his properties in Bread Street and Southwark to Collet and Browne for the supposed amount of the debts, £1,478. On October 8 he signed a bond in which he promised to pay Collet and Browne £2,500 if he did not perform the requirements of the mortgage. On October 10 he drew his will, providing among other things that Bodley and Browne should have various properties that they would sell, including the house in St. Peter's Hill, where all this was taking place. On the same day he signed a document making his mortgage of three days before look like an absolute sale, doubtless at the insistence of Bodley, who had decided that he should control the properties until he had reimbursed himself for the debts out of the profits. He had grown nervous about the widow-to-be's ability to make the estate yield enough money over a reasonable time to cover the debts, and he knew the trouble he would have extracting the money from the estate through the courts should she fail. On October 11, Nicholas conferred with Bodley about the arrangements for the second son, which were manifestly inadequate.[27] And on October 12, at the age of forty or forty-one, the first owner of the Globe died.

Collet and Browne acted merely in trust for Bodley, and in any event, Browne died within two years and Collet formally sold his interest in the scheme to Bodley in 1608. Bodley collected the rents in Bread Street and Southwark from October 10, 1601, and otherwise managed the properties there.[28] From that day, therefore, it was he who effectively owned the Globe. The widow, meanwhile, lived with the children at West Molesey, which she would control until the heir came of age.

As the years went by, the family grew increasingly unhappy about these arrangements, and eventually spent a great deal of time and money over them in the law courts. The family thought that Bodley should have got more than he did for the properties sold to raise the portions—none the less so, perhaps, because the principal purchaser was a Peter Collet.[29] The family also came to believe that Bodley could have been more zealous in extracting money from the Bread Street and Southwark properties, and Bodley came to think of the mortgage on those properties as a sale, which according to the crucial document it was. But in the meantime, the King's Men had no trouble about their lease, and Margaret Brend took some interesting steps.

In 1602 or early 1603, she tried to collect the money due for her father-in-law's bond of £400 which secured a debt of the lord admiral's. Nicholas Brend had tried in vain to collect the money from Richard Drake, so his widow tried the lord admiral himself. She caught him one day as he was at the royal palace of Oatlands, near West Molesey, preparing to follow the queen, who had just left for Hampton Court. He said that he thought the debt had been paid, but he offered her £100 for the bond. Evidently she insisted on more and he refused to pay more, for in 1606, Richard Drake having died three years earlier, her next husband sued the son and heir, Francis Drake, at common law for the full value of the bond.[30]

If Margaret's previous marriage had been curious, her next, as Thomas Brende would have seen it, verged on the bizarre. In about 1605, she took as husband a man named Sir Sigismond Zinzan, who in several ways rivaled the King's Men in theatricality.[31] She brought him a portion of £1,000 "& vpwards," raised out of Brend properties and matched, one supposes, by a suitable jointure.[32] Sir Sigismond settled in as master of the lands at West Molesey and as foster father to the five Brend children, who were successively joined by seven Zinzan children: Henry, Sigismond, Robert, Charles, Margaret, Elizabeth, and Letticia. To this busy household, Dame Margaret Zinzan (as she now was) eventually brought two others, a brother, Henry Strelley, and a sister, Mary Strelley, who had been born in 1592 and hence was not much older than the oldest Brend children.[33]

The Zinzans were of Italian ancestry, or so some of Sir Sigismond's relatives and descendants thought (they occasionally called themselves Zinzano), as did Anthony Wood.[34] Sir Sigismond's father was Sir Robert Zinzan, who was born in 1547 or early 1548, joined the royal service in 1558, became (like Richard Drake) one of the queen's equerries, and was, according to the king of Scotland, a "discreet . . . gentleman." He battened on royal gifts (given "in Consideracione," as was said of one, "of his faithfull obedient longe & good service done vnto yor highnes"), acquired interests at Walton (near West Molesey) in 1589 and at the end of his life lived there, was knighted like hordes of others in the early days of James' reign, and died late in 1607.[35] From the 1540s until at least the 1640s, most of the male Zinzans of whom sufficient record survives were professional horsemen in the royal service. A Hannibal Zenzant, or Zenzano, was farrier to Henry VIII and Edward VI.[36] Sir Robert must have been a

40

leading person in the royal stables. His brothers, Andrew and Alexander, were also royal equerries, as were both his sons alive in 1607, Henry and Sir Sigismond. A William was another in 1599, as, later, was Henry's son Richard. His other son, Joseph, sought to conduct a riding school in the 1640s, and a "Signor Alex: *Zinzano*," who was "his Majesties *Cavalerizzo*," trained a horse for the diarist John Evelyn in 1643. Sir Sigismond's son Robert may have been yet another royal equerry.[37]

All the Zinzans, at least from Sir Robert and his brothers forward, gave themselves also as Alexander, or even merely as Alexander. Because members of the family occasionally had to do with Scotland, one is tempted to think that the family acquired some valued connection in the middle of the sixteenth century with the Scottish house of Alexander out of which the earls of Stirling were to come. And in the 1630s, if not eighty years earlier, the Zinzans did acquire such a connection, when Sir Sigismond's eldest son, Henry, married a woman whose sister was to be countess of Stirling. That connection seems to be the only one, however, and a historian of the Scottish Alexanders convinced himself that the Zinzans used the name because an Alexander Zinzan of the mid-sixteenth century found that his Christian name was easier on English ears than his family one.[38]

Sir Sigismond had known the Brends from about 1598, when he would have been in his late twenties or early thirties, not yet knighted, and the second son of a very well-placed person both at court and in the horse business. He was proceeding in both himself, as was his brother, but along a line rather different from that of the father.[39] They were making themselves expert in the aristocratic sport of running at tilt. Their father had run at tilt, too, but not frequently and not, apparently, expertly. He took part in a famous tilt of 1581 and in the tilt of 1590 in which Sir Henry Lee, the queen's champion, resigned the "honour" and by way of explanation offered the queen the now-celebrated poem that begins, "My golden locks time hath to silver turned."[40] When Sir Sigismond came to marry Margaret Brend in about 1605, he and his brother had established themselves as a team of expert and probably professional runners at tilt, and very likely he had been knighted. He was about as old as the lady's previous husband had been at her marriage to him ten or so years before. She was, of course, a widow who had five children to look after, but she was also lady of the manor of West Molesey.

Tilts were often run at important royal festivities, and from about 1587 they were almost invariably run at the annual celebration of the monarch's accession, Accession Day—November 17 in Elizabeth's time, March 24 in James'. These Accession Day tilts occurred in the tiltyard at Whitehall and were lavish affairs that must have made the goings-on at the gorgeous Globe seem squalid by comparison. In 1621, Prince Charles alone spent £3,352.6s.6d. to participate (of which a John Shakespeare received £22.1s.0d. for providing bits to go with new saddles). He appeared with no fewer than thirty-six men, including six trumpeters, in his colors of white, green, and yellow, and as the year before, perhaps, with a tent of damasks of the same colors for his repose. When the earl of Rutland ventured his first appearance in these tilts in 1613, he paid William Shakespeare 44s. for composing an impresa and Richard Burbage, who was a painter as well as an actor, the same amount for "paynting and making it."[41]

Sir Sigismond and his brother performed in a tilt of 1601, probably that of November 17.[42] In June, 1603, they tilted with the earl of Cumberland at Grafton in an entertainment that he gave for the new king and queen, who had just met there, she traveling south from Edinburgh to join in the coronation and he north from London to meet her. The earl may have defended the new royal house (he had succeeded Sir Henry Lee as royal champion) and the Zinzans challenged it. If so, the earl may have shown more zeal for that house than was required by the game, for as his daughter, Lady Anne Clifford, wrote, he hurt Henry Zinzan "verie dangerouslie." Tilts were run on or about every Accession Day of James's reign except in 1617, 1619 (when the queen had just died), 1623, and 1625 (when the king himself lay dying). The Zinzans took part in at least sixteen of these tilts, including those of 1613, 1620, and 1621, and they very likely took part in the other three as well (1604, 1606, and 1608). Sir Sigismond excelled in 1613. The Zinzans are the only people who tilted so regularly from 1601 onward. Their names appear on all nine surviving complete lists of tilters on Accession Day in James' time, nearly always together at the end, suggesting, no doubt, that they were socially inferior to the other tilters but also, probably, that they were the players and the others the gentlemen.

Beginning at least in 1610, the Zinzans were paid £100 (once specified as £50 each) a few days before March 24 of every tilting year "to furnish themselves wth necessaries against this Tiltinge," as their privy seal of 1613 reads, "for asmuch as that service is vsually a charge to them wch we of or Royall disposicion are pleased to defray," as that of 1622 adds. The money was paid to them as a "free gift" for which they did not have to account. They did not even have to go anywhere to collect it, for the officers of the Exchequer were ordered to deliver it to them. No one else received such payments for tilting. It must be reasonable to guess that they were not only something like professional runners at tilt but organizers and managers of tilts. Indeed, in 1613, Chamberlain in listing the tilters remarked as he came to the last of them that there were six knights, named them, and then added, "besides" the Zinzans. Though Sir Sigismond was also a knight, apparently he was part of the help.

The Zinzans also ran in at least two other tilts, for one if not both of which they were paid, and both have literary associations. The first occurred on June 6, 1610, as part of the three-day celebration of Prince

Henry's becoming Prince of Wales, which may well have to do with the writing of *Winter's Tale*. The second was part of Ben Jonson's entertainment "A Challenge at Tilt" on January 1, 1614, which was for the earl of Somerset's marriage to Frances Howard.[43] They must have taken part in other martial games as well, and Sir Sigismond joined in the Prince's "challenge" of about 1610. If they did have a hand in the management of these affairs, one of their duties would have been to see that no harm befell the great nobles who took part, especially the king. So it is that one finds Henry Zinzan in about 1625, his tilting days finished, seeking royal relief because of "long service and extreme hurts he has received by Prince Henry and His Majesty," not to say the earl of Cumberland, "which now grow grievous unto him." Evidently he was believed, for he was given a patent to tax the transport of calf skins from Boston and Lynn.[44] They had to do, too, with less festive and dangerous ceremonials. In the great funeral procession for Prince Henry in 1612, each led a horse that represented an important part of the crown the prince might have worn, Henry's horse the dukedom of Cornwall and Sir Sigismond's the kingdom of Scotland, "covered with blacke cloath, armed with scuchions of that Kingdom, his cheiffron and plumes."[45] They signed themselves like this:[46]

Sir Sigismond was apparently a theatrical man of both kidney and choler. He disapproved, for example, of a clergyman whom Francis Drake had appointed to a living near West Molesey. Drake, therefore, must withdraw the man and appoint one of Sir Sigismond's choosing. Drake refused, remarking that Sir Sigismond's man "was given to drink and notoriously unfit." Sir Sigismond then wrote "two scandalous and libellous letters, touching Drake in his place of justice of the peace" and "disturbed" Drake's man as he was about to conduct a service on a Sunday. Drake sought help from London, and Robert Cley arrived with a summons. Sir Sigismond, his brother-in-law, Henry Strelley, and probably others beat Cley "so that Cley was driven to run for his life into the Thames, where he continued for a quarter of an hour in the depth of winter." It may have been for this exploit that Sir Sigismond and thirteen others (not, however, Strelley) from West Molesey were fined in the Star Chamber in the autumn of 1609, he the huge sum of £500 and the others from £2 to £30.[47] He also managed to be outlawed for debt three times in 1612 and once more in

1619.[48] That is, he contemptuously refused to appear in court to answer the charges against him.

This ménage persisted at West Molesey, and John (Sir John after September, 1617[49]) Bodley persisted at the Globe until the heir, Matthew Brend, came of age on February 6, 1621, when many changes had to take place. First of all, Matthew sued Bodley in the Court of Wards for the return of the Brend properties in London and Southwark, including the site of the Globe. Bodley argued that the document of October 10, 1601, was an absolute sale, and Matthew argued that however worded the documents might be, his father's transactions as he lay dying amounted to a scheme of trusts, not sales. The case was heard on November 10, 1621, and again on February 8, 1622. Matthew won the case, but the court found that Bodley was still owed £540 for Nicholas Brend's debts and awarded him another £210 for his pains and travel. If, that is, Matthew should pay Bodley £750, Bodley would have to return both properties. Though Bodley lost the case, the court excused him from paying costs because it also found that "hee hath bin a Careful husband in the well orderinge of the said messuages landes & tenements."

Matthew promptly paid the money, and Bodley, joined by Collet, turned over the properties on February 21, 1622.[50] Matthew Brend now owned the Globe. As if to afix a royal seal on this coming of age, the king knighted Matthew at Hampton Court on April 6.[51]

Once Sir Matthew had established his ownership of the Brend properties, the Zinzans had to establish their place in the new scheme of things. Sir Sigismond and his wife concluded, rightly, that she was entitled by dower rights to a third of the income from Nicholas Brend's freehold lands from the time of his death and to a third of all his personal goods. None of the income had been paid before Sir Matthew's coming of age, and since that time he had been paying sums informally. A reckoning was obviously in order, and Sir Matthew urged the Zinzans to negotiate one with him. It was a time of family harmony. Sir Matthew had convinced himself that the Court of Wards had given Bodley more than his due, and the whole family agreed: the Zinzans; Sir Matthew's brother, John; and his sisters, Jane (unmarried), Mercy (married to Robert Meese), and Frances (unmarried). In the winter of 1622–23, they all sued Bodley, arguing generally that Bodley had greatly enriched himself out of the Brend properties and specifically that he had collected too little rent from the properties set aside for the girls' portions and then sold them for far less than they were worth. This muster of Brends was increased by others who testified for them: Sir Matthew's aunt, Mercy Frobisher (now a widow); his mother's sister, Mary Strelley; and his stepfather's servant, William Fellowes.[52]

In this congenial setting, Sir Sigismond negotiated with his stepson, and before the end of the summer of 1623 they arrived at an amicable understanding. Sir Matthew would pay the Zinzans £140 a year for his mother's interest in all the Brend properties. The Zinzans would vacate West Molesey the following spring, taking with them most of the goods and implements but sowing the fields first so that Sir Matthew could reap them. Sir Sigismond would file one or more writs of dower against Sir Matthew, who would not contest it or them nor have to pay costs. Apparently this was a device to determine how much the Zinzans should have for past years and for Dame Margaret Zinzan's interest in her late husband's personal goods. Sir Matthew guaranteed his part of the scheme by giving the Zinzans a bond of £3,000, and he agreed that the Zinzans could repossess West Molesey should he not pay whatever was due to them.

This harmony was ruined by love. Sometime during the summer of 1623, Sir Matthew conceived a passion for Frances Smith, the daughter of Sir William Smith of Theydon Mount in Essex. He wanted desperately to marry her, possibly bewitched by her wit or person or both, but openly by her considerable portion, with which he though he might get his affairs into better order. He had had, no doubt, to borrow most of the £750 paid to Bodley and could have to borrow also whatever might be due Sir Sigismond. Smith was willing to give £2,000 with his daughter, but he and his two sons demanded a very convincing jointure in return, and this jointure would make parts of Sir Matthew's agreement with Sir Sigismond inappropriate and unenforceable.[53] They wanted the lady to have ownership during her lifetime of two of the most important pieces of Sir Matthew's estate, the properties in Bread Street in London and those at West Molesey, and they would suffer neither to be encumbered by the dower rights of Sir Matthew's mother. Sir Matthew, that is, would have to give up these properties if he was to bring the marriage off, and, as he convinced himself, he would also have to give the Smiths a general impression of wealth that he did not really possess.

During late August and the first three weeks of September, 1623, Sir Matthew negotiated with the Smiths, and in the midst of this time he turned to Sir Sigismond, whom he summoned to his lawyer's office in Gray's Inn. In lieu of his mother's dower rights in the properties at West Molesey and in Bread Street, he offered the Zinzans ownership of the properties in Southwark, including the Globe, for her life. He proposed that the Zinzans lease these properties back to him for £100 a year, and, when the rents above that sum reached a total of £1,000, that he give the Zinzans two-thirds of this total and keep a third himself. In the meantime, they would strive to increase the rents. He suggested that the rest of their previous agreement remain unchanged: the Zinzans would leave West Molesey in the spring and Sir Sigismond would file the writ or writs of dower. He wanted to give the Smiths the impression that the goods at West Molesey were his, but Sir Sigismund could quietly take what he liked when he left. Sir Matthew also wanted to give the impression that he and

Sir Sigismond would share the money yielded by the writs of dower, but Sir Sigismond would have it all.

Sir Matthew protested that the Zinzans would lose nothing by this new scheme, but Sir Sigismond saw his £140 a year shrinking to £100 and his wife's claim on the other major properties disappearing together with their right to repossess West Molesey should Sir Matthew not pay. So Sir Sigismond refused to agree and "went forth of the said Chamber downe the stayres." Sir Matthew "followed him into the Gallery," where he "much vrged and importuned." If Sir Sigismond did not agree, the marriage would not take place, and Sir Matthew "should bee vndone thereby and [he] did then wth teares and deepe oathes and imprecacions faythfully vowe and affirme" that Sir Sigismond would lose nothing by agreeing. Evidently, Sir Matthew promised that the Zinzans would get their £140 a year, though for the sake of impressing the Smiths the documents would mention only £100. Sir Sigismond was moved to agree, but only after extracting the promise of a further bond of £6,000 payable to his son, Henry, to guarantee payment of the first bond of £3,000 should Sir Matthew's performance fall short of the former agreement.

So Sir Matthew and his lawyer set about drawing up the documents, which amounted to a marriage contract, and they suggested that Sir Sigismond seek legal counsel for his part of the transaction from Simon Wiseman, who was to prove a good deal cleverer than they thought he was. All was ready on September 22. The Zinzans joined Sir Matthew in conveying the properties at West Molesey and in Bread Street to Frances Smith's trustees, and Sir Matthew conveyed those in Southwark to his mother for her life. Both conveyances were by foot of fine, a process that required three law terms. The properties would formally change hands, that is, in Easter term, 1624. A contract was drawn providing for the Zinzans' leasing the properties in Southwark back to Sir Matthew and for the Zinzans' withdrawal from West Molesey.

Late in the winter of 1623–24, as the Zinzans prepared to leave West Molesey, Sir Matthew gained his Frances and her portion at an altar, but not before the Smiths had winkled one further concession out of him. They presuaded him that he should increase the lady's jointure by adding the Globe to it, in return for which they would add £100 (less than half its worth) to her portion. Evidently there was no time to draw up a document before the wedding, so the Smiths settled for the promise, and the lady's glad husband drew one up later, on March 12, 1624, separating the Globe and its appurtenances at last from the other properties in Southwark and conveying it to her for her life—after, of course, the death of Dame Margaret Zinzan.[54] If Sir Matthew's life at this critical moment could be complicated by the demands of in-laws, so could Sir Sigismond's, and in a much more theatrical, and dire, way.

On Sunday evening, March 14, after Sir Sigismond had left for London—probably to see about the tilt to be performed in ten days (his and his brother's privy seal for their stipend that year is dated March 16)—his teenage daughter, Margaret, covertly took a teenage husband in the house at West Molesey. The groom was William Shelley, son and heir of Sir John and Lady Jane Shelley of Michelmore in Sussex, a family of great pretension and extensive Catholic connections.[55] Lady Shelley called Sir Sigismond's daughter "cousin Megg," and the Zinzans had just kept Christmas with the Shelleys at a house of theirs in Kew. Young Shelley was nineteen years old, the bride younger. In two years he would be master, he thought, of £1,000 a year, at least sixteen times what Meg might have been mistress of if Sir Sigismond could indeed have given her £650, as the locals thought. Both knew that the Shelleys energetically disapproved of the match and that Sir Sigismond would not have allowed it. But William had been a soldier in love's army for some time—he and a friend, for example, "had binne . . . in some Taverne . . . drinking of ye said Mris Margaretts health on there knees & . . . they did striue & contend together wch of them two did best loue her," and he had vowed to friends that "he would marry wth her, although he went A begging wth her." So the parish priest, Israel Ridley, was summoned with his wife, Alice, for a witness to the upstairs room, called the chapel chamber, and, doubtless remembering her own daring and not unsuccessful exploit with marriage thirty years before, Lady Zinzan sent up a servant, John Barton, to give the bride away. Wisely, she did not go herself. The ceremony over, the bride and groom called some friends who happened to be in the house (including Henry Strelley) to the same chapel chamber, where a small banquet was served. Eventually bride and groom went to bed, also in the chapel chamber, and, "in naked Bedd as man & wife," called their friends back to show that they intended to consummate their marriage. The next morning the groom, having sworn everyone to secrecy, took horse and rode away and, as it turned out, lived with his bride no more, for William Shelley proved no Nicholas Brend. Lady Zinzan presently found that the marriage had been consummated "to the full, for there were," she said, "such manifest toakens thereof in theire sheets that shee was faine to hide them from her seruants."[56]

Perhaps Sir Sigismond found out about all this at once. Certainly he knew in June or so, when he declared that he would tell the Shelleys, and the groom pleaded with him for a chance to do so himself. Marriage or no marriage, however, Sir Sigismond had to devote himself to carrying out his agreement with Sir Matthew Brend. The Zinzans left West Molesey two weeks after the marriage, at the end of March, 1624, and moved temporarily into a house in Covent Garden, near Drury Lane, where they stayed until the end of May, when they moved into permanent quarters in Chiswick.[57] Sir Sigismond filed one writ of dower against his stepson, who, according to the plan, acquiesced in it.

Then Sir Sigismond went abroad, leaving his lawyer, Wiseman, to look after the agreement with Sir Matthew Brend. He was taking up a new career at a likely time, for, as events were to prove, in 1624 he and his brother Henry had run at tilt on Accession Day for the last time. A year later the king would be mortally ill, so that there could be no tilt, and thereafter the new king would banish tilting from Accession Day, apparently to reduce expenses at court. The brothers Zinzan had come, therefore, to the end of their careers as professional runners at tilt. Perhaps sensing that tilting was in decline, perhaps restless after removing from the manorial premises at West Molesey, perhaps in need of money, Sir Sigismond undertook to run at real enemies, as did two others from the house at West Molesey, his son Sigismond and Henry Strelley. The English government had agreed early in June to raise and maintain four regiments of English foot soldiers to help the Dutch. Sir Sigismond acquired the command of a company among them, as captain at £15 a month in the regiment of the earl of Essex. The troops left for the Low Countries in July and August, Sir Sigismond among the first; he landed at Delft on July 13. His son went to the Palatinate as a lieutenant sometime during 1624, and Strelley, during the winter of 1624–25, joined the ill-starred English army that Count Mansfeld tried to lead to Germany.[58]

At Midsummer Day and Michaelmas, Sir Matthew paid first and second quarterly installments of the rent for the properties in Southwark, but only £25 each time, as though the rent were £100 a year rather than £140. Wiseman protested, and, it seems, more money was forthcoming. Moreover, Wiseman got £780 out of the writ of dower, which was much more than Sir Matthew had expected to pay, and to Brend's great annoyance he soon had a judgment issued in Sir Sigismond's name for that amount.

Sir Sigismond was back in England probably late in the autumn, when, in addition to reporting these triumphs to him, Wiseman explained some other aspects of the case. Sir Sigismond had not yet executed the lease for the properties in Southwark, nor had Sir Matthew executed the bond for £6,000. Furthermore, Sir Sigismond's contract with Sir Matthew, closely read, allowed but did not require the lease. Sir Sigismond, that is, owned those properties if he chose, as he decided he did. So with Wiseman's help, no doubt, he got the undersheriff of Surrey to put him in possession of them, including the Globe, and to instruct the tenants to pay no more rents to Sir Matthew. Enter, late in the autumn of 1624, Sir Sigismond Zinzan as owner of the Globe in the interest of his wife. And enter Sir Matthew Brend pleading in the courts to "secure his life from Sir Sigismond Zinzan . . . who resisteth ordinary justice."[59]

Presumably Sir Sigismond meant to keep the Southwark properties only until he could realize £780 from the rents and his stepson guaranteed to pay £140 annually. Though the rents had probably increased lately, they could hardly have amounted to more than £225 a year (which in his successful lawsuit against Bodley Sir Matthew had insisted they were really worth), and they probably amounted to less (Bodley insisted upon £90).[60] Hence Sir Sigismond might well have had to hang on to the properties for ten or fifteen years to get £780 out of them in addition to £140 a year. In December of 1624, perhaps on the third, his stepson applied to the Court of Chancery for relief, hoping mainly that the court might recalculate the debt to the Zinzans and also require them to lease the Southwark properties to him. He argued that the £750 he had paid Bodley should be taken into account (since the money was for his father's debts, and his mother and later Sir Sigismond were his father's executors), as should all the rents which the Zinzans had collected through the years at West Molesey and the various items which they, he said, had sold or taken away from the place.

Sir Sigismond answered on February 4, 1625. He had a good case. He protested that his wife could not be expected to pay her previous husband's debts because he had given her neither jointure nor enough money otherwise, and that she and he should not have to account for the rents at West Molesey because the courts had given her control of the properties there in her own right and not in trust for her son. He added that the contract of September, 1623, allowed him to lease the Southwark properties to Sir Matthew but did not require him to do so. Sir Sigismond must have thought that a good case deserved repetition, for ten days later he countersued in Chancery, raising many of the same matters. This repetition should have been in vain, however, for as Sir Matthew soon pointed out, his stepfather had not removed the four judgments against him for which he had been outlawed. Outlaws could defend themselves in the courts, but they could not seek relief in them. Because of the strength of his stepfather's case, perhaps, Sir Matthew did not take his lawsuit beyond bill and answer. Sir Sigismond, therefore, probably continued in control of the Globe and other properties in Southwark, and eventually he and Sir Matthew probably negotiated toward a new bargain providing for a cash settlement of somewhat less than £780 and a new guarantee of £140 a year.

Sir Sigismond expected to return to his command in the Low Countries or some other command during the spring of 1625, but in mid-February Prince Charles ordered him to remain in England "for our service." That service kept him in England for eighteen and a half months, until the end of September, 1626. He was probably wanted for a tilt on Accession Day in March and, when that was canceled because of the king's illness and death, for the elaborate ceremonials that should have followed— the funeral on May 5, the coronation on February 2, 1626, the queen's coronation (eventually given up), and a great procession through the City (planned for the summer of 1626 and also given up).

The royal order came at a good time. It gave Sir Sigismond a chance to negotiate personally with his stepson and, what was more urgent, personally to defend his daughter. For having learned of their son's marriage with Margaret Zinzan, the Shelleys did not propose to end the matter as Thomas Brende had done with Nicholas, by removing him as executor of their wills. They strove mightily to get the ecclesiastical authorities to annul the marriage, and Sir Sigismond responded with equal energy. In March, 1625, Archbishop Abbott recommended to one of the secretaries of state that the Shelleys and Zinzans take their quarrel to the Star Chamber, because "what one affirms the other denies, and without swearing of witnesses, the truth cannot be found." There followed for thirty-two months a voluminous case in that court in which the Shelleys argued that the Zinzans had conspired against their son, and the Zinzans argued that young Shelley had loved the girl for some time and married her more than willingly. Sir Sigismond and his daughter had the help of many people from the house at West Molesey who testified for him: his children, Henry and Elizabeth; his stepson, John Brend; his in-laws, Henry and Mary Strelley; and various servants and visitors. The case was heard on November 23, 1627. The Star Chamber dismissed the charges of conspiracy against the Zinzans and refused to interfere with the marriage, but it came down very heavily on those who were present when the marriage took place. The priest was fined £50, his wife £3.6s.8d., and the servant who gave the bride away £10. Moreover, it awarded the Shelleys costs of £120 against the three of them. The servant managed to pay the fine, but the costs were beyond him, so the Shelleys sent him to jail and kept him there for several months. As for their son, he seems to have boasted to some of his friends that if his mother were dead all the world would not keep him from living with Margaret Zinzan, and to others that "if I cann putt of this gentlewoman," meaning Margaret Zinzan, he could now have a wife who had £1,000 a year in lands and £10,000 in ready money.[61]

While Sir Sigismond was thus engaged with the Shelleys in Star Chamber, his stepson, Sir Matthew Brend, was busy in Chancery, foolishly pursuing Sir John Bodley and occasionally protecting himself against his brother, John Brend, who had sued him and Bodley in December, 1624, for a larger share of Nicholas Brend's estate. Still convinced that the Court of Wards had been much too generous to Bodley, Sir Matthew pressed on with the family lawsuit of 1623 and launched at least one other. He was trying, in effect, to get Chancery to recalculate how much was due to Bodley for the return of the properties in Bread Street and Southwark, though he could not clearly say so in his argumentation because that matter had already been decided, the money paid, and property returned. He drove the case on in the names of all the plaintiffs long after at least two of them, Sir Sigismond and John Brend, could have had much interest in helping him, and he reached a hearing on June 26, 1626. He lost ignominiously, for his case was so tortuously drawn that the court could not see how it legally affected him. The court threw it out and awarded Bodley £10 in costs, which Sir Matthew argued about until the end of January,

1627.[62] His brother had better luck. Though Sir Matthew for a time thought the case aimed at him and a connivance of Bodley's "for vexacion & for revenge & malice," it proved in the end to be aimed only at Bodley, and John Brend actually got, on June 2, 1627, a recalculation of some of Bodley's dealings with Nicholas Brend's property.[63]

At the end of September, 1626, King Charles, as he now was, no longer needed Sir Sigismond's services in England. Presumably he returned to his post on the Continent (the regiments were now aiding the Danes), and presumably he was back in England during the following winter. He may well have arrived at an agreement then with his stepson about Lady Zinzan's dower rights, for Sir Matthew borrowed some £600 from a linen-draper early in December.[64] Sir Sigismond would then have executed the lease of the Globe and other properties in Southwark to Sir Matthew, thereby, in effect, returning them to him. Sir Sigismond would have owned the Globe for about two years, living most of the time at Chiswick while attending on royal commands about festivities and ceremonials and negotiating his wife's dower rights with her son, but probably devoting most of his energies to his daughter's defense in the Star Chamber. His interest in the Globe ceased altogether about six months later when, some-time before June 20, 1627, his wife, Dame Margaret Zinzan, died.[65] The new owner then was Dame Frances Brend, Sir Matthew's wife, and she remained owner until the Globe was no more. That lady was, it seems, as effective at bargaining with Sir Matthew as her father and brothers had been, for in June, 1633, he increased her jointure yet again by giving her the properties it comprised, including the Globe, not merely for her life-time, but forever.[66]

From mid-1627 on, Sir Sigismond Zinzan fell increasingly into difficult times and eventually into what he saw as poverty and obscurity. He was cut off from Brend money and from tilting regularly in glittering surroundings. Somehow he had lost his pay as a royal equerry, though he still had the title. He had three daughters who needed portions and one who also needed an expensive legal defense. Presently he ceased campaign-ing in the Low countries, perhaps finding it at £15 a month no pathway to riches. In 1628, probably, he pleaded with his old tilting companion, the king, to pay him for the eighteen and a half months in 1625 and 1626 when, at the royal command, he had stayed in England and earned no pay in the Low Countries. After an official inquiry in February, 1629, estab-lished that he had earned £227.10s.0d., the king was pleased (as the privy seal read) in July, 1630, to allow him at his humble suit £277.[67] The ink must have been scarcely dry on that document when Sir Sigismond pleaded again for money. This time the king granted him a pension of £100 a year to begin at Christmas, 1631, and to run not for life but during the royal pleasure. The pension, as this privy seal read, was "for the better accomodacion of the prsent Accions" of Sir Sigismond and for "good and faithfull service heretofore done vnto or late Deare and Royall father . . . and since vnto vs." This generosity, however, was not enough, either, and Sir Sigismond soon began assigning portions of the payments to merchants to whom he owed money.[68]

He returned to the king, asking now that the pay and allowances for his equerryship be restored. He wrote a florid and humbling petition. Because of the loss of his pay and allowances, he began,

> I was forced to such importunitie as had almost brought me to be insensible of All modestie and Ciuillitie, and had not yor sweete and Princelye nature pardoned manie great infirmities that want and dispayre brought vpon me, I might haue lost my selfe in a iust neglect deseruedly to haue ben cast vpon me in all my hopes presented in dayly peticions to yor Matie. But such was yor Princely goodnes and bounty towards me (when my great wants were truly diserned and knowne to yor Matie) as I am dayly releiued by a yearely guift of 100li, or otherwise I had either rotted in Prison, or perrished with want.

Alas, he went on, that gift was being collected by others "to pay ould and Clamorous debts," so that he still felt "such wants as fewe can beare, with that patience I indure them." His pay and allowances would enable him "to appeare amongst Horsemen,"

> whereas nowe I spend my time in a retyred way not able . . . scarce to walke abroad for debt much lesse to ride[,] a misery to great to accompany ould age that is otherwise pinched with greater wants then Horses. But patience and dayly hopes of yor Mats greater Compassion towards me sweeten my afflictions, and bringe me to peticion this grace and favor towards me presented with my prayers to the rewarder of all good Deedes to recompence yor Princely bounty towards me.

Some twenty years later Sir Sigismond implied that the princely bounty was awakened yet again.[69]

Meanwhile, the Star Chamber had by no means ended the question of Margaret Zinzan's marriage. The Shelleys proceeded vigorously in the Ecclesiastical Court to get it annulled, arguing mainly that their son had been drunk at the time. Sir Sigismond presented much convincing evidence that he had not, including a remark by the priest that young Shelley did not "stammer, stumble, or lispe in speech more then he usuall[y] doth."[70] But eventually the Shelleys were successful, and Sir Sigismond appealed to the Judges Delegates. He was heard by six judges presided over by the archbishop of Canterbury, Laud. The judges divided three to three, and Laud resolved the question by siding with the Shelleys but allowing Sir Sigismond his full expenses as costs. When Sir Sigismond presented a claim for £2,000, however, Laud decided that £200 should suffice. So it was that William Shelley married again in 1636, the bride this time one of the

French ladies of the queen's privy chamber, Christienne Marie de Luz de Vantelet, as she gave herself when she was denizened on February 23, perhaps to facilitate the marriage. Whatever other financial inducements to marriage she may have had, she had a royal pension of £150 a year, which hereafter she collected as Lady Christiana Shelley, the groom having been knighted on March 28, perhaps also to facilitate the marriage.[71] She bore the Shelleys an heir, Charles, and less than four years after the marriage both she and her husband had died, he before November 22, 1639, and she in Paris, describing herself as a Catholic, in January, 1640.[72]

Far from rendering Margaret Zinzan's case ancient history, these deaths caused new interest in it, even though she, too, had married (a Robert Thomas of Kingston on Thames), for now the Shelley estates were directly at stake. If Sir Sigismond could establish that his daughter was legally young Shelley's widow, he and she might come off very well. So he took the matter to the House of Lords in March, 1641, but apparently without success, the Lords having more urgent business before them, like Strafford's attainder and the Army Plot.[73]

Though he must have been in his seventies when the English Revolution began in earnest in the summer of 1642, Sir Sigismond Zinzan rushed to the colors—of his former chief, the earl of Essex, and the Parliament rather than of that king upon whose sweet and princely nature he had called a few years before. He joined the cavalry regiment of Arthur Goodwin, Hampden's friend, late in July as sergeant-major. He was also given the command of a troop as captain a month later, on August 27, and remained with the regiment in both capacities until January 8 and as captain until March 24, 1643, presumably taking part with the regiment (which was part of Essex's army) in engagements at Daventry, Marlborough, Wantage, and Brill. This campaigning gave him the chance to appear among horsemen again, and it was considerably better paid than that in the Low Countries had been. When he was both sergeant-major and captain, his net pay was £8.8s.0d. a week. It would have been £3.10s.0d. more a week had he supplied his own horse, as captains were supposed to do. Instead, he paid the deduction and rode a government horse.

Both Sir Sigismond and his brother, Henry, grew to be very old men, living, as they thought, on the edge of starvation. Sir Sigismond pleaded with Cromwell for relief in August, 1654. He wrote of "being fill'd with many infirmities and weaknes of old age" and of being "reduced to extremity of poverty and want, yea to such necessity that he is ashamed to expresse it, and without speedy supply must inevitably perish." He wrote that his pension was no longer paid. In his service under Essex, he said, he had used £4,000 of his own money to pay his troop, and the arrears of his salary came to £3,000. Whatever the truth of the rest of his plea, this last was the cry of a foolish, fond old man fourscore and upwards. Cromwell's men had the records searched and found that Sir Sigismond had actually been overpaid for his soldiering by £306.11s.0d. Yet they, too, like the king before them, decided to relieve him. They gave him a pension of 20s. a week beginning May 10, 1655, little more than half his royal one, but they saw to it that it was paid.[74] Henry Zinzan made a similar plea. Because he "hath been allwayes faithfull to the Parlamt and yor Highness," that is, Cromwell, "and is a very aged man, being 92 yeares of age, and reduced to a very great want and misery, being ready to perish," he asked for "such allowance as may preserve him from starving, during the short remaynder of his dayes (wch cannot be many)." He, too, got 20s. a week, beginning February 22, 1656.[75]

Little more than a year after the Restoration, on July 16, 1661, the restored king restored Sir Sigismond's pension of £100 a year because of "his long service and Great Age." It was to recommence at Christmas, 1660—Sir Sigismond, that is, was to have a half year of it at once—and it was now for life rather than the royal pleasure. But it was too late. He died about then, probably over ninety years old, and it was his daughter, Letticia, his administratrix, who collected his £50.[76]

It is worth noting that both Puritans and Royalists were willing to help Sir Sigismond Zinzan, and that Royalists were the more generous, though they could easily have despised him as a traitor to their cause. Neither could have thought it remarkable that he had for a time owned the Globe or soldiered in the Low Countries and England. But perhaps neither could have thought it right that the more notable of the two best equestrian sportsmen of a vanished age in England should end his days in misery.

Despite the broils among the owners, the King's Men had infinitely less trouble about their lease in Southwark than their predecessors had had about the one in Shoreditch. One reason must have been that the Brends, unlike Giles Allen, had unchallenged title to the land. Other, probably more important, reasons must have been that the Brends and other owners of the land were single-mindedly interested in the rents and not, like Allen, in converting the playhouse to more decent uses, and that the King's Men could afford to pay their rent and even (though not, as we shall see, without a fight) to see it increased. In short, the King's Men were a more secure financial enterprise than the Lord Chamberlain's Men had been, and they had more reasonable landlords.

We have been told that the King's Men had one legal quarrel with the Brends, but we have known little about it and have been reluctant to accept that little. On April 30 and May 1, 1914, C. W. Wallace published an article in the *Times* (pp. 9-10; 4) in which he declared that he had found many new documents concerning the Globe. He mentioned some of their contents but without giving citations. He promised one day to publish the documents properly but did not keep the promise. Braines eventually identified and used nearly all the documents in his book about the Globe, but one eluded him. It specifies, according to Wallace, that in 1609 John Bodley claimed and got £20 from the King's Men to recognize the lease that Nicholas Brend had given them; that on October 26, 1613, after the Globe had burned down, the King's Men acquired a new lease from Bodley extending the old one for six years, until Christmas, 1635; that on February 14, 1614, Cuthbert and Richard Burbage and John Hemings traveled to West Molesey and persuaded the fourteen-year-old Matthew, his mother, and his uncle to sign a document extending the old lease to 1644; and that in 1615 the King's Men paid Bodley £2 for permission to build a house adjoining the Globe. Then, according to Wallace, in about 1633 Sir Matthew Brend (as he now was) refused to honor the extension to 1644. He argued that he had signed the document as a minor, hence that it was not valid, and he tried to find a new tenant willing, presumably, to pay more rent. The King's Men sued him in what Wallace called a "long and lively sequel." Chambers took Wallace's word for these things, and with them partly in mind he guessed at how much the King's Men paid as rent during the several stages through which their lease went (2: 426–27). But Bentley ignored Wallace's account (6: 178 ff.).

That there was such a lawsuit has been known for a century because there are three cryptic allusions to it in the so-called sharers papers of late spring and summer, 1635. These allusions place the lawsuit in the Court of Requests. Wallace had evidently found a bill, perhaps with other documents attached, which lies among the thirty thousand and more such filed in that court during the reign of Charles I and now kept in some 347 unindexed bundles. I have not found Wallace's bill, but I have found ancillary documents that tell us how the lawsuit proceeded, how it concluded, and what, at last, the rent really was, for Chambers' guess was quite wrong.

The three principal shareholders in the Globe at the time, Cuthbert Burbage, Richard Robinson, and William Hemings, filed the bill against Brend late in 1633, and the case continued one way or another until late 1637. The shareholders wanted their lease extended for nine years and were willing to pay more rent. Brend refused to negotiate with them for a time but in November, 1634, agreed in court to extend the lease for nine years in return for a greatly improved rent. Then he dealt with the shareholders as he had done with Bodley in the 1620s. He decided that he ought to have done better. Rather than extend the lease as he had agreed, he haggled with the shareholders for two years and eventually took the matter back to the court. There Brend ended as he had done with Bodley, in defeat.[77]

The original rent for the Globe property was £14.10s.0d. a year for the period of the lease, until Christmas, 1629. Glancing at both Wallace's remarks and the sharers' papers, Chambers guessed that Bodley raised the rent to £20 when in 1613 he extended the lease to Christmas, 1635 (payable, presumably, from 1629, but Chambers did not say) and that the court raised it to £55 when extending the lease to 1644. The new documents, however, say several times that the rent remained £14.10s.0d. a year until Christmas, 1635, and that the rent the court ordered the King's Men to pay during the final extension was £40 a year. The new documents also say several times that the final extension was for nine years from the end of the former extension, hence, until Christmas, 1644. So those guesses are also wrong in which Chambers, T. W. Baldwin, and others shortened the extension so that Brend could pull the Globe down on April 15, 1644, as the dubious document mentioned earlier in this essay has him doing. If Brend did indeed pull it down then, he had got possession not because the lease had run out but because the King's Men had given it up and ceased paying rent.

A person to be noted, finally, in the history of the Globe is George Archer, a porter who was born in 1562 or 1563. He was Sir Matthew Brend's rent-gatherer in Southwark, had probably been Bodley's before that, and, since he was in the house in St. Peter's Hill when Nicholas Brend died there in 1601, may have been his as well. He lived in one of the Brend houses in Maid Lane from at least 1602, perhaps the one "conteyning three severall roomes with a yard" which he occupied there on a lease from Sir Matthew in January, 1636.[78] He surely collected rents at the Globe, possibly for much of its history. The acquittances the Burbages and their associates received, therefore, perhaps bundles of them, bore this signature:

Appendix: Elizabethan and Jacobean Tilts

E. K. Chambers has a list of Accession Day tilts in Elizabethan and Jacobean times in his "Court Calendar," in *The Elizabethan Stage* (Oxford, 1923),4: 102–30 (he omits that of 1611), and Bentley carried the list on in vol. 7: 36, 39, 43, 44; 4: 655 (he omits those of 1618 and 1624 and gets the year of another wrong). For the years in which there were no such tilts, see *The Letters of John Chamberlain,* ed. N. E. McClure (Philadelphia, 1939), 2: 67, 225, 487, and John Nichols, *The Progresses . . . of King James the First* (London, 1828), 3: 259–60; 4: 838, 1028–29. The Zinzans received their payments directly out of the Exchequer from 1610 onward. Before that they could have received payments out of one of the branches of the royal household, whose payments are less well recorded than those of the Exchequer. I list below the sources that seem the most useful for their participation in and payment for each tilt. In most cases there are other sources, especially for payments.

1601—Historical Manuscripts Commission (H.M.C.), *Salisbury*, 11: 540 (a list of tilters of 1601 including "Lord North," who did not achieve that title until Aug. 10, 1601).

1603 (Cumberland)—Nichols, *Progresses*, 1: 189.

1605—H.M.C., *Salisbury*, 17: 107.

1607—Nichols, *Progresses*, 4: 1076.

1609—Thomas Birch, *The Court and Times of James the First* (London, 1848), 1: 92. Nichols (*Progresses*, 2: 287) mistakenly gives the year as 1610. "Sir Richard Preston" appears on the list but had become Lord Dingwall by Accession Day, 1610.

1610—E.403/2561/f.279^v.

1610 (Prince Henry)—Nichols, *Progresses*, 2: 361; H.M.C., *Downshire*, 2: 315–17.

1610[?] (Prince's "Challenge")—B.M., Cotton Vesp. XIV, L–W, f.285.

1611—E.403/2561/f.297.

1612—S.O.3/5/Mar. 1612.

1613—*Chamberlain*, 1: 440; E.403/2601/f.103^v.

1614 (Somerset)—Nichols, *Progresses*, 2: 729; S.O.3/5/Dec. 1613 [1st item].

1614—E.403/2602/f.16.

1615—*Chamberlain*, 1: 590; Nichols, *Progresses*, 3: 76; S.O.3/6/Mar. 1615.

1616—Nichols, *Progresses*, 3: 135; E.403/2602/f.72^v.

1618—*Chamberlain*, 2: 152; S.O.3/6/Mar. 1618.

1620—*Chamberlain*, 2: 298; E.403/2602/f.170^v.

1621—S.O.3/7/Mar. 1621.

1622- –Nichols, *Progresses*, 4: 754; E.403/2562/f.55^v (postponed to May 18).

1624—E.403/2562/f.112.

Charles Rogers, *Memorials of the Earl of Stirling and of the House of Alexander* (Edinburgh, 1877), 2: 175, cited "the Warrant Book of the Exchequer," 2: 141, as recording that the Zinzans were paid £100 for the Accession Day tilt of 1608, but I cannot identify the book nor find any other indication that they received such a payment out of the Exchequer in 1608. Nichols (*Progresses*, 2: 287n.; 3: 78n.) reported that the Zinzans received additional payments of £1,000 in 1614 and 1615, apparently out of the Exchequer, but I cannot verify these payments in the records of the Exchequer, either.

III. *The Value and Feasibility of Reconstruction*

C. WALTER HODGES

*I*t may be useful to begin this paper by making clear what we are to understand by a *reconstruction*. The word may be used in many senses. I have recently read an article by a journalist well known for her coverage of feminist affairs, writing about the options open to women whom she called "reconstructed housewives." A policeman, on the other hand, may think of reconstruction as the mock re-creation of a crime, an attempt to discover its method as a means of exposing the criminal. Thus, in a way, it verges upon drama. Did not Hamlet use just such a reconstruction in his play of the Mouse-trap, wherein he caught the conscience of a king? We come, therefore, to the point where we must ask ourselves whether a reconstruction is a work of science or of art, what proportions of art may be allowed to it, or what rigors of science ought to be maintained. Perhaps we ought also to ask, what is the morality of it? What, in that light, is the real relation of a reconstruction to its original?

Let me take an example. Noah's ark, as the Bible tells us, was constructed of gopher wood. I do not know how long gopher wood survived—nor, now, does anyone, for all supplies of that material ran out long ago—but if the ancient ark had been religiously preserved and venerated for all time by some sect (called, let us say, the Diluvians, or the Forty-Day Delugists), and if, as the original gopher pieces decayed, and, no more being available, they were replaced by some other wood—cedar of Lebanon perhaps, or common oak—it would not have been very long, measured by biblical time, before the entire ark would have been a replacement in another material. Add to that the religious devotion of the Diluvian sect, which in the course of time covered the ark with beaten gold and enclosed it in a huge temple, the gates of which were opened to the faithful once a year on Rainbow Day, and one might well ask in the end what sort of relation this cult object could be supposed to have to the original. Devotees of another sect, the possessors of, say, the original golden calf, a very beautiful object in its own right, a museum piece, might well deride

58

the venerable ark as a sham; and certainly there would be a strong body of puritanical opinion which held that it was a waste of money and effort to go on mending and rebuilding the old thing, which was no longer at all useful for keeping animals in and was by this time a very doubtful floater. It was, they would say, an object of sentimental interest only.

We might well agree to the attribution of sentiment. We would also surely agree to the interest. But I for one would take exception to the final "only." I will be bold enough here to put in a strong claim for sentiment as having a very powerful and legitimate influence in making decisions about building, and especially about *re*building. Let me leave this fairy-story about the ark, and give you a real example of more recent date.

On July 14, 1902, at eight minutes to ten in the morning, a building that for over four hundred years had been one of the most famous landmarks of any city in the world, none other than the great campanile in the Piazza di San Marco, in Venice, suddenly gave up the ghost and collapsed in a heap on the ground. Fortunately, no one was hurt, for there had been a little warning; enough, in fact, to give an enterprising photographer time to set up his camera and wait for the event, of which, when it came, he took a truly remarkable picture. In the days following, after the dust had settled, the heap of beautiful Venetian-pink rubble became a tourist attraction in its own right.

What was then to be done? Could there be any question? In so famous a city, and with such a famous landmark, there was surely no alternative; the great campanile must be rebuilt as quickly as possible. It had long ago been surveyed. It was fully documented. Even the money would not be hard to find. So what problem could there be? None, surely . . . but there was. A strong body of intelligent and articulate opinion argued that the piazza had never for centuries looked so well as it did now, without that great, blundering campanile that had been so much too big for its site and had stood so much too long in the way of the view of San Marco and the Doge's Palace.

It was, as it happens, a very good argument. The piazza did indeed look very fine without the campanile. The campanile was indeed too large. But, true as that might be, how could such a cool esthetic judgment possibly prevail? Venice, in the historic record, is, visually, above all the city of Canaletto and Guardi. It has to be granted that these two painters themselves found the oversized campanile an embarrassment in their compositions, and they tended either to avoid it or to scale it down just a little, to make it fit. Nevertheless, this great building, which had towered over Casanova, Goldoni, Byron and Napoleon, Wagner and Browning, and Ruskin and Henry James, had become so much a part of Venice that it could not possibly be allowed to disappear. To abolish it would be like abolishing navels from stomachs: whether they are nice or not is not a proper question to ask. Therefore, the campanile was soon rebuilt, so exactly as it had been before that hardly a soul could tell the difference; and how many visitors to Venice who are seeing it today, even at this very moment, realize that what they are looking at is actually a reconstruction? Sentiment demanded a reconstruction, and sentiment prevailed, I think, on the whole, rightly.

Or, while we are about it, take another case—another famous campanile. What about the Leaning Tower of Pisa? I hasten to reassure you that the leaning tower of today is not a reconstruction, but the original. It was built true and upright in 1174, but fairly soon thereafter it began to lean, and it has been leaning more and more, little by little, throughout all its long life. It is now seventeen feet out of the perpendicular. Much work has been done, and more is planned, to prevent it from collapsing; nevertheless, it may still eventually do so. Now suppose the tower does collapse, and suppose, as well might happen, it were then decided to rebuild it stone by stone; and suppose you were in charge of the reconstruction. What would you do? Would you not seize with both hands this glorious opportunity to straighten the thing up at long last? It really would look much better in its setting, and in relation to the other buildings of its group, if it were standing upright. That was, after all, the original intention.

Well, you might think so and you might even say so, but in the end would you be allowed to do so? I doubt it. Once again I think arguments of sentiment, of all the emotion gathered during centuries of wonder and admiration, would prevail over arguments of ordinary sense. To take one question only, what would you do about Galileo? Who does not know the story of Galileo standing at the top of the Leaning Tower of Pisa, dropping stones of different weights from the leaning edge, to prove that they would all fall at an equal speed? Would you, could you, so easily banish the ghost of Galileo? You could not. The tower is more than a piece of architecture; it is also a monument in the history of elementary physics. Those beautifully mounting galleries of Romanesque arcading are all very fine in their architectural way, but at Pisa, in the end, it is the leaning that counts.

I have had a purpose in these observations, which are really not so whimsical as they many seem. I have been trying to demonstrate a balance of two values, of sentiment and authenticity, in the reconstruction or preservation of ancient buildings, and to suggest that sentiment plays a stronger part than we may imagine. By sentiment I mean a powerful complex of associative historical emotions, not simply sentimentality. Buildings are more strongly infused with such emotions than most other objects human beings make, perhaps because they are, in a sense, shared by everyone. They are our historical guarantees, our tangible pedigree. Henry Ford is on record as having said—on his oath, too, in a witness-box, in his libel action against the *Chicago Tribune* in 1919—that history is bunk. Well, he said it, but (witness-box or no) did he really believe it? If so, he had a very strange way of showing it, for it was one of his greatest personal pleasures to collect old American buildings, especially those with strong historical associations, and have them faithfully re-erected for posterity in a park of their own, in Greenfield Village, just nine miles from downtown Detroit. It was Ford's personal tribute to the history he said was bunk, and he was rightly proud of it.

So far so good. We are agreed that nobody really wishes historic buildings to disappear. Wherever possible, when they are damaged or destroyed, we try to repair or reconstruct them. But this assumes either that they are the original buildings or that we know exactly what they were like. Suppose we do not know, or are not sure? That, especially in the case of buildings of particular significance, does not seem to diminish our desire to restore them, but rather the contrary.

Take, for example, the famous tomb of King Mausolus of Caria, the original Mausoleum, built in the fourth century B.C. at Halicarnassus, on the southwestern coast of what is now Turkey. In ancient times the Mausoleum was counted one of the Seven Wonders of the World. Of those seven only one, the Great Pyramid at Giza, still remains. But the Mausoleum at Halicarnassus apparently survived until the fourteenth century A.D., when it was at last destroyed in an earthquake. Its stones were then carried off and used for other purposes, except for a few bits and pieces of sculpture that were acquired by the British Museum in the nineteenth century. With these, and with the descriptions by ancient authors such as Pliny and Vitruvius (who had either themselves seen the famous building still standing or had known people who had, who gave them specific descriptions and dimensions of it), the desire among modern scholars to reconstruct the Mausoleum became more and more irresistible. Scholars from all over the world have worked on this project, with all sorts of different results, for more than a hundred years, and the work is still going on. Today, with the most sophisticated modern methods of archeological scrutiny and new excavations on the site, a team of Danish archeologists, under the direction of Professor Kristian Jeppersen, assisted by Dr. Geoffrey Waywell of King's College, London, and Dr. Brian Cook of the British Museum, have at last produced a reconstruction that would appear to be definitive, it is so careful, so logical, and so ingenious.

I say that the reconstruction "appears" (to me) to be definitive. However, when I asked one of the officials in the Department of Greek and Roman Antiquities at the British Museum if it were, he at once became guarded, and I felt that I had asked a naive, if not a vulgar, question. The reconstruction of the Mausoleum, for all its finesse, for all its elegant deductions from the analysis of fragmentary carvings, for all its achievement in presenting what now appears to be a final and conclusive result, is and ultimately must remain an abstract exercise in scholarship. There could be no useful purpose in actually re-erecting the thing at full size (as a lodging in afterlife for some other dead grandee), nor would anything be learned from it that could not be learned in this case equally well from a model. Indeed, full-size reconstruction would be impossible because the outstanding feature of the Mausoleum, the thing that made it so famous in its day, was the wealth of fine sculpture with which it was ornamented, and that has all disappeared (except for the few fragments in the British Museum). The sculptures were all broken up and burned to make lime, centuries ago, and one cannot "reconstruct" original art. Even so, there has remained an obsessive curiosity about what the Mausoleum was actually like. The time and money spent in research has been well spent, and our knowledge is the richer as a result. But since conjectures have had to be employed, and since the building by its very nature is not connected with any living practice, there is no point in drawing a line under it and saying the reconstruction is finished. Classical scholarship would prefer simply to call it a conjecture, and leave it at that.

Conjecture. Now of course there is nothing wrong with conjecturing; indeed, the general study of history could hardly be carried on without it. But how much of it you allow and how you use it depends on what you want it to do and how it affects the value of the work as a whole. In the case of the reconstruction of a historic object at full size, involving, as it may, some degree of conjecture and/or modification, it is reasonable to ask what value or values we should expect such a reconstruction to have.

I suggest that it ought to have three particular values: it should be an aid to learning, a stimulus to discovery and further thinking, and a source of imaginative pleasure and recreation. In that last case reconstruction may sometimes go further and take on the quality of art in its own right, as I hope soon to show. But first let us consider some recent (or fairly recent) examples of the reconstruction of historic places and objects, all of them things that had completely disappeared from the world, taking with them, for better or worse, much of the knowledge and experience of the people historically associated with them. We are to judge whether the reconstructions of these things pass or fail under the three headings I have proposed, to which I would simply add: do we like them, or do we not? Are we glad or sorry they were made?

In the United States the first example that inevitably comes to mind is the restoration of Colonial Williamsburg in Virginia. It is, I suppose, the most extensive, elaborate, and carefully executed historical reconstruction ever embarked upon. It covers 130 acres. Eighty-three of the surviving old buildings of the town were fully restored, all modern buildings were demolished or removed, and 413 houses of the appropriate historic type were reconstructed on their original foundations. A continuous and devoted study of its architecture and history has controlled the development of Colonial Williamsburg since its beginning in 1926. The idea of the reconstruction was initiated by a local clergyman, Mr. William Goodwin, who inspired John D. Rockefeller, Jr., to finance the project. The cost, in its time, was something over $62 million. In terms of esthetic attraction and of public response to it, and in the sheer popularity of historical reconstruction-making where a reconstruction is truly well made, this example could hardly be bettered; and in terms of money it must long ago have bettered its investment. But Colonial Williamsburg is a remarkable project, rather beyond the comparative simplicity of what we have here in mind. Let us turn to something equally imaginative, but on a smaller scale.

The re-creation of the original Pilgrim settlement, Plimouth Plantation, in Massachusetts, supposedly as it appeared in or around the year 1627, was begun in 1957. Its purpose was clear: it was to be a memorial to the beginnings of a nation and also (presumably) to pay for itself with an honest source of revenue from tourism. But was it well done? Was it worth doing? In my opinion it was, and if it had not been well done it would not have attracted either the attention or the respect that it sought and has earned. All the buildings were fully researched by the architect in charge, Mr. Charles Strickland, and his colleagues—who incidentally discovered, among other things, that the Pilgrims did not build their houses in the log-cabin style that had always been supposed and was taught in schools, a style that was actually imported to America from Sweden very much later, but by a timber frame and board system, partly imported from England and partly invented by the Pilgrims on the spot. This had not been brought to light before, simply because there had never been any reason to inquire; only the decision to build an actual full-scale reconstruction provided that. The reconstruction of Plimouth Plantation earns part of its living by giving little theatrical performances of life at the time of the original settlement, with Pilgrims and Indians and the rest, so it is possible to say that in one of its aspects the whole thing is a sort of theatre or stage setting, but built for reality in real materials. But if so, it is a very good one, especially when, in the background, out in the bay, you can see the full-scale reconstruction of the *Mayflower,* itself built for reality in England and sailed across the Atlantic to her moorings at Plimouth Plantation in 1957.

More recently the *Mayflower*'s example was followed by a reconstruction of Sir Francis Drake's *Golden Hinde,* the first English ship to sail around the world. This reconstructed vessel made her Atlantic crossing in 1974. Her captain reported when she arrived in Barbados that she had "rolled like an old bucket," which may be something that was learned, if it had not already been suspected. But the captain's cabin, high up in the poop, was, as the *Mayflower*'s captain had discovered in the earlier voyage, by far the most uncomfortably rolling berth in the ship. It also came as a surprise in both these voyages (because no one had thought of it before) that with the big sail set on the bowsprit, you could not see anything ahead from the deck, so a forward lookout had to be kept on the foremast cross-trees. Incidentally, the *Golden Hinde*'s officers used Elizabethan navigational instruments on the voyage, and found them remarkably accurate.

I suppose the most famous, and the most scientifically valuable, historic reconstructions of any kind were two reconstructed ancient seagoing craft—three really, because one of them had to be built twice—launched, respectively, in 1947 and 1970, by (shall we say) a cranky theorist from Norway. When the world first heard that six men were at sea with the intention of crossing the Pacific Ocean on a raft made of soft and spongy balsa wood, it drew its own conclusions about the sanity of these men; and of course, as was very soon learned, the world was wrong. When, twenty-three years later, Thor Heyerdahl set out again, this time to cross the Atlantic on a ship made of bundles of reeds, the world knew better than to laugh at him a second time. The stories of the *Ra* and *Kon Tiki* expeditions are too well known to detain us here, except for three things that ought to be emphasized. First, I asserted that these reconstructions were scientifically valuable, and I hardly need remind you that they proved, among other things, in the most dramatic way possible, theories about the migrations of ancient peoples, about their knowledge of navigation, and about the dissemination of cultures at the dawn of human history that would otherwise never have been known or believed. Next, I want to point out that Heyerdahl designed and built his balsa raft and his reed ships following his belief in the reliability of ancient traditions and ancient works of art as being good witnesses in practice. He took the old traditions and the old pictures at their face value and copied them. Finally, we ought not to forget that his reconstructions were made in dead earnest, for Heyerdahl and his crews were reconstructing not only ships but voyages, and these they were reconstructing at the risk of their lives.

This brings me to yet one further and final aspect of the theory of reconstruction that I would now like to pursue: reconstructions of events by the use of live people.

I have already referred to the systematic reconstruction of crimes by the police for the purpose of crime detection, with a sideways glance at Hamlet and his Mouse-trap play. I indicated that at this point reconstruction begins to take on a life of its own, to become art in its own right. It is becoming drama. Take, for example, the reconstruction of one particular crime. The Elizabethan play *Arden of Feversham* has its place in the textbooks as the first example of an English domestic tragedy. But what was it in its own day, before it became a piece of literary history? It was the reconstruction on the stage of an actual and notorious murder, which had taken place within living memory—a sort of Lizzie Borden or Maria Martin shocker. Consider, too, the lively reconstruction of biblical events: to keep them fresh in mind, to be an aid to learning and a stimulus to further thinking as well as a source of imaginative recreation, was, as we well know, one of the most important functions of all early drama, which was

64

supported by the church itself for the teaching of religious doctrine (as, later, the state was to use drama to teach nationalist doctrine). Thomas Nash, in his pamphlet *Pierce Penilesse, his supplication to the Divell* (1592), defended the whole business of play-acting on just such grounds. Referring to history plays, in 1592 (the same year that *Arden of Feversham* was published) he wrote:

> Nay, what if I prove plays to be no evil, but a rare exercise of virtue? First, for the subject of them (for the most part) it is borrowed out of our English Chronicles, wherein our forefathers' valiant acts are revived, and they themselves raised from the grave of Oblivion, and brought to plead their aged Honours in open presence: than which, what can be a sharper reproof to these degenerate and effeminate days of ours? . . . How would it have joyed brave Talbot (the terror of the French) to think that after he had lain two hundred years in his Tomb, he should triumph again on the stage, and have his bones new embalmed with the tears of ten thousand spectators at least (at several times) who, in the Tragedian that represents his person, imagine they behold him fresh bleeding?

Now, we know who it was that made brave Talbot triumph again and die again on the stage in just such a way as that at just that time: it was Shakespeare. We also know that Shakespeare earned a great part of his early fame and fortune by his artistic (and politically tendentious) reconstructions of "our English Chronicles" upon the stage. And not English chronicles only, but classical ones. He arranged, did he not, a notable reconstruction of the assassination of Julius Caesar, even leaving those famous last words *Et tu, Brute?* in their original Latin for the sake of greater authenticity. (This particular reconstruction was not thought good enough by Ben Jonson, however; considering himself a better hand in the classical line, he promptly wrote a dramatic reconstruction of the fall of Sejanus to demonstrate how well such a thing could be done, providing it with all the academic paraphernalia of footnotes and quoting his sources from the ancient writers to show how reliable his reconstruction was.)

As we know, one of the last works in which Shakespeare had a hand was a living re-creation of *The Famous History of the Life of King Henry the Eighth.* Of this Sir Henry Wotton wrote to his nephew in July, 1613, that the King's players at the Globe playhouse had "a new play . . . representing some principal pieces of the reign of Henry VIII, which was set forth with many extraordinary circumstances of pomp and majesty, even to the matting of the stage; the Knights of the Order with their Georges and garters, the Guards with their embroidered coats, and the like. . . ." The actor presenting the Prologue of that play, addressing the audience from the stage, bids them: "Think ye see the very persons of our noble story, *as they were living.*" And remember, too, that the play as presented was not at that time known by the title *Henry VIII*; as Sir Henry Wotton tells us, it was called *All Is True.*

And of course, as we also know, it was during a performance of this play that the famous playhouse in which it was being presented, the Globe, was accidentally set on fire and burned to the ground, on June 13, 1613, at, I suppose, about a quarter to three in the afternoon.

Only the foundations remained intact, and upon them the Globe was reconstructed without delay. It stood for another thirty years and was then pulled down in the course of what is nowadays called redevelopment. Our task here is to consider how—bearing in mind the factors I have tried to set before you: the sway of sentiment; the needs of scholarship and their furtherance by practical investigation; the undoubted popular appeal; and the special place of the Globe, not only as a theatre for making historical reconstructions of its own but as the historical beginning, the very detonator, of the cultural explosion that is the phenomenon of drama in modern society—to consider how it may now, itself, be suitably reconstructed for a second time.

It has been by a somewhat roundabout route that we have at last arrived at the Globe. Having examined, and I hope justified, a general attitude in favor of making historical reconstructions, I would add only that if there is any lost building at all, from any period in history, whose reconstruction, from both a scholarly and a popular point of view, would surely be welcomed and acclaimed, that building is beyond all question the Globe playhouse, "the most famous theatre the world has ever known," as I recently heard it described on a BBC program. I will pass on now from the question of the value of reconstruction, to the next: its feasibility.

Is a reconstruction of the Globe feasible? We do not have complete information about it; but do we have enough to work with? In my opinion we have, and, short of the emergence of some miraculous discovery, like the Dead Sea Scrolls—which we have neither right nor reason to expect, and if we wait for it we may have to wait forever—short of that, the next step toward obtaining further information is to make practical use of what we have, and of our deductions from it, various as these may be, by actually building at full size. The time has come to do that.

Now I must ask your indulgence. I am naturally very proud to think that a symposium of distinguished scholars has been assembled under the auspices of a great university partly as a result of a proposition put forward in a book by me. However, I am not so vain as to think that everything I wrote in *Shakespeare's Second Globe* is right. I said at the end of that book that I offered it as "a contribution and a beginning," and I meant that: this volume is a continuation. Neither am I so vain as to suppose that more than a few specialists have read my book. So the indulgence I ask is to be allowed to describe, quite briefly, the proposition I put forward there, with some explanation of how it came about.

Some years ago I was approached by two English businessmen

("projectors," as Ben Jonson and his contemporaries would have called them) who asked me to advise them about a project to rebuild the Globe in London as the central feature of a sort of trading and entertainment complex. In the end the scheme never came to anything, but at the time it gave me an opportunity to do professionally the sort of research I had long wanted to do but could not, lacking the time, and owing to the pressures of other work. But on this occasion I accepted with pleasure, and settled down to think. What should I advise them to do?

As most readers of this volume will know, there are two basic contemporary pictures of the Globe, of which we are bound to take note. One is a detail in the foreground of a long panorama of the City of London published in 1616 by the Dutch engraver Claes Janzoon de Visscher. I think of this, rather whimsically, as the windmill picture, for no better reason than that it reminds me of a truncated windmill. The engraver is not known ever to have been in England, and he probably worked either from other people's sketches, which may have been rather fumbling, or from verbal descriptions. The description of a polygonal building made of wood might have called to his mind, in Holland, the (to him) familiar image of a windmill, which may have nudged him subconsciously into giving his Globe this unlikely upright shape. Be that as it may, in other respects the picture does have quite a number of verifiable features.

The other picture of the Globe is again a detail from a panorama of London, this time from the hand of an excellent and very reliable topographical engraver, Wenzel (or Wenceslaus) Hollar, a Bohemian, who did live in London, who did actually see the Globe, and who made a drawing of it, on the spot, which he used some years later for the detail of the Bankside portion of his famous *Long View of London*. I think of it as the "Sphinx" picture, because, for over 330 years, there it has sat, looking like one of those creatures that Shakespeare in *The Tempest* called "Strange Shapes," unassailable, unloved, unbelieved-in, and therefore largely avoided by all inquiry, guarding its own mystery, like the Sphinx. Otherwise, the only thing wrong with it is the title "Bear-Baiting h" (for house), which applies not to this but to the building next door on the right, which is titled "the Globe." Unfortunately, the two titles have been accidentally reversed. It is the right hand building which is the bear-baiting ring, though it had in fact been built and used as a playhouse in earlier days, being in those days called the Hope.

There is one other picture of an Elizabethan playhouse that must not be omitted, a sketch of the interior of a public playhouse and the only such interior to have been drawn for the record. The sketch is copied from a drawing at first hand by one Johannes de Witt (see fig. VII-1 below), who visited the Swan in 1596. It is a drawing reproduced in all the schoolbooks in the world. It has been the subject of endless comment and analysis, and I do not propose to say more about it here except to quote Sir Edmund Chambers, who wrote that "with all its faults, the drawing is the inevitable basis of any comprehensive account of the structural features of a playhouse."

Very well. Now if you were to take that drawing of the Swan interior and sketch it out again in a rather more sophisticated style, we would get something such as is shown in figure III-1. It is not a measured reconstruction, being intended only to give the general effect of a simple, plain, open-staged playhouse, with a roof over the stage held up by two great posts. Very well again; but I have been inclined, for reasons I need not go into here, to advance from this very simple position and to add one or two other things, such as the little porchlike arrangement standing out from the stage rear wall, which is represented in figure III-2. It could be a very useful arrangement, and it is here shown serving, rightly or wrongly, as the "monument" in which Cleopatra, Charmian, and Iras have taken refuge at the end of *Antony and Cleopatra.* I have also been inclined, for reasons that I think will not be bitterly quarreled with, to give the whole interior of a typical fine playhouse such as the Globe a far richer appearance, more decorated, even perhaps gaudier than the drawing of the Swan by itself would seem to suggest (see fig. III-3). This is the sort of Globe playhouse I was prepared to design for my friends the projectors, and indeed would have enjoyed doing. It had their full approval. But then came the snag.

"Of course," they said, "it will have to have a roof. We cannot use it without a roof."

The need for a roof is a familiar injunction in proposals to reconstruct the Globe, and one that has to be faced squarely. In northern latitudes it cannot be said to be an unreasonable condition. But of course, to roof the Globe over is to modify one of its best-known historical characteristics, and therefore if that modification must be made, it must be made in such a way that the conditions prevailing at the original Globe should at the least not be lost sight of. And it must be done with style and discretion. (To begin with, I do not think the thing ought to be called a roof. Call it, say, a skylight, and we may approach the problem on better terms.) However, that is all by the way. My friends made the expected injunction, and for the sort of site they were proposing I really could not think it unreasonable. But how could it be done? One sees in de Witt's sketch, and in my sophisticated adaptations of it, the awkward shape that has to be covered. Bear in mind that a translucent roof—a skylight—must somehow be fitted in without being seen from outside the building (which would greatly damage the authentic effect) and must somehow not seem too clumsy within. Above all, what about rainwater and snow? What about gutters? What about that *thatch?*

The thatch of the Globe: it was that which caught fire and burned the place down in 1615 and, perhaps even as a result of that it has had a sort of historico-hypnotic effect on Globe reconstructions ever since. That thatch is so simple and rustic and familiar, one almost feels one can reach across the centuries and pluck straws from it. That thatch is legendary. It is not only authentic; it is lovable.

But one could not keep the thatch *and* put another roof (or skylight) into it, and one could not add gutters to it. I concluded regretfully that it would have to go. It would have to be replaced by tiles.

A simple enough solution, but what followed from it illustrates very nicely what I had in mind when I said above that the way forward now, to obtain any of the further knowledge we want, is to be brought face to face with the actual job of building at full size. Without an actual building in view the thatch-versus-tile problem, as such, might never have come into my head; and without that problem, the ultimate solution, which is so simple and, I believe, so unquestionably right, and which has been staring us all in the face for years and years, would probably never have come into my head either. The solution was, and is, to leave the first Globe, with its picturesque thatch, alone, and to reconstruct instead the second Globe, the Globe of Hollar's picture, of which we have not only his etching but his original on-the-spot drawing as well, from which the etching was made—the Sphinx that has for so long puzzled everybody, which some have said is useless as evidence, which few have tried to make sense of, and which has waited patiently for over three hundred years to be needed. For the second Globe *was* roofed with tiles; our reconstruction of it would *have* to have tiles, and thus could have gutters. Also, however we were to manage adding the skylight, the geometry of it would have to deal only with a simple half-circle, not with all those picturesque ins and outs we associate with pictures of the first Globe and the Swan.

Having suddenly been illuminated by this flash of insight, I was at once reminded of something else I ought never to have lost sight of (but I had been wrapped up in my own mind's-eye image, formed long before upon the first Globe and, I suppose, based initially upon Visscher's engraving, as well as upon the known dimensions given in the existing contract for building the Fortune playhouse, which have hitherto provided a baseline for all Elizabethan theatre reconstructors). I had not sufficiently heeded a clear voice that had been telling me, telling us all, for a long time and very persistently, that more attention ought to be paid to the second Globe, especially with regard to its proportions. It was the voice of Richard Hosley, whose primacy in this insight I gladly take this opportunity to acknowledge.

So let us take on the Sphinx. We have at least her reliable exterior; but all her riddles are concealed within.

I did try once, a long time ago, to make a reconstruction drawing of the interior of the second Globe. When I did it I became aware of a number of questions that I touched upon but did not follow up at the time.

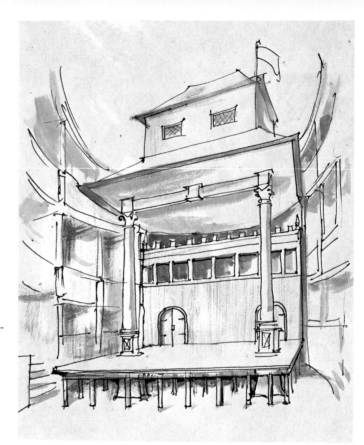

Fig. III–1. The stage and tiring-house of the Swan: sketch interpretation of the drawing by Johannes de Witt (see fig. VII–1 below).

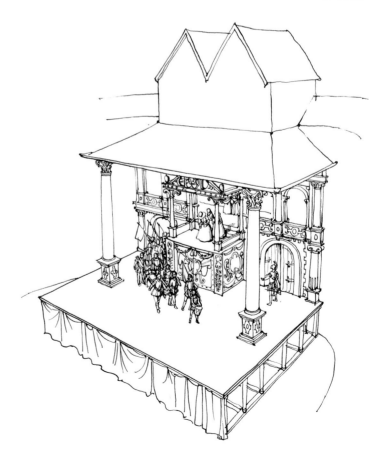

Fig. III–2. Stage with "porch" structure added to tiring-house wall.

Fig. III–3. Interior of the first Globe, showing suggested enrichment of decoration.

It was clear to me that the ceiling over the stage had to be raised as high as the eaves of the surrounding galleries, to allow sufficient light onto the stage and to avoid increasing the sense of oppression which that large, impending, double-gabled house over the stage already has. (Bring it down even a little lower *into* the yard area and the oppressive effect would be well-nigh doubled.) In any case, Hollar's picture shows clearly that the ceiling comes to the eaves. Thus, to support this overstage house, the posts on the stage would have to be increased in height. Thus, they would have to be more massive. Thus, they would be more in the way; and so on. There was also the problem of where they should stand. Because they have so much weight to carry, I felt that they could not be left in the "traditional" halfway-up-the-stage position that we had inherited from the drawing of the Swan. So I brought them right down to the front of the stage, and then edged them away toward the sides to get them as far out of the way of the actors as was possible. But I was not very happy with this solution.

You will also note on the left of this drawing that, where the sweep of the great roof comes down to its junction with the top gallery at the eaves, I have lightly sketched a continuation of a sloping member, a principal rafter, of the roof, as if to lock it in there more securely. That was the beginning of an idea that then went to sleep for a long while. I will not go into any of the intervening details, but will jump forward at once to the solution that gradually forced itself upon me. I use the word *force* because the idea at first seemed to me outrageously revolutionary. I was not seeking to be outrageous; nor was I trying to be revolutionary. Indeed, I have sometimes been very critical of scholars who have put forward what I took to be unwarrantably revolutionary innovations, and I did not want to be found in that position myself. But in this case so many things seemed to me to be rushing together pointing in the same direction, things I had not looked for or at first suspected, that in the end I decided to go for it, and give the idea its head.

The question I asked myself about that big, double-gabled house structure hanging over the stage, presumably laying all its dead weight on only two pillars, was, what was it doing up there? What was it for? It did not seem to me that it could be for some vast increase of overstage flying machinery, or for offices or dressing rooms, or even for storage; for why build so expensively up aloft to hang a great weight of storage over the arena, when it would be far cheaper and more convenient to build a shed outside on the ground at the back? The company had enough land there. Furthermore, the form of that roof was in itself suggestive of some structural purpose. That interlocked scissor-truss of a double gable, reaching down at each side to the wide frame of the galleries, 12 feet wide or more, into which again it could lock itself, suggested that under certain circumstances the roof *could hold itself up,* and the question of where to place the supporting posts could be solved by answering that there were none; that the roof was designed to be self-supporting. But the "certain circumstances" that would make this possible would be that the whole superstructural edifice was not the "house" it seemed to be, but only an open timber roof with a screen wall at the front, the whole thing being designed as a weather cover for as large an area of the playhouse as possible. There was no floor in it. Its appearance as a house was deceptive.

There are other reasons, very seductive ones, that contribute to this notion; I will come to them shortly. But first let us consider, is this possible? Or, rather, was it possible at that time? Could a Jacobean builder have conceived such an idea? The span he had to cover was, at its widest (the diameter of the yard) according to my calculation in my book, 64 feet, a very wide span for unsupported timber construction, and I have been told by Richard Hosley and John Orrell that I have underestimated that span. So was it possible? Let me say that for the supporting central truss of the roof that I designed for my book I was careful not to use any remarkably long members of timber. I preferred to use short or shortish lengths, limiting myself to 16 feet, in order not to exaggerate the possibilities in my favor. The result is perhaps rather "bitty." By using longer timbers one would do better.

Yet whatever an English carpenter might have done, as an exceptional case, to bridge a span of 65 feet or more without supporting posts, we do know that at that time in other countries carpenters could bridge wider unsupported spans than that. For example, a famous theatre of Renaissance Italy, the ducal theatre in the Farnese palace in Parma, built by Aleotti in 1617 (just three years after the second Globe was completed in London) has an unsupported roof span of no less than 105 feet. However, the method by which that span was achieved was not commonly, if ever, practiced in England. In Parma, the great transverse roof beams were composite, made up of shorter timbers bound together with iron straps. English carpenters never used iron in this way (even though English wheelwrights certainly had the art of shrinking iron tires onto wooden wheels). It must be allowed that even in Italy this grand theatre built for the duke of Parma was an exceptional building. But then, who is to say that a new playhouse being built for the king's own company of players in England may not have been in its own way an exceptional building, possibly even making use of foreign ideas?

Two factors, which I described just now as seductive, seem to me to contribute a certain force to the open-roof idea. For the first, I show an outline analysis of Hollar's etching of the Globe, with, below, a projection from it onto a ground plan. Notice on the plan that the little turret with its domelike top is positioned not over a back part of the surrounding gallery structure, as one might have expected, but over a void where we must suppose the stage to be. In a similar analysis of Hollar's drawing this

73

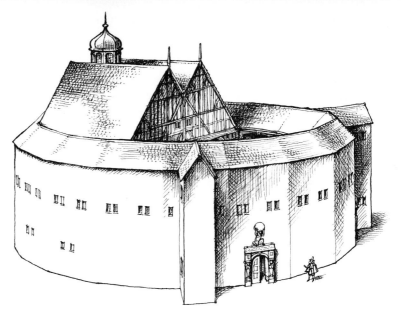

Fig. III–4. Reconstruction exterior of the second Globe as in Hollar's *Long View of London*.

Fig. III–5. Reconstruction of Hollar's Globe, viewed from the rear.

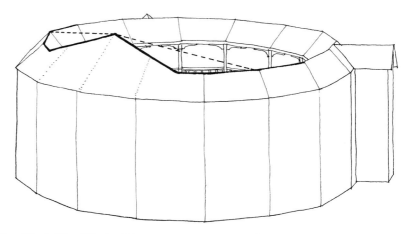

Fig. III–6. Fig. III–5 with superstructure removed.

positioning is even more pronounced. Now the question is, what is this domed thing? What is it for? After examining all the possibilities, I could think of one, and only one, that seemed to me tenable. The thing is a lantern, an architectural device to let daylight into a large enclosed space with a floor a long way below. (It is most unlikely that such a thing would have been built, certainly not in that position, to light a loft or attic, which could have been lit better, more cheaply and easily by other, more conventional, means.) Therefore, if it is a lantern, it must have been put there to give additional light to the back of the stage (for the big roof over the stage, though it was very sheltering, was also very shadowing). And if that was so, there cannot have been any intervening floor or ceiling between the lantern in the roof and the stage below.

The other factor is rather more complicated. I show on page 74 a series of drawings of which the first (fig. III-4) reconstructs Hollar's Globe from the viewpoint presented in his etching—that is, as seen from the tower of St. Saviour's church (now Southwark Cathedral), the position from which Hollar made his original study drawing. It was next necessary for me to visualize the building as seen from the back. Assuming that the carpenters of this timber-frame building had adopted the simplest and most direct way of dealing with a certain problem they had, in marrying the square-plan roof of the superstructure to the round-plan roof of the surrounding gallery frame, their solution is given in figure III-5. Next, I would have you imagine that for some reason (which need not concern us here; several are possible) the big superstructural roof was eventually taken down. What would then have remained is shown in figure III-6, where a curious peak, which was once an extension of the gallery roof, bringing it up to the point where it could join the wall of the superstructure, is now left on its own. Assuming, next, that this now vestigial hump is mended or patched up where it stands, the result is shown in figure III-7 and, from Hollar's original viewpoint on the cathedral tower, in figure III-8. The result is remarkably like the mysterious peak that Hollar has depicted at the back of the building he calls the Globe (but which we know is really the bear-baiting house, formerly known as the Hope playhouse).

Now, the contract for building the Hope has survived, and one of its provisions is that the builder must make a roof (or "heavens") to go right across over the stage "to be borne or carried without any posts or supporters to be fixed or set upon the said stage," a necessary condition because the stage was to stand on trestles and be easily removable. The roof over the stage was, however, certainly a fixture, because it was fitted with lead gutters, and therefore presumably it was, like the rest of the house, tiled.

What is suggested, therefore, is that the second Globe and its neighbor, the Hope, which were both built at the same time, both had "heavens" superstructures built (as the Hope's certainly was) without the

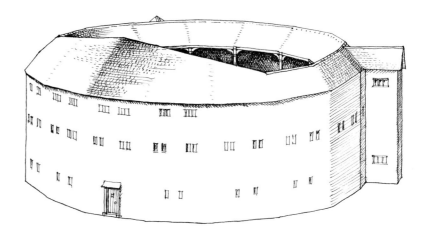

Fig. III–7. Rear view with new, mended roof line.

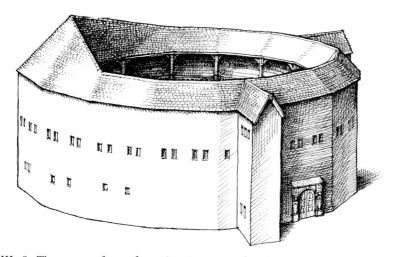

Fig. III–8. The new roof seen from the viewpoint of Hollar's *Long View*.

support of posts standing upon the stage. Later, I suggest that, when the Hope ceased to be used as a playhouse, the "heavens" there was removed, leaving only a vestigial stump, patched over, and showing what Hollar shows, a curious peak.

To sum up, I have suggested that the peculiar nature of the Globe's twin-gabled superstructure denotes an exceptional response to an exceptional problem: how to get rid of the roof posts standing upon the stage. They were certainly got rid of somehow at the nearby Hope, a playhouse of comparable size, built at the same time, and I have suggested that it was done by devising a self-supporting open-timber roof, with hammer beams and a scissor-truss. That there was no floor, or at least no complete floor, in this upper structure seems to be confirmed by the position of the cupola, which, as I have indicated above, can be no other than a lantern and which therefore seems intended to throw light down onto the stage. All these things, independent and dissociated though they may in the end turn out to be, nevertheless, by some cunning collusion, do appear to pull together in the same direction; and whether one agrees with my conclusion or not, it must surely be agreed that the theory is remarkably seductive. If I have thereby fallen into error I will say at least this in my defense: no one that I know of has yet presented a better explanation to account for that strange peaked-up arrangement at the back of Hollar's Hope.

Such, then, are the leading themes of my personal offering on this subject. The major theme, that a reconstruction of the Globe should take the form shown in Hollar's picture, I think few would quarrel with. Although it holds mysteries, they are mysteries that are accessible to analysis and solution in terms of building practice, rather than, as is necessary with other types of evidence, chiefly by the analysis of theatre literature. Thus a new and fruitful field of discovery is open to us. Moreover, let us not forget that if the Globe itself, or any part of it, had survived, it would have been the one in Hollar's picture and no other. It is our nearest and strongest link with the physical appearance of Shakespeare's theatre.

For my second theme I have advanced the hypothesis that the big double-gabled roof was a self-supporting structure, which did away with the need for posts standing on the stage (fig. III-9). If this can be shown to have been practical, then I think it will have been shown to be true; once again we are in an area where yes or no can be judged in structural terms, irrespective of other kinds of evidence. To my mind it is a critical judgment, which may be found ultimately to depend upon the width of the diameter of the playhouse yard and the span that has to be bridged as a consequence. If it turns out that that span is too wide for any sort of unsupported structure, then we shall be back again with our problem of the roof-supporting posts upon the stage, and the question of where to put them. Shall we prove that Jacobean audiences and actors did not object to having great supporting posts (and how many of them?) in a forward position on their stages? In fact, it makes quite a nice drawing here, which is why I am not at all reluctant to present it. But what sort of a theatre would it make? Would it have been acceptable to Shakespeare and his companions the actors, when they were rebuilding *and improving*—and we know they improved it, because we have a document that tells us it was "new builded in far fairer manner than before"—when they were improving their famous and successful playhouse?

In conclusion, I maintain that, with Hollar and with all the evidence that scholars have been bringing together now for more than a hundred years, we at last have material enough to build a serious and sensitive reconstruction of the Globe. Certainly, where we find gaps in our knowledge we shall have to fill these by conjecture, though Shakespeare and the Elizabethans would have used a shorter word for that. They would have called it *art*. Ultimately, we might expect that our reconstruction would have the quality of a work of art in its own right, one that Shakespeare and Burbage, if they could walk into it, would recognize for their own. As for the future, if scholars then should find fault with, or wish to modify, what we may build, their own researches will benefit from it as it stands. Our proceedings will be on record for them to study. They will know why we did what we did; and if by following us they can then do better, well, God bless them.

Meanwhile, "nothing will ever be attempted if all possible objections must be first overcome." That high-minded quotation from Samuel Johnson has always appealed to me, with its nice balance of gravity and aspiration, and I thought it would provide a fine moral flourish for me to end with. But as I had only known it from hearsay, I took the precaution of checking my reference, and I was a little dismayed to find that these splendid words are put into the mouth of someone whom Dr. Johnson clearly intends us to regard as a ninny. They occur in *The History of Rasselas, Prince of Abyssinia*. The prince and his tutor, in the course of their adventures, meet with a person described as an artist (that is, an artificer), who is entirely wrapped up in building what is, for Dr. Johnson, a ludicrous machine for an obviously impossible purpose. When Prince Rasselas questions this manifest simpleton about the value and feasibility of his project, he defends himself, in his simpletonian way, by saying, "Nothing will ever be attempted if all possible objections must be first overcome."

But may I remind you that if Dr. Johnson were alive today he might have thought differently about this silly artist of his; for what was it, after all, that the poor fellow was trying to do? He was trying to build an airplane.

So, on reflection, I think I shall not withdraw my quotation from Rasselas. It is very apt. Let it stand.

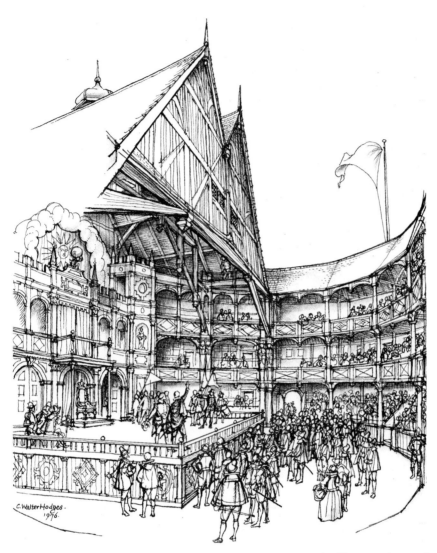

Fig. III–9. Interior of the second Globe, showing suggested self-supporting roof.

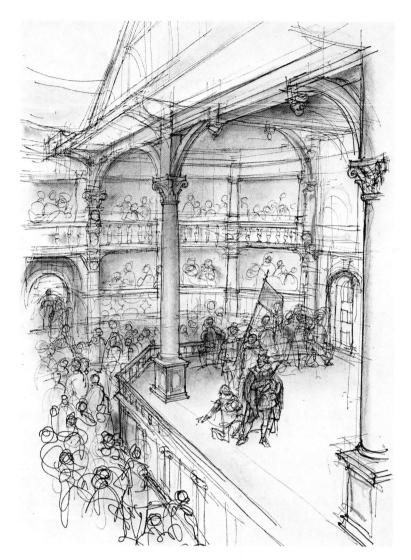

Fig. III–10. Interior of second Globe, with supporting posts (first reconstruction).

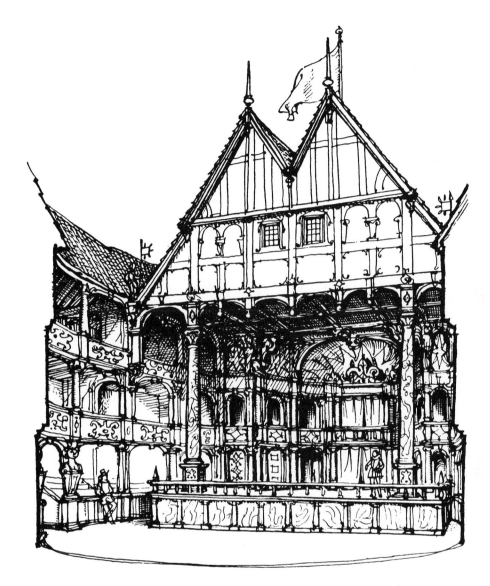

Fig. III–11. Second Globe interior. Sketch reconstruction with posts (second version).

IV. *The Shape and Size of the Second Globe*

RICHARD HOSLEY

In 1975, in the course of an essay on the first Globe, I suggested that the second Globe was a 24-sided building measuring about 100 feet in diameter.[1] In the present essay, in view of the recent researches of John Orrell, I now propose the more specific hypothesis that the second Globe was a 24-sided building having a diameter of 99 feet measured between opposed exterior faces, or 99 feet 10 inches measured between opposed exterior corners. The second Globe is necessarily the focus of inquiry because of Hollar's superb depiction of it in his drawing the *West Part of Southwarke toward Westminster* (ca. 1640), and again in his etching the *Long View of London from Bankside* (1647). However, conclusions regarding the shape and size of the second Globe (built in 1614) apply equally to the first Globe (built in 1599) and to James Burbage's Theatre (built in 1576) because the second Globe, having been erected on the foundations of the burnt-down first, was of the same shape and size as the first Globe,[2] and that playhouse, having been constructed of the timbers of the dismantled Theatre, was of the same shape and size as the Theatre.[3]

The suggestion that the Globe had a diameter of about 100 feet was based on the argument that Hollar draws the frame of the second Globe approximately three times as wide as its height to the eaves and that its height to the eaves was presumably, as at the Fortune, about 33 feet. The conclusion cannot be made more specific because of inescapable ambiguities in the evidence, chief among them being that Hollar's depiction of shrubbery at the base of the Globe makes it impossible to take an objective measurement of the height of the building for comparison with its measureable width. Happily, however, John Orrell has now succeeded, in chapter 5 of this volume, not only in demonstrating the remarkable reliability of Hollar's horizontal measurements but also in estimating the width of the Globe by trigonometry. He concludes that in the drawing Hollar depicted the second Globe as 103.35 feet in width, including a correction for anamorphosis.[4] This figure, since Hollar cannot be expected to have represented the width of the building exactly to scale, may be considered a generalization: the Globe, Hollar tells us, was about 103 feet in diameter. How can we make this generalization sufficiently specific to support a reconstruction, whether in drawings, a scale model, or a full-scale replica, without resorting to uncontrolled conjecture?

Orrell himself provides an answer to this question, for in an earlier study he demonstrates that the ground plan of the second Globe was laid out *ad quadratum*—that is, in accordance with the method of the square.[5] In this method the builder, using a three- or four-rod surveyor's line, stakes out on the ground a square of given dimensions. Having done so, he checks its rectangularity by running a line first between one pair of opposed corners of the square and then between the other: if its diagonals are equal, the square will be true. (If they are not equal, the builder makes them so by appropriate adjustment of the layout of the square.) The intersection of the diagonals incidentally establishes the center of the square, and the builder marks it by pounding a stake into the ground at that point. Next, running his line from the center of the square to one of its corners (much as on paper one would extend a pair of compasses), the builder circumscribes a circle about the square passing through its corners. The procedure so far is illustrated in figure IV-1*A*. Next the builder constructs a second square each of whose sides is tangent to the circle and parallel to one of the sides of the first, or inner, square. Then, finally, he circumscribes a second circle about the outer square passing through its corners. The resulting configuration is illustrated in figure IV-1*B*.

I have described the last two steps of the method as they exist in theory. In practice, as Orrell points out, the builder would proceed to draw the outer circle immediately after drawing the inner, since, as will be explained below, he already knows the radius of the outer circle. Thus he would in fact establish the corners of the outer square by simply extending the diagonals of the inner square until they intersect the outer circle. The variant procedure may be traced in figure IV-1*B*.

The *ad quadratum* configuration has several useful properties, two of which are of special relevance to the present inquiry. First, the radius of the outer circle (R in fig. IV-1*C*) equals the length of one of the sides of the inner square. Thus, in laying out the ground plan of a round building, the builder can easily predict the size of his outer circle: if he wishes an outer circle with a diameter of 99 feet (hence with a radius of 49 feet 6 inches), he simply makes his inner square 49 feet 6 inches on a side. Second, the diameters of the inner and outer circles, being, respectively, equal to a side and the hypotenuse of the same right isosceles triangle, are related in the ratio of $1:\sqrt{2}$. Thus either diameter can be readily calculated from the other: if one knows the diameter of the inner circle, multiplying it by 1.414 will produce the diameter of the outer

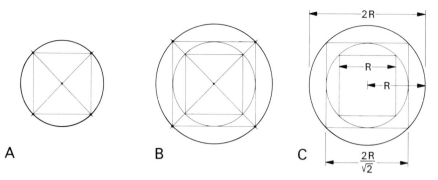

Fig. IV–1. The *ad quadratum* method of laying out a circular ground plan.

circle; or, if one knows the diameter of the outer circle, dividing it by 1.414 will produce the diameter of the inner circle. In figure IV-1C, in order to link the two noticed properties of the *ad quadratum* configuration, I have expressed the diameters of the outer and inner circles in terms of a double radius (2R).

Orrell shows, by reference to the plan projected by C. Walter Hodges from Hollar's depiction of the Globe in the drawing,[6] that the ground plan of the Globe was laid out with *ad quadratum* proportions: the inner diameter of the building, allowing for the builder's use of dimensions taken on post centers where Hollar would presumably have recorded dimensions between outer corners, stands in relation to its outer diameter in almost exactly the ratio of $1:\sqrt{2}$. And Orrell suggests, further, that the most likely significance of the observation that Hollar depicted the width of the Globe as about 100 feet (he had not yet calculated the width of the building as 103.35 feet) is that the builder (Burbage in 1576, Peter Street in 1599), using the traditional three-rod surveyor's line, made his inner square 3 rods, or exactly 49 feet 6 inches, on a side, thus producing an outer circle with a diameter of 6 rods, or 99 feet, and an inner circle of 70 feet (99 feet divided by $\sqrt{2}$; see fig. IV-2A). These dimensions would be on post centers, for inevitably a builder must think in such terms. If we next suppose that the first-storey posts of the Globe frame were 10 inches square, like those called for in the contract for building the Hope playhouse (1614), it follows that the Globe would have had an outer diameter of 99 feet 10 inches measured from one corner of the building to the corner opposite, and an inner diameter of 69 feet 2 inches measured in the same fashion (fig. IV-2B). Precise values for the face-to-face diameters, since these depend on the number of sides of the chosen ground plan, will be suggested after consideration of evidence for the shape of the building.

In view of Orrell's subsequent calculation of the width of the Globe in Hollar's drawing as 103.35 feet, the hypothesis of a diameter of 99.83

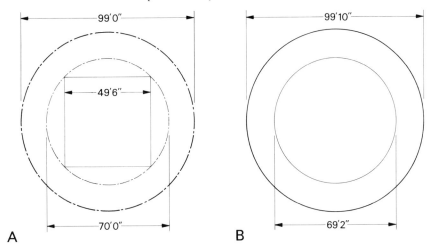

Fig. IV–2. Outer and inner diameters of the Globe frame. (*A*) Measured between centers of opposed principal posts. (*B*) Measured between opposed corners.

feet between corners requires the assumption that Hollar inadvertently exaggerated the width of the building by 3.52 feet, or 3½ percent— somewhat more than the 2 percent margin of error observed by Orrell in his analysis of the intervals between identifiable landmarks on the north bank of the Thames.

Pictorial evidence for the shape of the Globe is provided both by Hollar's drawing and by his etching. In both illustrations Hollar depicts the Globe as fully round—that is, in the terminology of geometry, as a right circular cylinder. However, the timber construction of the Globe would have required the building to have plane faces, and in fact it is represented as having plane faces in such pictorial sources as Visscher (1616) and Merian (1638). Thus it is clear that the Globe must have been a right regular prism of so many sides that from a distance it gave the impression of being cylindrical. Viewing the building from nearly a quarter of a mile away, Hollar appropriately represented it as fully round.

Although the form of the Globe was a many-sided prism, the builder, in preparing for construction, would naturally have thought of it in terms of a many-sided polygonal ground plan, and we may conveniently approach the problem in the same way. A polygon of how many sides? At the beginning of my study of this question I postulated four possible shapes: polygons of 16, 18, 20, and 24 sides. My investigation suggested that the Globe could not have been a 20-sided building, that it probably was not an 18-sided one, that it might have been (but in fact was not) a 16-sided one, and that it probably was a 24-sided one. Since it seems unnecessary to publish negative analyses of the 18- and 20-sided shapes of ground plan (each of which is admittedly attractive on theoretical grounds), I shall

85

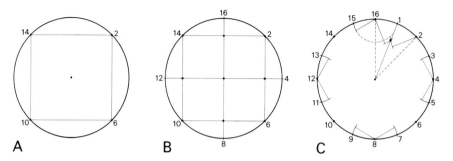

Fig. IV–3. A method of laying out a 16-sided ground plan.

content myself (and, I hope, the reader) with a short general statement about their deficiencies in a footnote toward the end of this essay. The situation is rather different in the cases of both the 16-sided and the 24-sided shapes of ground plan, and I shall therefore discuss them in some detail. Each of these shapes seems especially deserving of consideration since the one is known, the other supposed on good grounds, to have been used for a theatrical building of the period: the 16-sided shape for the temporary banqueting house built by Henry VIII in Calais in 1520,[7] the 24-sided shape for the Swan playhouse built by Francis Langley on Bankside in 1595.[8] In what follows I examine the relative convenience of each of these polygons for an Elizabethan builder who evidently used the *ad quadratum* method of laying out a basic ground plan consisting of a pair of concentric circles and who presumably used no instrument other than a three-rod surveyor's line in "inscribing" the required polygon in those circles.

To construct a 16-sided polygon on paper by Euclidean methods, one twice bisects each of the four central angles of a square. The method is essentially the same on the ground, and just as simple. A builder using the *ad quadratum* method would already have circumscribed a circle about a square (the second or outer square of the method) whose corners could serve as points 2, 6, 10, and 14 of the desired hexadecagon (fig. IV-3A). Presumably he would then bisect each of the central angles of the square by locating the midpoint of each side and then drawing a diameter of the circle through each pair of opposed midpoints (fig. IV-3B). Thus he would establish the 4 remaining corners of an octagon, or points 4, 8, 12, and 16 of the completed hexadecagon. Finally, the builder would bisect one of the central angles of the octagon by striking arcs of equal radius from the two circumferential points defining that angle (let us say, as shown in fig. IV-3C, *16* and *2*) so as to establish a 9th corner of the completed hexadecagon (point l); and he would then apply the chord lying between that point and one of

86

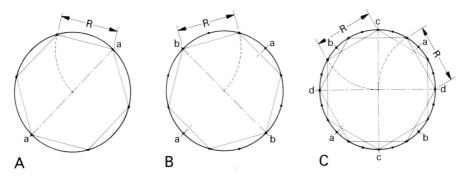

Fig. IV–4. Use of the radius of a circle in constructing polygons of 6 (*A*), 12 (*B*), and 24 (*C*) sides.

its adjacent points (let us say, 16) seven times round the circumference of the circle: once in each direction from points 4, 8, and 12, once counterclockwise from point 16. Thus he would establish the 7 remaining corners of a hexadecagon: points 3, 5; 7, 9; 11, 13; and 15.

To construct a 24-sided polygon on paper by Euclidean methods, one twice bisects each of the six central angles of a hexagon. This can easily be done on the ground since a hexagon is easily constructed, each of the sides of that figure being equal to the radius of the circumscribed circle (fig. IV-4*A*). But a builder using the *ad quadratum* method would have had other resources because of the uses to which the hexagon can be put. The basic geometry is simple. Let us define the hexagon of figure IV-4*A* by establishing the axis *a–a*. Next, as in figure IV-4*B,* let us construct a second hexagon with an axis *(b–b)* running at right angles to the axis of the first hexagon. Thus we will have inscribed in a circle two regularly intertwined hexagons whose corners will constitute the corners of a dodecagon. Finally, as in figure IV-4*C,* let us construct a third and a fourth hexagon having axes *c–c* and *d–d* running at right angles to each other and at an angle of 45° to the axes of the first two hexagons. Thus we will have inscribed in a circle, all told, four regularly intertwined hexagons whose corners will constitute the corners of a 24-sided polygon.

The *ad quadratum* builder would already have circumscribed a circle about a square (the outer square of the method) whose corners could serve as points 3, 9, 15, and 21 of the desired 24-sided polygon (fig. IV-5*A*). Presumably he would then bisect each of the central angles of this square by locating the midpoint of each side and then drawing a diameter of the circle through each pair of opposed midpoints (fig. IV-5*B*). Thus he would establish the 4 remaining corners of an octagon, or points 6, 12, 18, and 24 of the completed 24-sided polygon. Finally, from each of the 8 established points the builder would measure off the length of the radius of the circle in both directions along its circumference. Thus he would establish, in eight successive pairs, the remaining 16 corners of a 24-sided polygon: points 23, 7; 2, 10; 5, 13; 8, 16; 11, 19; 14, 22; 17, 1; and 20, 4. In making this constuction the builder, using the geometry described in the preceding paragraph, would in effect have inscribed in a circle four hexagons with axes successively separated from one another by an angle of 45°. Moreover, in marking off the sides of each hexagon (R in fig. IV-4), he would have been making repeated use of the same measurement (presumably 3 rods) that he had earlier used as the radius of the outer circle and as the sides of the inner square of the *ad quadratum* method (R in fig. IV-1C).

In sum, both the 16-sided and the 24-sided forms of a ground plan measuring 99 feet in diameter can be easily laid out by a builder using the *ad quadratum* method and no instrument other than the traditional three-rod surveyor's line.

The pictorial evidence for the shape of the second Globe consists of two features shown by Hollar: the row of windows extending round the building at the level of the middle gallery and the near staircase, which in the drawing is seen at about midpoint of the perceived half-circle of the building but which in the etching (because of a slight alteration of the point of view toward the left) appears a bit to the right of center (see figs. IV-8 and IV-9 below). In the drawing Hollar shows the windows on both the right and the left sides of the near staircase, whereas in the etching he shows them only on the left, either because his heavy shading of the right side of the building precluded representing windows to the right of the staircase (the drawing is unshaded) or because his executed representation of the windows was obscured by the shading. But before further considering the evidence for shape, we must briefly consider Hollar's variant siting of the staircases in drawing and etching. The evidence is set out by Hodges in projections of the playhouse plan from both pictorial sources, printed on pages 38 and 39 of *Shakespeare's Second Globe*.

The projections indicate that Hollar located the staircases 100° apart on centers in the drawing but 90° apart on centers in the etching. As in other instances of variation between drawing and etching, the question arises whether the representation in the etching was Hollar's inadvertent error in transmitting information correctly recorded in the drawing or his deliberate correction of an ascertained error in the drawing. Here we may consider the relative effectiveness of different possible orientations of the 16- and 24-sided shapes of ground plan in accommodating the observed variant sitings of the staircases. The 16-sided shape, if we orient the major axes of the building so that they run through the middles of opposite bays (fig. IV-6A), provides staircase sites 4 bays or 90° apart, whereas this

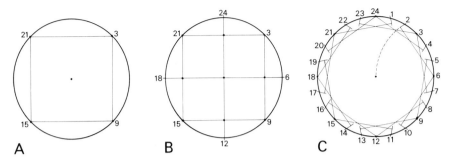

Fig. IV–5. A method of laying out a 24-sided ground plan.

shape, if the major axes are oriented so as to run through the junctures of opposite pairs of bays (fig. IV-6B), provides sites 5 bays or 112½° apart. Correspondingly, the 24-sided shape, if the major axes of the building run through bay middles (fig. IV-7A), provides staircase sites 6 bays or 90° apart, whereas the same shape, if the major axes run through bay junctures (fig. IV-7B), provides sites 7 bays or 105° apart. Thus the orientation of axes through bay middles in both shapes of ground plan provides staircase sites 90° apart, as in the etching (figs. IV-6A, IV-7A), whereas the orientation of axes through bay junctures in both shapes fails to provide staircase sites 100° apart, as in the drawing, exceeding the mark by a central angle of 12½° in the case of the 16-sided shape (fig. IV-6B) and of 5° in the case of the 24-sided shape (fig. IV-7B). It therefore appears that in the matter of staircase location the etching is more likely to be correct than the drawing. Thus, in accordance with this interpretation, I suppose that Hollar, in depicting the near staircase in the drawing, located it by eye instead of by a measurement on his drawing frame and thus was able to err in its location by a central angle of 5° (half the difference of the angular separation of the staircases in the two sitings), and that, in later depicting the near staircase in the etching, he was able to recognize and correct his error because, knowing that the staircases stood 4 bays apart in a 16-sided playhouse or 6 bays apart in a 24-sided one, he knew also that they must have butted up against bays of the frame exactly 90° apart on centers.

The hypothesis that the siting of the near staircase is probably correct in the etching but erroneous in the drawing bears on our inquiry into the shape of the Globe. Accepting this hypothesis, we should expect to find that the location of the near staircase in the etching corresponds closely with its location in the plan projected from the etching, but that the location of the staircase in the drawing does not correspond closely with its location in the projection from the drawing. Needless to say, our expectations in this matter would be reversed if we were to adopt the alternative

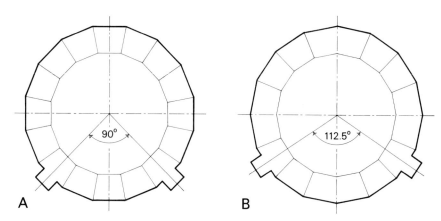

Fig. IV–6. Possible sitings of the staircases in a 16-sided Globe. (A) Major axes of the playhouse frame oriented through bay middles. (B) Major axes of the frame oriented through bay junctures.

hypothesis that it is the drawing rather than the etching that comes closer to correctly locating the near staircase.

I turn now to the number of windows depicted by Hollar. To the left of the near staircase he shows 9 windows in the drawing (fig. IV-8), but he also leaves a blank space at the far left which could have accommodated 2 or 3 additional windows if we allow for incremental narrowing of the interval between windows as they approach the perceived edge of the "round" building. Thus it seems clear that the arc of the building extending from the staircase to the left edge of the building could have accommodated 11 or 12 windows. The interpretation is confirmed by the etching (fig. IV-9), where Hollar, now omitting the blank space, shows 12 windows between the staircase and the left edge of the building. To the right of the staircase Hollar shows 7 windows in the drawing, but again he leaves a blank space at the far right which could have accommodated 2 or 3 additional windows if we again allow for incremental narrowing of the interval between windows as they approach the edge of the building. (Stigmata caused apparently by a tear in the drawing are misleadingly reproduced in fig. IV-8, made from a photostat; compare the better reproduction in fig. 16 of *Shakespeare's Second Globe*.) Thus it seems clear that the arc of the building extending from the staircase to the right edge of the building could have accommodated 9 or 10 windows. (Unfortunately the etching, in which the right side of the building is heavily shaded, is silent on this question.) Combining the information of our two sources, we may conclude that Hollar depicts a building that had or could have had 21 or 22 visible windows in half of its circumference, 12 to the left of the staircase and 9 or 10 to the right.

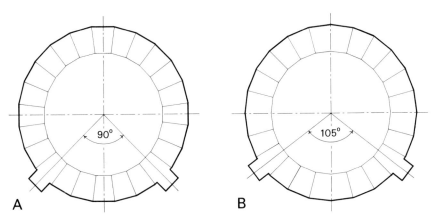

Fig. IV–7. Possible sitings of the staircases in a 24-sided Globe. (*A*) Major axes of the playhouse frame oriented through bay middles. (*B*) Major axes of the frame oriented through bay junctures.

It is necessary to add to the preceding paragraph a brief coda about a puzzling aspect of Hollar's technique in representing the windows. In the drawing (fig. IV-8), as we should expect, Hollar incrementally narrows the interval between successive windows as they extend from the staircase round the building to the left, perhaps not depicting the last three windows because they would have had to be shown so extremely close together as to make execution difficult with the thick penpoint he was using. (To the right of the staircase he inadvertently widens and then slightly narrows the interval between windows.) In the etching (fig. IV-9), however, Hollar depicts uniform intervals between the windows except for the last interval on the left, which he does represent as slightly narrower than elsewhere. This apparently unsophisticated treatment, which is especially surprising in view of Hollar's having incrementally narrowed the corresponding intervals in the drawing, is difficult to explain. One possible explanation is that Hollar here deliberately defied perspective in order to emphasize the precise number of windows in the arc of the building in question. Another possible explanation is that he assigned the work of etching the windows to an assistant who carried out his task without considering that the conventions of perspective required him to show an incremental narrowing of the interval between successive windows as they approached the edge of the building.

In order to relate Hollar's representations of the Globe to the ground plans of both a 16-sided and a 24-sided building, I have prepared projections from drawing and etching for each of the four cases (figs. IV-10–13 below). I am indebted to Hodges for the basic idea of the projections, and especially for the all-important angle of orientation of the axis of each projection. Instead of tracings, however, I have used photo-

RICHARD HOSLEY

Fig. IV—8. The number of windows of the frame depicted in Hollar's drawing of
the Globe.

copies of Hollar's illustrations, and in other respects my presentation differs
from its model because of a different purpose: in each case I have substi-
tuted a polygonal ground plan (including a plan of the stage) for Hodges'
true-circular roof plan (including a plan of the superstructure roof); and I
have exchanged his general reference lines for reference lines relating the
windows and near staircase as shown in each projection to the windows and
staircase as shown in drawing or etching. I have also related the pertinent
bays of each ground plan to each of Hollar's illustrations by "gathering
together" each pair or trio of window reference lines by means of a horizontal bar, the number of lines so gathered depending on whether 2-window
or 3-window bays are in question. And I have, finally, inserted in each
reproduction of Hollar a pair of short dimension lines indicating the horizontal interval in both illustration and projection between the left-hand
edge of the near staircase and the approximate centerline of the first window of the bay immediately on the left of the staircase.

In the case of the 16-sided shape (figs. IV-10–IV-11), 4 bays of
the projection (numbered *1–4* in the diagrams) fall within the quarter-
circle of the playhouse lying between the near staircase (butting up against
bay 5) and the left edge of the building. If each bay had 3 windows, 12
windows, separated from one another by a central angle of $7\frac{1}{2}°$ on centers,
would thus have been visible from Hollar's point of view. So it is in the
etching (fig. IV-11), although with some displacement resulting from Hollar's depiction of a uniform interval between windows as they approach the
left edge of the building. In turning to the drawing (fig. IV-10), we

92

Fig. IV-9. The number of windows of the frame depicted in Hollar's etching of the Globe.

note from the projection that 8 bays of the plan fall within the observed half-circle of the building. The 7 windowed bays, if we assume 3 windows per bay, would have shown a total of 21 windows: 12 in the 4 bays (*1–4*) to the left of the staircase, plus 9 in the 3 bays (*6–8*) to its right. So it is, potentially, in the drawing, where 21 or 22 windows either are depicted or could have been depicted in available blank space at the edges of the building: 12 to the left of the staircase, plus 9 or 10 to its right. Displacement of the staircase, attributable to a presumed error of 5° in its siting in the drawing, may be disregarded.

So far the correspondence of pictorial sources and projections is very close. In the matter of one additional feature, however, the correspondence is faulty. The projections differ considerably from the illustrations in the width of the interval between the near staircase and the first window of the bay immediately on its left: in each projection, as the inserted dimension lines indicate, this interval is more than twice as great as in the corresponding illustration. Presumably the reason for this discrepancy is that the faces of a 16-sided building of the assumed diameter (99 feet) have too great a width (19 feet 6 inches) to permit the near staircase, centered on the face of one bay (5), to stand as close to the first window of the immediately adjoining bay (4) as would have been possible in the case of a 24-sided building, in which the faces have a much smaller width (13 feet). Moreover, we may not interpret Hollar's rightmost window in the etching as a window of the staircase bay, for in that case the number of windows remaining in the perceived arc of the building (11), corresponding to 4

93

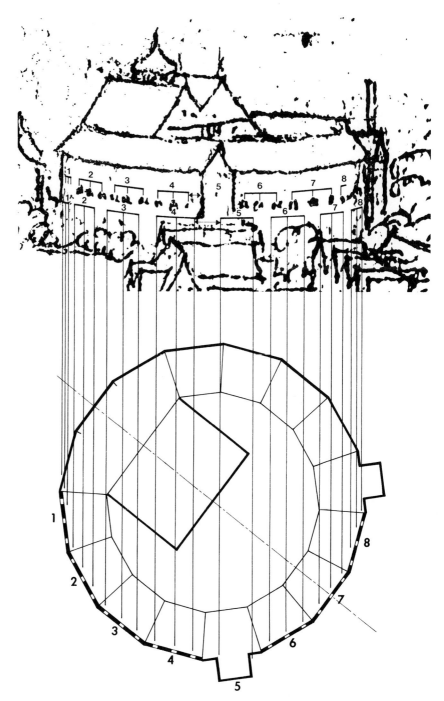

Fig. IV–10. The correlation of windows, bays, and near staircase in Hollar's drawing of the Globe and in a 16-sided plan projected from it.

94

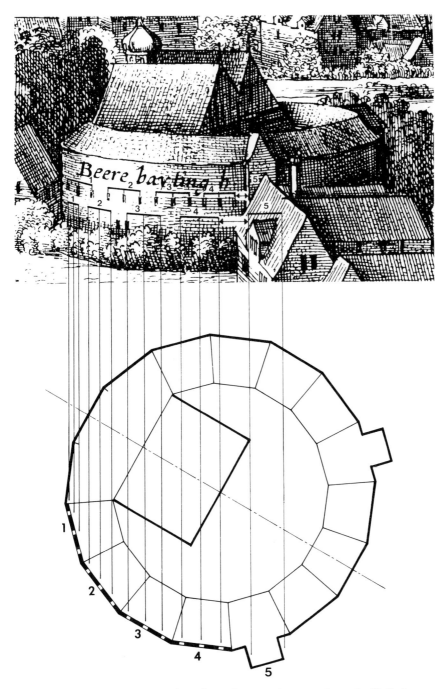

Fig. IV—11. The correlation of windows, bays, and near staircase in Hollar's etching of the Globe and in a 16-sided plan projected from it.

bays of the frame, would fail to agree with the number (12) required by the plan. We may conclude that Hollar's evidence, although in part consistent with a theory that the Globe was a 16-sided building, is in part inconsistent with such a theory.

In the case of the 24-sided shape (figs. IV-12–IV-13), 6 bays of the plan (numbered *1–6* in the diagrams) fall within the quarter-circle of the playhouse lying between the near staircase (sited next to bay 7) and the left edge of the building. If each bay had 2 windows, 12 windows, separated from one another by a central angle of $7\frac{1}{2}°$ on centers, would have been visible from Hollar's point of view. So it is in the etching (fig. IV-13), although with some displacement resulting from the depiction of uniform intervals between the windows. In turning to the drawing (fig. IV-12), we note from the projection that 12 bays fall within the observed half-circle of the building. The 11 windowed bays, assuming 2 windows per bay, would have exhibited a total of 22 windows: 12 in the 6 bays (*1–6*) to the left of the staircase, plus 10 in the 5 bays (*8–12*) to its right. So it is, potentially, in the drawing, where 21 or 22 windows either are depicted or could have been depicted in available blank space at the edges of the building: 12 to the left of the staircase, plus 9 or 10 to its right. Again, displacement of the staircase, presumably due to an error of 5° in its siting in the drawing, may be disregarded.

So far, as in the situation of the 16-sided ground plan, the correspondence of pictorial sources and projections is very close. Here, however, in contrast to the situation of the 16-sided ground plan, the correspondence is fairly close in the matter of the observed additional feature. The projections and the illustrations agree, in general, on the width of the interval between the near staircase and the first window of the bay immediately on its left: that interval, as the inserted dimension lines indicate, is almost exactly the same in the drawing as in the plan projected from it, about 30 percent smaller in the etching than in the plan projected from it. Presumably the reason for this general agreement is that the faces of a 24-sided building of the assumed diameter (99 feet) have a small enough width (13 feet) to permit the near staircase, centered on the face of one bay (7), to stand appreciably closer to the first window of the immediately adjoining bay (6) than would have been possible in the case of a 16-sided building, in which the faces have a much greater width (19 feet 6 inches). We may conclude that Hollar's evidence is consistent, in general, with a theory that the Globe was a 24-sided building.

To summarize. One feature of the pictorial evidence, the number of windows depicted in the perceived round of the Globe, is as consistent with the theory of a 16-sided building as with that of a 24-sided one. However, another feature of the evidence, the interval depicted between the near staircase and the first window of the immediately adjoining bay on the left, is inconsistent with the theory of a 16-sided building, although consistent in general with the theory of a 24-sided one.

Another kind of evidence for the shape of the second Globe consists of the proportions in plan of nonscenic rectangular stages of the period. We know the horizontal dimensions of three such stages, one in a public playhouse, another in a private playhouse, the third in a temporary court playhouse fitted up in a hall. The public playhouse stage, that of the first Fortune (1600), measured, according to the contract for building that playhouse, 43 feet 0 inches wide by 27 feet 6 inches deep.[9] The proportions of width to depth of this stage may be described by an arithmetical ratio of 1.564 or by a fractional ratio (approximated to a norm of 3:2) of 3.1:2.0 (see fig. IV-14A). The private playhouse stage, that of the Phoenix or Cockpit (1616), measured, according to the designs by Inigo Jones preserved at Worcester College, Oxford, 22 feet 6 inches wide by 15 feet 0 inches deep.[10] The proportions of width to depth of this stage may be described by an arithmetical ratio of 1.500 or by a fractional ratio of 3:2 (fig. IV-14B). And the temporary court stage, set up in the Hall at Woodstock in 1621 ("the scholars of Oxford being to act a play before the King"), measured, according to a record in the Declared Accounts of the Office of the King's Works, 24 feet wide by 16 feet deep.[11] The proportions of width to depth of this stage may also be described by an arithmetical ratio of 1.500 or by a fractional ratio of 3:2 (shape not illustrated). The three stages, having width-to-depth ratios that deviate only slightly from a mean of 1.521, have such strikingly similar proportions that we may, conceding the danger inherent in generalizing from so small a body of evidence, suppose that nonscenic rectangular stages of the period were traditional in conforming to a width-to-depth ratio of about 3:2 (arithmetical ratio about 1.500). I shall make a further point, about the strength of the tradition in question, at a later stage of the present argument.

Before continuing that argument, however, I must call attention to two assumptions that I make about the relationship of the Globe stage to its containing polygonal building. Both assumptions are standard ones, accepted in practically all reconstructions of "round" public playhouses that employ the concept of a rectangular stage.

The first is that the front edge of the stage (viewed in plan) ran along what may be called the transverse axis of the playhouse. This assumption is based both on the evidence of the Fortune contract that the stage of that playhouse extended "to the middle of the yard" and on the evidence of the Swan drawing (ca. 1596) that the stage of that playhouse did the same.

The other assumption is that the rear edge of the stage (viewed in plan) ran between inner corners of the polygonal playhouse frame. This assumption is a conclusion based on the following premises: (1) the tiring-

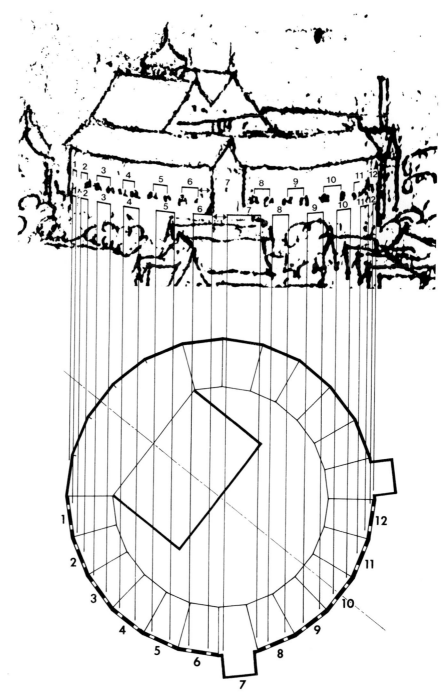

Fig. IV–12. The correlation of windows, bays, and near staircase in Hollar's drawing of the Globe and in a 24-sided plan projected from it.

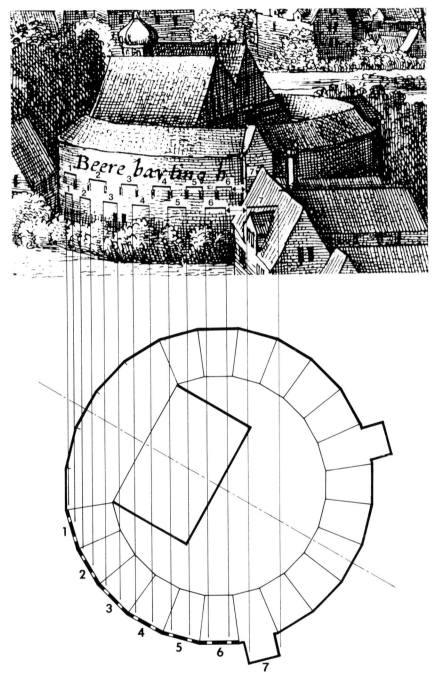

Fig. IV–13. The correlation of windows, bays, and near staircase in Hollar's etching of the Globe and in a 24-sided plan projected from it.

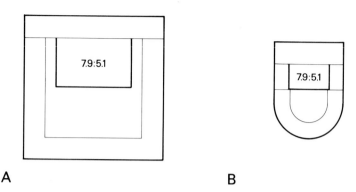

Fig. IV–14. Two known ratios of width to depth of stage. (A) Stage in the Fortune playhouse. (B) Stage in the Phoenix playhouse.

house façade must have run (in plan) between inner corners of the polygonal playhouse frame; and (2) the stage presumably did not extend laterally beyond the ends of the tiring-house façade, for if it had done so the bays of the frame on either side of the tiring-house would have encroached upon the rear corners of the stage and thus altered its rectangular character.[12]

If we accept these two assumptions, it is clear that the width and depth of a rectangular stage fitted into a polygonal playhouse frame will vary in accordance with the location (variable from one polygonal ground plan to another) of the inner corners of the frame chosen to accommodate the rear corners of the stage. Or, to put the matter in more general terms, the geometrical pattern of the polygon chosen as the ground plan of a "round" playhouse will determine the proportions of a rectangular stage fitted into that ground plan. *Ut theatrum, sic proscaenium.*

Thus a rectangular stage fitted into the frame of a 16-sided playhouse, where there are conveniently located inner corners 3 bays apart (central angle 67½°), will have proportions of width to depth that may be described by an arithmetical ratio of 1.336 or by a fractional ratio (approximated to a norm of 3:2) of 2.8:2.1 (fig. IV-15A). This ratio (1.336) deviates considerably from the mean (1.521) of the ratios of our three model stages. It is thus clear that the 16-sided form of playhouse enforces a rectangular stage having proportions appreciably narrower and deeper than those that have been suggested as traditional. On the other hand, a rectangular stage fitted into the frame of a 24-sided playhouse, where there are conveniently located corners 5 bays apart (central angle 75°), will have proportions of width to depth that may be described by an arithmetical ratio of 1.535 or by a fractional ratio of 3:2 (fig. IV-15B). This ratio (1.535) is very close to the mean (1.521) of the ratios of our three model stages. Evidently, the 24-sided

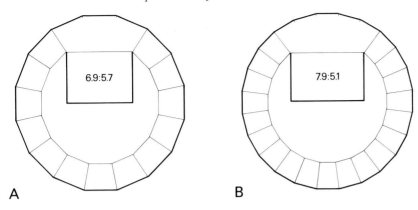

Fig. IV–15. Two hypothetical ratios of width to depth of stage. (*A*) Stage in a 16-sided Globe. (*B*) Stage in a 24-sided Globe.

form of playhouse enforces a rectangular stage having proportions almost exactly the same as those that have been suggested as traditional.[13] The cited dimensions and ratios are listed in the table.

Dimensions and Width-to-Depth Proportions of Some Known and Hypothetical Nonscenic Rectangular Stages

Stage	*Dimensions*	*Arithmetical ratio of proportions*	*Fractional ratio of proportions*
Stage of hypothetical 16-sided playhouse	. . .	1.336	2.8:2.1* (2.828:2.116)
Stage of second Globe (1614) as here reconstructed	41'6'' × 27'8''	1.500	3:2 (3.000:2.000)
Stage of Phoenix playhouse (1616)	22'6'' × 15'0''	1.500	3:2 (3.000:2.000)
Temporary stage set up in the Hall at Woodstock (1621)	24' × 16'	1.500	3:2 (3.000:2.000)
Stage of hypothetical 24-sided playhouse	. . .	1.535	3:2 (3.035:1.977)
Stage of first Fortune playhouse (1600)	43'0'' × 27'6''	1.564	3.1:2.0* (3.062:1.958)

*Approximated to a norm of 3:2.

The influence of variant polygonal playhouse forms on the shape of the rectangular stages they contained gives perspective to our evidence for the shape of nonscenic rectangular stages of the period. A rectangular stage fitted into a 24-sided playhouse frame in the manner suggested would have been forced to have width-to-depth proportions of 3:2. But our three model stages, having been fitted into rectangular rather than polygonal architectural contexts, would have suffered no such constraining influence on their proportions. Thus the designer of each of those stages was free to employ whatever proportions he chose. That each designer, despite this freedom, chose proportions exactly or very nearly in a ratio of 3:2 suggests that the tradition of such proportions was a strong one.

In sum, if we suppose that the designer of the Globe stage utilized traditional proportions of width to depth, our evidence suggests not only that the second Globe was not a 16-sided building but also that it was a 24-sided one.

The foregoing arguments regarding the shape of the second Globe may be briefly synthesized. The ground plan of a 16-sided building, for which there is a theatrical analogue in Henry VIII's temporary banqueting house at Calais, could easily have been laid out by Euclidean methods requiring (in the case of a 99-foot diameter) only a three-rod surveyor's line. However, the 16-sided shape of building does not harmonize in general with Hollar's pictorial evidence, and it would presumably have enforced a stage with untraditional proportions of width to depth. On the other hand, the ground plan of a 24-sided building, for which there is a theatrical analogue in the Swan playhouse, could also easily have been laid out by Euclidean methods requiring (in the case of a 99-foot diameter) only a three-rod surveyor's line. Moreover, the 24-sided shape of building harmonizes in general with Hollar's pictorial evidence, and it would presumably have enforced a stage with traditional proportions of width to depth. In short, all of the evidence at present available accords with the hypothesis that the second Globe was a 24-sided building.[14]

I turn now to a more detailed consideration of the size of the second Globe. If we combine the hypothesis that the Globe was a 24-sided building with the hypothesis that it had a 99-foot outer diameter measured between centers of opposed principal posts, and if we assume that the posts in question were 10 inches square, as called for in the Hope contract, we find that the outer diameter of the Globe would have measured 99 feet between opposed faces of the building.[15] And, if we assume that the inner diameter measured 70 feet between centers of opposed principal posts, we find that the inner diameter would have measured 68 feet 6 inches between opposed faces of the building. The two sets of diameters are illustrated in figure IV-16, together with a third set established earlier, the outer and inner diameters measured between opposed corners of the building (99 feet 10 inches and 69 feet 2 inches). In accordance with the proposed face-to-

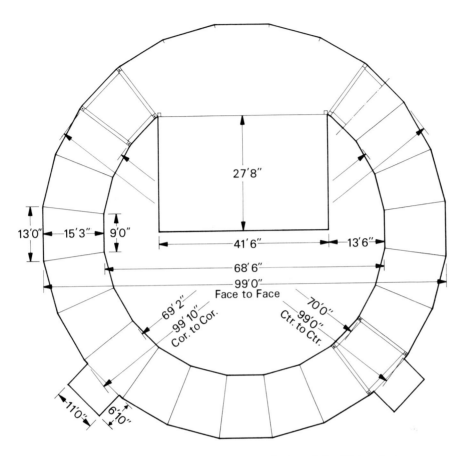

Fig. IV–16. Proposed dimensions of the ground plan of the Globe playhouse.

face diameters, the depth of the frame would have measured 15 feet 3 inches between the outer and inner faces of each bay; and in accordance with the proposed corner-to-corner diameters, the outer and inner faces of each bay would have measured, respectively, 13 feet and 9 feet between corners (fig. IV-16).

The conclusion that the frame of the second Globe was 15 feet 3 inches deep may be compared with the requirement of the Fortune contract that the frame of that playhouse was to be 12 feet 6 inches deep in the first storey. Clearly, the Globe differed from the Fortune in having considerably larger galleries. Moreover, the Globe frame differed from the Fortune frame in another important respect. Our knowledge of the *ad quadratum* proportions of the Globe frame derives from Hollar's depiction of the depth in plan of the roof, hence in effect from the depicted depth in plan of the third storey. Yet *ad quadratum* proportions must have been used by the builder in laying out the ground plan of the building. It follows that the first and third storeys of the Globe frame had the same depth in plan and thus that the

103

Globe, unlike the Fortune, did not have "jutties forwards" in the upper storeys of its frame. In this connection we may note the apparent absence of overhangs from de Witt's depiction of the frame of the Swan playhouse.

The noted differences in horizontal dimensions between the frames of the Globe and the Fortune are part of the larger question of the differences in ground plan between a round and a square playhouse of the dimensions given: compare the superimposed plans of the two playhouses in figure IV-18 below. In respect to vertical dimensions of the frame, however, there is no reason to suppose that the round and the square forms of playhouse were in any way different; and there is reason to suppose they were similar, since our contract for building a round playhouse (the Hope) concurs with our contract for building a square one (the Fortune) in requiring that the first storey of the frame be 12 feet high. Thus it is reasonable to suppose, not only that the first storey of the Globe frame was 12 feet high as called for in the Fortune and Hope contracts, but also that the second and third storeys of the Globe frame were, respectively, 11 feet and 9 feet high as called for in the Fortune contract (the Hope contract being silent on the latter question). Presumably the heights of frame called for in the Fortune contract include the thickness of constructional timbers in all three storeys. Thus, assuming that the Globe foundation rose one foot above ground level (as suggested by the Fortune contract), we find that the height of the Globe frame would have measured 33 feet from ground level to the top of the wall-plates. The proposed vertical dimensions are illustrated in an axonometric projection of two bays of the skeleton of the Globe frame reproduced as figure IV-17. The scantlings of the depicted members of the frame are those called for in the Hope contract, except where, the contract being silent, it has been necessary to resort to supposition. The most important of the supposed scantlings is a 12-inch depth of groundsill. This dimension has the effect of setting the tops of the first-storey joists at an elevation of 2 feet above ground level and of making the floor-to-floor height of the first storey the same as that of the second (11 feet).

Earlier in this essay I defined my two basic assumptions about the Globe stage: that its front edge ran along the "transverse" axis of the playhouse frame and that its rear edge ran between two inner corners of that frame—specifically, between corners separated by 5 bays or a central angle of 75°. When we consider the second assumption in detail, however, it becomes clear that precise location of the points defining the rear edge of the stage—and thus the points from which the sides of the stage would have extended forward—depends on the precise manner in which, at the chosen corners of the frame, the tiring-house façade joined with the faces of the bays of the frame that stood immediately on either side of the tiring-house. Requirements both of construction and of architectural styles make it unlikely that the system of rectangular posting of the tiring-house façade could have used, at the juncture of that façade with the face of each

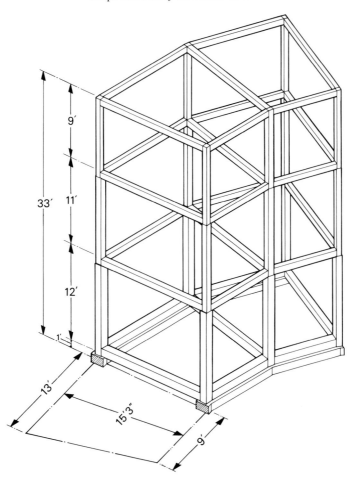

Fig. IV–17. An axonometric projection of the skeleton of the Globe frame, with vertical dimensions taken from the Fortune contract and scantlings of structural members taken from the Hope contract.

adjacent bay of the frame, the same principal post as did the system of polygonal posting of the frame. I therefore assume that there were two principal posts at each of the corners of the frame chosen to define the rear edge of the stage, one such post serving the posting system of the tiring-house, the other that of the frame. Presumably the two posts of each pair would have been (so far as possible) contiguous, linked by pins or ties of some sort at convenient points where they did not overlap in the vertical dimension. The conception is illustrated in plan in figure IV-16 above. A practical effect of this arrangement is that each of the side edges of the stage would presumably have extended forward, not from the exact corner of the frame in question, but from a point approximately 5 inches removed from that corner, namely, from the outer edge of the end post of the

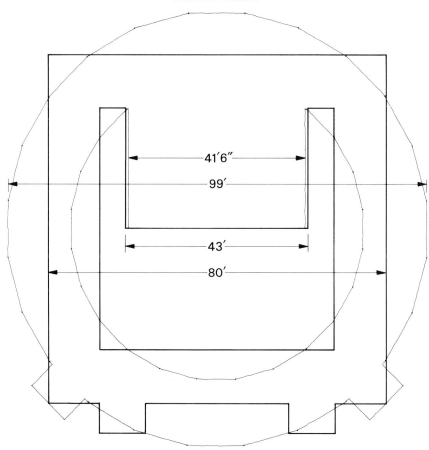

Fig. IV–18. The proposed ground plan of the Globe compared with the known ground plan of the Fortune.

tiring-house façade. Thus we may hypothesize that the Globe stage measured 41 feet 6 inches in width by 27 feet 8 inches in depth (fig. IV-16). As it happens, the width and depth of such a stage stand in a ratio of 3:2 or 1.500—exactly the same as the ratio of two of the three nonscenic rectangular stages cited above and very close to that of the third (3.1:2.0 or 1.564). The various dimensions and proportions cited may be compared in the table given above, and in figure IV-18 the proposed size of the Globe stage may be compared with the known size of the Fortune stage.

My last topic is the ground plan of the staircases. In his drawing of the west part of Southwark, Hollar depicts the near staircase of the Globe as about one-ninth the width of the playhouse frame (fig. IV-8 above). Thus, assuming a playhouse width of 99 feet 10 inches, we may suppose that the width of the staircase was about 11 feet. (In the etching, fig. IV-9, Hollar shows the near staircase as about one-eleventh the width of the playhouse frame; thus the width of the staircase would have been about 9 feet.) This is of course an external measurement; by subtracting 10 inches for the assumed thickness of principal posts in each of the two sides of the staircase frame, we arrive at an internal width of 9 feet 4 inches. Since this is too short a dimension to accommodate a "straight" flight of stairs rising about 11 feet (the largest required rise between landings), it is clear that the stairs must have been of the winding variety, fully contained within the staircase. Thus we may suppose that the depth of the staircase frame was 6 feet: that is, 3 feet for the length of treads rising in one direction and 3 feet more for the length of treads rising in the opposite direction after the turnaround (thickness of the newel included).[16] This is an internal measurement; by adding 10 inches for the thickness of principal posts in the front of the staircase, we arrive at an external dimension of 6 feet 10 inches for the depth of the staircase. I therefore suppose that the Globe staircases were built to a ground plan measuring 11 feet by 6 feet 10 inches "from outside to outside" (fig. IV-16) and that the stairs proper were contained within a ground plan measuring 9 feet 4 inches by 6 feet.[17]

V. *Wenceslaus Hollar and the Size of the Globe Theatre*

JOHN ORRELL

*I*n an article shortly to be published in *Shakespeare Survey*, I argue from the evidence of the Fortune contract that both the Fortune and the Globe were so designed that their plans could be laid out on the ground by the skilled and economical manipulation of a traditional three-rod (49 feet 6 inches) surveyor's line. The most direct way to establish the ground plan of the Globe (doubtless used initially by Burbage at the Theatre in 1576) was to inscribe its polygon within a circle whose radius was three rods and whose diameter was therefore six rods, or 99 feet, between the post centers of the outer part of the frame. Such a theatre would be about 100 feet wide overall, not including the attached staircase turrets. Before writing the article, I tried to discover whether the familiar drawing of the second Globe made by Hollar in the 1630s could be coaxed to yield confirmation or disproof of my theory, but was forced to adopt an unsatisfactory method of estimating that had previously been used by C. Walter Hodges and Richard Hosley, with divergent results.[1]

This method begins with the assumption that the height of the second Globe's frame was similar to that specified in the Fortune contract and proceeds to a conclusion by comparing the width of Hollar's Globe to its height. There are several reasons why this method will not do. First, there is no very precise agreement on what height the slightly ambiguous terms of the Fortune contract actually do stipulate, the estimates ranging from 33 feet to 34 feet 6 inches. Of course there can be no certainty that the Globe was the same height as the Fortune in any case. Next there is the lamentable fact that Hollar's drawing is imprecise in just this matter of height, the visible left-side wall being fringed with bushes at its base so that we cannot see where it springs from the ground. Finally, there are questions that must be asked about the very nature of the drawing and the validity of measurements taken from it, and to some of these questions the present essay is addressed. The aim is to find a satisfactory way of measuring the width of the Globe as it is shown by Hollar, avoiding if possible the treacherous comparison of width to height which has so far yielded such debatable results. In the following pages I outline very briefly a reliable method of direct measurement.

The drawing over the rooftops of Southwark is of course our best piece of visual evidence about the Globe, but it is often forgotten that it has a companion piece (fig. V-1), a view made at the same time from the same place and by the same technique, also over the rooftops, but eastward toward Greenwich. This Greenwich drawing is obviously a study of the most mechanical sort: its composition has no center of interest, its roofs make uncouth orthogonal assaults on the picture plane, its margins—edges, rather—cut abruptly across important objects with no sense of framing, like an unskillfully cropped photograph or a snapshot.

There is reason to believe that this view toward Greenwich is indeed the seventeenth-century equivalent of a photograph—that it was composed at a drawing frame whose effect is to offer a mechanical survey of the real scene, not an artist's composition. Such a drawing frame consists of a rectangular frame graticulated with strings—lute strings, often—forming a grid that enabled the artist to measure the horizontal and vertical elements within the scene he surveyed. A fixed eyepiece forced him to adopt the single unmoving point of view required for a linear perspective composition. Alberti explained how the thing worked in the fifteenth century: how a perspective view was nothing but a plane intersection of the visual pyramid of rays whose apex lies in the observer's eye, and how the drawing frame (or *velo* as he called it) represented just such a plane.[2] Measures taken from the frame could be transferred to the drawing board by means of a pair of compasses, or else the frame itself might be filled with glass and the drawing made directly on it with a pen or small brush.[3]

If Hollar did on occasion use a drawing frame it should follow that some of his sketches will betray that fact by their exact consonance with reality; we should expect the intervals between major landmarks to be as precisely stated as they would be in a carefully surveyed map. To check this all we have to do is to establish the point from which the drawing was made, then rule on a modern Ordnance Survey map the sightlines from it to the various points Hollar shows. In any view of London before the fire of 1666 many of these will be landmarks that have subsequently disappeared or been rebuilt, so some historical investigation will be necessary. But once the sightlines have been drawn on the map it is simply a matter of discovering whether the intervals as given by Hollar really can be found along a straight intersection of them. If they can, the line of intersection thus established will represent a line parallel to that of the drawing frame as the artist had set it up. Of course, as we draw it even on a large-scale map it will be much further away from Hollar's precise point of view than his actual drawing frame was, but the geometry of similar triangles shows that

Fig. V–1. Wenceslaus Hollar, *East Part of Southwarke, Greenwich.* (Paul Mellon Collection, Yale Centre for British Art.)

the ratio of intervals marked along it will be the same as those originally found at the frame itself. Provided that the drawing offers enough information for at least four points of intersection to be established the matter can be proved.

In the view toward Greenwich there are not enough identifiable landmarks to make this sort of demonstration very convincing, so I have chosen instead a little sketch of Hollar's now in the British Library showing London as seen from the foreshore by Durham House.[4] We can clearly identify a broad range of landmarks all across the drawing, from St. Sepulchre to the left to the White Tower at the right. Choosing landmarks at fairly even intervals across the view, we identify them and plot the sight-lines on a map. Then we find whether the intervals as recorded in the sketch are consonant with these real intervals; it is simply a matter of juggling the drawing across the lines of sight until it fits, which it does on a bearing of 167° from true north (fig. V-2).

Here, then, is a sketch in which no fewer than nine identifiable landmarks are precisely stated as they would be on a drawing frame. We must conclude either that Hollar used such a frame or that his eye and hand were so accurate that he had no need of one but nevertheless composed as if he were using one, for we must notice that the precision here is entirely a matter of rendering a *plane* intersection of the visual pyramid. He is not putting down on paper a simple record of the relative distances apart of the

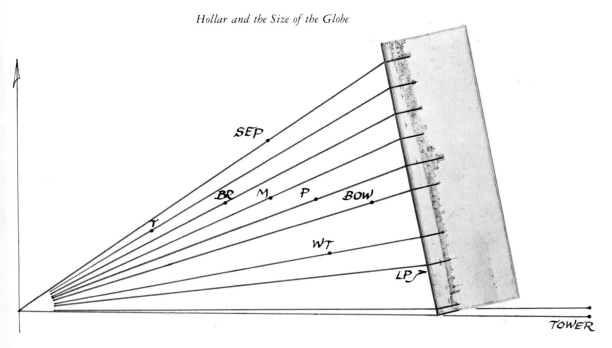

Fig. V–2. Wenceslaus Hollar, *London and Old St. Paul's*, plotted on sightlines drawn to positions traced from a modern map. The landmarks located are:

T	Temple	*WT*	Bulmer's water tower
BR	St. Bride's	*BOW*	St. Mary-le-Bow
SEP	St. Sepulchre	*LP*	St. Laurence Poultney
M	St. Martin's, Ludgate	*TOWER*	White Tower
P	St. Paul's crossing		

landmarks as seen radially from his point of view. Such a landscape presupposes a more or less segmental arc of intersection and results in intervals quite different from those yielded by the plane intersection. The intervals in the drawing are exactly consistent with the use of a drawing frame and not at all with freehand estimating. They constitute a deliberate measurement of the landscape akin to a survey.

John Norden's panorama of London, the *Civitas Londini* of 1600, shows a little figure atop St. Saviour's waving a pair of compasses in the air beneath the legend Statio Prospectiva: "Point of View." The compasses suggest a surveyor's attitude to accuracy, and of course Norden was a surveyor by profession. There is evidence that the views of the north bank of the Thames in the three famous panoramas—Norden's, Visscher's and Hollar's—were composed at the drawing frame, each artist covering the more-than-180° of the whole scene in a series of "takes" which he spliced together in the studio. Some of the evidence shows that Norden and Visscher used a common survey, though Hollar seems to have made his own.[5] We should note that the veracity of such a survey consists in its statement of the relative positions and the lateral extent of the objects in

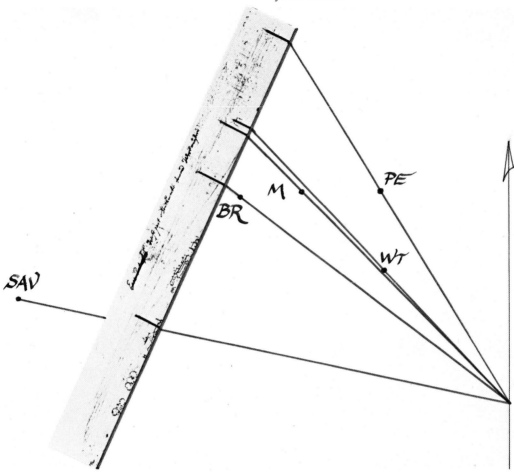

Fig. V–3. Wenceslaus Hollar, *West Part of Southwarke toward Westminster*. (Paul Mellon Collection, Centre for British Art.) The sketch is here plotted on sight-lines drawn from St. Saviour's tower to the following landmarks:

PE	St. Paul's east end	BR	St. Bride's
WT	Bulmer's water tower	SAV	Savoy: southwest corner of
M	St. Martin's, Ludgate		river front

Hollar's markings along the north bank are very faint and do not reproduce well.

view, not in details of their appearance. In the little drawing in figure V-2 the interval between St. Paul's (say) and the Tower is exactly stated, but one would hardly want to vouch for the size of the lantern on the roof of the Middle Temple hall. The intervals are a matter of measurement, taken presumably by compasses at the frame itself. They are mechanical; but the details are the topographical artist's own way of seeing things.

We now turn to the familiar view toward Westminster. Was this also composed at the drawing frame? Like the Greenwich view it seems

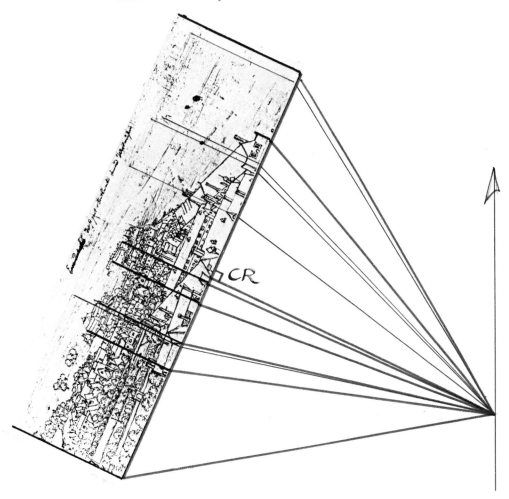

Fig. V–4. Same as figure V–3, but here the bearings of the Globe, the Hope, and the eastern gable of Winchester House have been deduced from the drawing.

ill-composed, uncomfortably overstating the foreground like something from *Les Toits de Paris*. But here the theatres do give a center of interest and make the whole seem less mechanical. Notice that there is a horizon line, ruled with a straight-edge all across the drawing. It can be seen just above the actual horizon to the left and just below it to the right. Onto this line, as is proper to a linear perspective view, all horizontals in the sketch converge. But to discover whether the drawing was made at a frame we must find enough identifiable landmarks—we need a minimum of four—to check against a map of sightlines. Because the theatres themselves are the objects of our interest we must not use them for this purpose, or we may be guilty of a circular argument. Fortunately, dimly though the background is presented to us now after centuries of rubbing, it does give more than four locatable points.

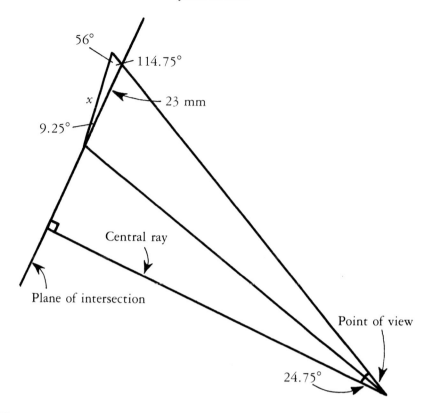

Fig. V–5. Method of calculating the width of the gable end of Winchester House (x) as shown by Hollar:

$$\frac{\sin 56}{23} = \frac{\sin 114.75}{x} \quad \text{where } x = 25.19 \text{ mm}$$

$$335 \times \frac{25.19}{306} \times 2 \tan 34.3 = 37.62 \text{ feet}$$

To work from the right. The east gable of St. Paul's is most exactly stated, with very fine lines, its peak just above the horizon line (just above, that is to say, Hollar's level at the top of St. Saviour's). Then, to the left, there is no mistaking the outline of Bevis Bulmer's water tower, built in the 1590s at Broken Wharf. It burned in the fire of 1666 but was rebuilt on the same site, as the Fire Court records show, and is marked on Ogilby and Morgan's map. We can therefore place it on a modern map too. Above and to the left is St. Martin's, Ludgate, a tower which stood a few feet further to the south and west than Wren's present flèche. Further left still, above the sketchy outline of Baynard's Castle, is the heavy tower of St. Bride's. Left of that again there is nothing much recognizable until we come all the way to a point just above the right-hand side of the Globe. Here, very faintly but also recognizably, is the outline of the Savoy, with

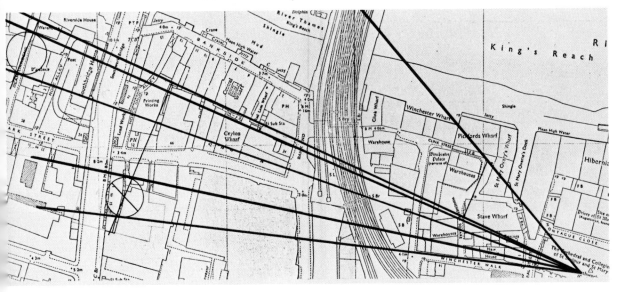

Fig. V–6. An enlargement of the Bankside section of figure V-4, showing the bearings of the theatres and the gable of Winchester House. (Based upon Ordnance Survey map, with the permission of the Controller of Her Majesty's Stationery Office, Crown copyright reserved.)

two turrets to the right and one to the left. In most reproductions this outline is very dim indeed, but the dense photograph published by Richard Hosley in the *Revels History* shows it clearly.[6]

Here, then, are our five identifiable landmarks, four of them well spaced across the range of view. As before, we juggle their intervals across the map of sightlines and discover that they are indeed exactly consistent with the geographical facts and a picture plane on a bearing of 25.25° from true north. The overall arc of the view can also be measured as 68.6°.

I should stress that the diagram (fig. V-3) is only a shortcut to the truth. The demonstration is better made through trigonometry, whereby the very great precision of Hollar's drawing becomes evident; but lack of space prevents the inclusion here of the rather lengthy calculations.

If the positions of St. Paul's east end, the water tower, St. Martin's, St. Bride's, and the Savoy are all consistent with a straight picture plane of 25.25°, it follows that other places represented in the view are likely to be similarly accurately stated, including the two theatres and Winchester House (fig. V-4). The drawing may therefore be used, in conjunction with a modern map, to calculate the sizes of the objects it represents. It is a matter of expressing the width of each object as a proportion of a plane running through it, parallel to the picture plane and coextensive with the arc of the view. Thus, knowing from modern maps that such a plane running through the nearer gable of Winchester House was 335 feet distant from the observer, and knowing also that the gable was inclined at 9.25° from that plane, we may calculate the width of this architectural feature as it is shown by Hollar. From our plotting we know that the whole arc of the view is 68.6°, equally divided by the central ray. At 335 feet from the observer, this arc spans 335 × 2 tan 34.3 feet. A simple calculation shows that where the gable end is 23 mm wide out of the 306 mm of the overall width of the view, its deviation from the picture plan reduces its visible width by a determinable amount. Once this is established, the actual width of the gable as shown in the drawing may be calculated as a proportion of the plane running through it parallel to the picture plane and terminated on either side by the limits of the arc of view. The result for the Winchester House gable end is 37.62 feet (fig. V-5). Parts of the building are still extant, and these have led the authors of the London County Council Survey of London to illustrate it in measured drawings as 38 feet wide.[7] Hollar is 1.0 percent off the mark.

We can use a similar technique to check the distances between the identifiable landmarks on the north bank, and these turn out to be accurate to within ±2.0 percent, but of course we should expect that to be so because it is on their accuracy that we have established the veracity of the drawing in the first place.

The most interesting part comes when we turn to the two theatres (fig. V-6). Here matters are complicated a little because a certain calculable distortion, known by the catchall name of anamorphosis, makes all spheres and horizontal discs stretch somewhat as they diverge from the central ray of a linear perspective view. The theatres are horizontal discs, so we have to consider this matter. There is nothing mysterious about it, but I find it impossible to explain in the space available and must refer the reader instead to B. A. R. Carter's concise exposition of it in the *Oxford Companion to Art*. Here I shall simply assert that the Hope is close enough to the central ray for anamorphosis to make little difference and that the Globe's width, lying between 12.5° and 17.5° from the central ray, will be overstated by 3.64 percent as it appears on Hollar's sheet.

Allowing, then, for anamorphosis, and taking our measurement of the distances of the planes through the theatres from our knowledge of their sites as determined by W. W. Braines[8] (and here a certain latitude introduces itself; I have assumed that the theatres were placed centrally on their sites as measured east and west, but that may not have been so), we may calculate their size.

The Hope turns out to be 99.29 feet wide, while the width of Globe is 103.35 feet (both excluding the staircases).[9] These results are so close to one another that I feel drawn to conclude that the "rounds" of both theatres were made to the same measure. The results I have noted are, I believe, accurate to within ±2.0 percent, the margin of error for the intervals along the north bank, and so are consistent with a common width of about 101 or 102 feet.

VI. *Appearance and Reality: A Carpenter's Viewpoint*

STUART EBORALL RIGOLD

$\mathcal{T}$his is an attempt to look, or to divine, beneath the skin. The frame of many framed buildings, whether of timber, steel, or any other material, is, from the exterior, entirely an endoskeleton. Among them, on all evidence, was the second Globe: however accurate and detailed for its scale is Hollar's drawing of just before 1644,[1] it shows not a stitch of framing save the finials of the two gables over the stage and, possibly, a jettied summer or heavy collar beneath their conjoined topmost triangles. There is no need to suppose this to be an omission in the interest of simplified massing; it agrees with all other early seventeenth-century views of London, engraved panoramas, and the few paintings, such as those of Claude de Jongh,[2] that show a certain amount of exposed close-studding but the walls generally rendered or otherwise covered. From this date the exposure of framing on old buildings or new becomes ever rarer in eastern England (such showplaces of late medieval framing as Lavenham, Suffolk, have been totally stripped of rendering in the last century); there, in contrast to the Welsh march, they continued to glory in ornate frames, to build them until early in the eighteenth century, to paint them a specious black and white, and, before that century was out, to paint simulated framing where there was none. A superfical feature, perhaps, but it is some gauge of the divergence of the metropolitan or cosmopolitan mind from the provincial, a divergence only half a pace less with the first Globe; it warns us to be very selective with our archeological analogues.

The theme set down for me, "English Timber-Framed Buildings in the Sixteenth and Seventeenth Centuries," can only provide my outermost parameters. My task is to isolate the small part of the subject that is relevant and to clear away what is distracting, even absurd, in the context. This includes, despite the straw thatch of the first Globe, all overtones of rusticity and "Old English" picturesqueness. If the vagaries of mannerism appeared to ages of purer classicism as grotesque and "antique" (as Wesley called Hatfield House), their constituents are Italianate. Nor are all the

117

traditions of English carpentry to be equated with the "vernacular." England through most of her history has been as much a land of timber building as New England. The diversity of manners and techniques has been correspondingly wide: in region, as we have seen; in patronage and purpose; in bold inventiveness or safe experience in the engineering field, where a climacteric, in many ways unsurpassed, lay back in the thirteenth and fourteenth centuries.[3] Timber buildings on a grand and urbane scale have always approached the standards of masonry, and stone buildings have generally called for the carpenter's craft, at the same level of elegance, for roofs and partitions.

In the Globe we are concerned with London, not with Chester or Shrewsbury, and with a uniquely cosmopolitan, competitive, and centripetal society. No doubt London carpenters had their conservative, restrictive, even vernacular side, but it was eastern vernacular, and in their craft, as in all other, they assumed that London was the point of impact for innovations and the trend-setter for all England, swaying first the most mobile and receptive clientele, not only the richest. The Globe of 1614 must be judged above all from a seventeenth-century standpoint, and as a whole, not as the sum of its parts. If certain parts had roots deep in the past, fifty years earlier a comparable, centrally planned auditorium did not exist, whereas fifty years later, however old-fashioned the Globe might have appeared in detail, it would have been judged among buildings of a widely familiar structural type. An inn-yard or a friary might have sufficed *faute de mieux,* but a theatre was purpose-made, for plays to be heard rather than seen, yet seen to be heard. It had two parts: accommodation for the audience and an acoustic center. Once these had been brought together, probably by and in the theatre, the combined type was used for other assemblages; some were called theatres, like the Sheldonian at Oxford,[4] but by far the most widely disseminated were galleried Protestant preaching-houses,[5] with their familiar and centripetal direction, which have preserved the type ever since. One contributory factor must have been the galleried commercial exchanges, appearing in London about the same time,[6] but already familiar in places like Bruges.[7] In any case it was in London that the problems of structure and scale were suddenly and successfully answered; in London that new and downright ideas on framing were available and applied; and largely from London that both were distributed through England and, in due course, the English-speaking world.

Whereas there is a great wealth of medieval and submedieval timber-framed buildings (covering most things until at least the 1570s) in the Lowland English countryside and its small towns, the major cities have lost proportionately much more and London most of all. What is recorded, photographically or otherwise, tells us little of the framing details owing to the almost universal covering of the buildings. In Paris it is even worse, since plaster of Paris is recorded for complete external rendering since the thirteenth century. We are reduced to arguments by analogy, with the *nearest* parallels, but there is widespread evidence for radical innovation in jointing; for a more economical use of timber, now in far shorter supply, with a readiness to use elm and softwood, both of which produce weaker tenons, as well as oak; and for a heavier nogging of the frame, so that it approaches a timber-laced solid wall, with stresses more evenly distributed than simply at the joints and main members of the frame.[8] All these points are noticeable from quite early in the seventeenth century; in London they were doubtless detectable earlier.

Before discussing what the carpenters had inherited from the older eastern English tradition and would normally have used without question unless directed otherwise (the "vernacular" element, in fact, of their equipment), it is useful to point to several abiding considerations that are valid for the older, the newer, or any manner of carpentry and that may show where we can justly seek our analogues if none is to be found in the right place. The first is that wall framing, floor framing, and roof framing—that is, framing of the sloping surface of the roof as distinct from its supporting trusses—are always closely related. In the most primitive form, where the floor joists are simply placed on top of the main beams, the rafters will normally be laid over the purlins and minor elements in the wall frame; occasionlly they are wrapped round the line of the wall posts.[9] In late medieval frames the joists, rafters, or wall studs are tenoned to the principal supporting members only, but are uninterrupted and as long as possible. In a well-built building of the seventeenth century they are in short lengths, pegged and tenoned to major and minor members of the frame, all brought into the same plane. By a like process, in the oldest buildings, the main posts or the duplicated principal rafters can be close to, but independent of, the surface of the roof or wall.[10] By the seventeenth century integration had long been complete, so that any columns in the round carrying the superstructure of the stage are more to be regarded as a projecting element of the substructure than part of the frame. Another instance of the same elaborate timber building has always imitated masonry; in the earlier phases it did this by using heavy moldings and boarded infils to give an appearance of solidity[11] and above all, in true Gothic fashion, by making architectural features of structural elements, particularly curved ones. Still, in the Elizabethan period it accommodated itself to Roman forms, to keystones and faceted courses, and these in their timber expressions hearkened back to Renaissance, or mannerist, masonry. But such treatment rapidly confined itself to the area of screens and internal façades, of which the front of the tiring-house would provide an ideal specimen. These are parts where even a stone house would need carpentry, and in a framed building they are more like grand-scale furniture than part of the frame. As the exterior came to depend more and more on an overall covering of plastic material, and the interior decor more and more on ultimately movable fittings, the frame was reduced to an armature, to be relied on but, as in modern framed buildings until the last few decades, not to be seen to do its work.[12]

Nevertheless, there are elements in framing inseparable from the relatively slender scantling and high tensile strength of timber, which can be neither eliminated nor disguised, particularly the bracing of angles in all directions and not least where the very plan is not rectilinear. In later medieval times the braces had generally been long and given a Gothic virtue by their curvature. In the second Globe we can assume that the short and straight bracing, almost universal by 1614,[13] prevailed throughout, especially in the vertical radial planes where long braces would have seriously impeded passage through the tiers, and that the sort of members needed to transfer the thrust of an arched structure to carry the "heavenly" superstructure through the galleries to the posts of the outer wall frame would have been an even greater interference.

In fact, the movement toward a rectilinear and fairly rigid frame had been the dominant one throughout the sixteenth century, with less emphasis being placed on the principal members of the building. The outer surface of a gable had become simply a piece of wall frame, whereas formerly it had been a variant of the roof truss within, so that the roof structure had been "readable" externally. Among forms of roof truss, one, the essentially rectilinear form (fig. VI-1) with a heavy collar and vertical queen struts, had practically replaced all others in southeastern England, and failing clear instructions to the contrary, the carpenters of the second Globe would have considered no other alternative from the utilitarian point of view. This form probably originated on the upper Thames or in Wessex and by the mid-sixteenth century had driven its principal rival, the tenacious and picturesque "crown-post" form, out of Kent and Essex, and therefore out of London, too. From the area of its dissemination a concomitant form of wall framing, in fairly large quadrilateral panes, its bracing reduced to short arch-braces within the panes, was also "on the march," but meeting strong resistance from the equally rectilinear close-studded form. This form was probably of east-country origin and was never common in Wessex. It can be traced at least to the early fifteenth century, as a rare, specialized, strong, and expensive form, and it spread throughout eastern England and the Midlands before 1500, at first with continuous studs, but later, and particularly in the second half of the sixteenth century, with the studs broken by and tenoned to a rail at half-height.

From Kent, I cite examples of ca. 1540 (the house built by Arden of Feversham for himself, ca. 1540, fig. VI-2) and another as late as 1621, Honywood's at Lenham, Kent (fig. VI-3). As in many Kentish examples, the form of framing is conservative but the amount of it exposed is selective in the later cases or in modifications to earlier buildings; in gales or refenestrated surfaces it is usually covered up. From the opposite end, toward the northwestern extremity of the southeastern quarter of England, where close-studding is common (as it is in Normandy), I cite the guildhall and grammar-school complex at Stratford-on-Avon. The form was certainly very familiar to Shakespeare and familiar in London, although, among considerable graphic evidence for it there, I can illustrate almost the only visible survivor, Staple Inn in Holborn, from 1586, a prestigious building but a sober and conservative one (it housed a legal institution) (fig. VI-4). All these but the last show the more traditional and more distinctively southeastern form, with the studs unbroken by a horizontal rail at half-height. It was certainly a form that might have been considered for the external frame of the Globe: it was strong, heavy, and needed less bracing, but it was also expensive and, in fact, a field for conspicuous waste. It is a better option for the first Globe than the second, since its popularity was waning markedly after about 1600; its advantages for display diminished with the amount of it that was rendered over, and in a building completely covered, as the second Globe almost certainly was, it would hardly have been cost-effective.

There are variants of close-studding that can be traced back quite early in the sixteenth century, but they would have been exotic in the London area. The most conspicuous and memorable almost forms a distinct northern variant of the manner, in combining diagonal close-studding, almost like multiple bracing, with upright. This is not unknown in the East and South: it may occur as one of the elements in various mixed and eclectic combinations of framing, predominantly Western and Midland, that appear in the Elizabethan period in urban as well as rural contexts. They have a certain provincial vulgarity about them, even when used with such panache as in Little Moreton Hall, Cheshire (fig. VI-5). In the metropolitan parts of England they are usually little patches of relief in a generally close-studded frame or are spread almost contrapuntally over a frame of large quadrilateral panes, as an ornament with little function as bracing. The fashion was neither learned nor in tune with carpentry as structural engineering, but represented a touch of wealth and show among a "middle-brow" clientele. In any case, it was recessive by 1600, and it is almost certain that the builders of, at least, the second Globe would have despised it.

The commonest form of this ornamental framing in the southeast uses short quadrant members passing through the square panes of the frame and adding up to circles when they cover four panes. It is the quadrilateral panes that really carry the structure; they may be quite small in these ornamented areas, but where they are relatively large, typically two to a storey and with little or no visible bracing, they form the most persistent, and ultimately dominant, alternative to close-studding. Almost by a process of elimination it can be deduced that the wall frame of the second Globe was of this kind. It is less easy to demonstrate this by distribution because the form is in fact widespread, used in default of more specialized

Fig. VI–1. House near Canterbury showing, in gable, roof truss with heavy collar, clasped side-purlins, and queen-struts; quadrilateral framing. (Photo K. W. E. Gravett.)

forms and most suitable where the frame was covered. It might be pleaded that the wide-pane framing, whether of squares or with one dimension slightly more extended, is absent from East Anglia, though not from the Thames valley, in J. T. Smith's pioneering study of the distribution of wall-frame types,[14] which is based on a large sample of visible frames. This raises what seems to be the only other solution worth considering—not close-studding, but a form that might be regarded as "close-studding with the seams let out," that is, storey-length studs with wide intervals and no half-height members, the form that appears on the market cross at Wymondham, Norfolk, as rebuilt in 1617.[15] In fact, however, broad quadrilaterals, even panes much broader than they are high, do occur, even in East Anglia (which is some distance from the London tradition), and the pattern is sometimes reproduced in the pargeting that covers the frame. A joinerly refinement has a square within a square (fig. VI-6).

The pattern of the normal, and ultimately all-conquering, quadri-

Fig. VI–2. Part of a house of "Arden of Feversham" built against the gatehouse to Faversham Abbey, Kent, ca. 1540, showing uninterrupted close-studding, exposed braces, and fascias on jetties. (Photo author.)

Fig. VI–3. Detail of Honywoods or High House, Lenham, Kent, 1621, showing uninterrupted close-studding, fascias to jetties, and frieze windows. (Courtesy National Monuments Record, England; photo author.)

Fig. VI–4. Staple Inn, Holborn, London, 1586, showing close-studding with interrupting rail and long windows. (Courtesy National Monuments Record, England; photo ca. 1920 by H. and V. Joel.)

lateral frame has its exact correspondent in a form of roof truss, which appears to have moved with it, gaining popularity as it moved, from Wessex and the middle Thames eastward into Essex and Kent. Both together were well established in the apparent area of dissemination well back into the fifteenth century and had conquered Essex, Kent, the East Midlands, and the north and the northwest of London by the middle of the sixteenth, to remain dominant and relatively stable for a century and more. They were certainly the most basic and neutral elements in framing throughout the earlier seventeenth century. The apparent line of attack was from the "near West," down the Thames and through London, but the surviving evidence from London itself is so scanty that the part of London in the dissemination may be underestimated, and the northward pressure, against a less assured resistance from the established modes, may have come relatively early, and from London. Shakespeare's "birthplace," which has a good case for acceptance as far as site is concerned, is essentially a building of broad quadrilateral framing. If it could be demonstrated that it was physically his birthplace and not, as I have long suspected and Mr. Richard

Harris has recently publicly contended,[16] a rebuilding, probably during his lifetime, it would become a useful piece of evidence in the spread of styles in carpentry. It is certain that by the end of Shakespeare's life there was in London a homogeneity and a responsiveness to what was acceptable in carpentry, at least at the bourgeois level and above, just as there was over metropolitan, or southeastern, England in many other aspects of civilization, in the widest possible sense of the word.

The form of roof truss which matches quadrilateral paned wall frames in that it includes a broad rectilinear element, fits well with its distribution and expansion but is also adapted to close-studded walls, and, from the middle of the sixteenth century, is the usual form of truss found in combination with these two is a "double-framed" roof. It repeats the distinct bays of the wall in its principal rafters, each couple of these carrying a horizontal heavy collar, with little or no camber, and supported by two vertical queen struts from the tie beam below, thus producing a dominant rectilinear feature. In its classic, elementary form it is extraordinarily widespread and persistent (fig. VI-1), incorporating or ignoring the variations that evolve with it. Particularly at first, the principal rafters may be diminished to the scantling of common rafters above the entry of the heavy collar, but structurally the effect of this is nil. It may be repeated, with two tiers of heavy collars, producing a more complicated transverse quadrilateral frame, as in the "Godbegot" building at Winchester, which has a typical quadrilateral-paned wall frame (apparently built just after the dissolution of the cathedral priory, but if so, rather conservative in concept).[17] The double-framed roof normally carries a side purlin in each slope, clasped between the principal rafters and the heavy collars, but later, and particularly in the London area—and unavoidably in a polygonal structure such as the Globe demonstrably was—the purlins are butted in relatively short lengths between the faces of the principals. Finally, but probably seldom before the seventeenth century, there may be intermediate principals within each bay, with the purlins broken into short lengths, each entering the principals at alternate levels. It is possible that the second Globe had its purlins thus fragmented; it is almost certain that in its time and place, each Globe had a roof of this general kind over the galleries, which would imply that it did not have a ridge piece, that it did not have king posts to the apex, and that it did not have angle struts reaching to the principals or the collars.[18]

Two elements, then, may be taken as statistically of the highest probability (if it is not in the interests of any specialized function to vary from the norm), and fundamentally adaptable to and economical for such a structure as the Globe: a quadrilateral-framed wall, matching the similar but functionally necessary internal façades, reticulated and perhaps discretely braced, but with no concentration of diagonal thrusts in its plane; and a double-framed roof, with heavy collars, purlins in the roof slope, probably wind braced unless in very short lengths, and almost certainly

Fig. VI–5. Little Moreton Hall, Cheshire, 1560s and 1570s, from the gatehouse, showing herringbone studding on quadrant braces superimposed on quadrilateral framing. (Courtesy National Monuments Record, England.)

with queen struts. These would suit what we know of it, either from visual evidence or from the very nature of its usage: that it carried an extensive and uninterrupted external covering, and that each stage of the galleries carried a heavy load of humanity, liable to thrust its weight inward and then suddenly outward toward the restricted stair turrets, to stamp its feet, but above all to press downward, calling for a pattern of discrete and largely untransferred vertical thrusts through all its stages.

Whatever may have been the difficulties in roofing the stage and tiring-house, roofing the relatively narrow galleries was a routine matter, and the flooring of the storeys below them called for no special comment in the theatres for which the contracts survive. In the outer ring of the second Globe we need expect nothing exceptional if we could find analogous galleried buildings in the London area to compare them with, save that, as a polygonally planned building, its structural logic necessitates what might be expected, but not demonstrable, in a rectilinearly planned one: that it was a building of butted bays and relatively short lengths of timber, far removed from the medieval tradition of long posts and long plates in the

Fig. VI–6. Post office at Milton Regis, Kent, ca. 1615, showing inner squares in quadrilateral framing and frieze windows in probable London style. (Photo K. W. E. Gravett.)

lines of greatest strain. Nothing in the known contracts[19] implies continuous posts passing through three storeys, and there is simply no place for horizontal members more than a bay long. The bay, in fact, is treated precisely as it is in the now "traditional" steel frame: it is preserved conceptually, with untransferred vertical compression, but is broken into short units and with diagonal bracing, wherever it is needed, kept to the minimum, as in the short, straight wind braces at the end of the purlins, quite unlike their wide-spreading medieval predecessors. This is the economy of a depleted timber supply, in tune with the permission, in the

127

contract for the Hope theatre,[20] to use softwood, rather than oak, in specified positions of less strain. It is within the spirit of such a contract to interpret it for our purposes in any material of the requisite tensile strength. Structurally, if not acoustically, steel or reinforced (not pre-stressed) concrete would serve, whereas in a medieval building, the nearest equivalent to steel framing, high-quality wrought iron, was not of the requisite compressive section, and was only used as a kind of super rope.

If the roof purlins were butted from principal to principal, as the polygonal plan would demand, and the common rafters tenoned and pegged to these in two sections, the floors below were no less likely of comparable form, with common joists, little more than six feet long, housed into it and tenoned. These were probably attached in like manner to the plates of the inner and outer frames, allowing entry at the same level, in a way that had been experimented with in the London area since the fifteenth century[21] but was contrary to medieval and traditional practice, which lodged the joists over the horizontals of the outer frame.

This assumes that neither face of the galleried parts was jettied, which should certainly be the first hypothesis. True, the contract for the Fortune theatre provides for a "forward" jetty of the upper two storeys to a mere ten inches, but it is hardly justifiable to extend this to the second Globe. "Forward" probably means externally, and Hollar's drawing clearly contradicts this in the case of the Globe, where the polygonal plan would make such treatment very difficult and more difficult still if the outer covering were firred out to make a circle. Had it been internal, it would have provided a little weather shade for a slight gain in floor space, a probable loss of strength and disturbance of the classic simplicity of a façade with superimposed orders most likely worked on the pilasters. Jetty-ing was recessive and often very shallow at this date, and ten inches would not provide the cantilevered strength of long, lodged joists, carrying the whole forward-set frame. The possibility, however, of something like the form found in New England, but rare in old England, in which the joists stop at the lower, inner plate and the forward wall is carried on a massive upper plate,[22] cannot be dismissed from the inner façade.

The quadrangular stair turrets are another feature with many extant parallels in domestic architecture. The stairs need not have been vises with awkward corners, though these are known.[23] There is not room, in some nine or ten feet square, for quarter landings and a square well as at Hatfield House, but there is space for a half landing and fairly steep, straight flights, which is usual enough in houses and would handle the crowds much more smoothly and safely than a vise. From this point both direct record and plentiful analogues cease, save in the double-gabled roof above the stage, which follows a very usual urban pattern at least where London fashion reaches, from early in the seventeenth century. The decor and the mechanics of the stage involve other lines of reasoning than the normal or probable practice of carpentry. Here we would wish the two precious surviving building contracts to be more specific, but they are not. Evidently there was already, by the end of the sixteenth century, a consensus about what was proper to a stage, and "teething troubles" had already been overcome. This was surely more than a matter of rapid adjustment to trial and error in London alone; the experience from Italy, France, and Spain must have contributed to it. To assess the contracts properly we must strip away what is common to all or most such documents in England and leave what is strictly relevant to the theatres.

The indenture for the Fortune theatre,[24] dated January, 1600 (New Style), is a very familiar and conservative type of document, following medieval precedents[25] in its strict specifications of scantling and quality of materials and its easy citation of a named prototype, but with few structural technicalities to let the layman into the "mysteries" of the carpenter's craft. It was intended as a safeguard for both parties in the absence of specific trade standards and codes of practice as we know them today. It was not an inhibition on further consultation, but normally left the carpenter to exercise his "tried and true" way in matters of detail. Less usually, certain subsidiary works, such as tiling and plastering, were not left to direct agreement with another trade but were presumably subcontracted. The "Articles" for building the Hope in 1613, though slightly simpler in legal form, are similar in content, again with a cited prototype or precedent. Both are, in fact, less detailed and freer from penalty clauses than many fifteenth-century contracts. What is "sufficient" or "workmanlike" is guaranteed by the carpenter's reputation in a society of highly organized crafts. No architect or agency other than he is answerable for anything, and as far as we know, no Elizabethan theatre ever physically failed from a structural fault. External risks were another matter, and though safety regulations in building already prevailed in the City, Bankside was outside it, and the risk was worth taking. The discretion of a London master was in itself the best insurance.

One thing not written into either contract and taken for granted by all parties was the basic resilience and flexibility of a heavy-framed building, particularly when not nogged with inflexible and also heavy material. Such a building was clearly able to withstand the shifting weight of a "full house" (however we interpret the available evidence about actual numbers), as a somewhat comparable, if provincial, courtyard building, Forde's Hospital in Coventry, withstood an air raid that killed many of its residents. The Globe was raised upon sole plates bedded on a ground wall of brick and mortar, like any normal frame building. This, indeed, is specified in the Fortune indenture, which also mentions piles, and the piles of the Globe are stated to have remained serviceable after the fire.[26] This is no surprise, for in neither case were they projecting piles, nor did they play any part in the frame, from which they were totally isolated. Any such usage is unknown in buildings proper at the date, though by Elizabethan times projecting piles, driven by improved rams, were made structurally integral with timber bridges (whereas in medieval bridges the posts also stood upon sole plates.)[27] The piles of the Globe, for which there is slight other evidence, were no doubt the substructure of the ground walls, short driven piles, themselves surmounted by a platform of rough boards, as had long been the practice for setting masonry structures in marshy or geologically variable soil. Those under the Jewel Tower at Westminster were well preserved where set in the silt of the tributary bounding Thorney Island, totally rotted where driven into gravel.

With regard to the apparatus of the stage we can only observe that neither of the contracts specifies much, that what was unsaid had presumably already been satisfactorily resolved in the prototypes, and that if the second Globe had any marked innovations, they went unrecorded. The distyle canopy, of no enormous depth considering the extend of the stage, is a fairly constant feature in most representations of spectacles, and one of its functions was to act as a resonator. We are in no position to argue about any adjustment of its proportions, or those of the back-stage structure, save that the claims to magnificence must refer mainly to these, and any form of classical frontispiece the age produced, relying on trompe l'oeil as much as on measurable depth, in screenwork or title pages,[28] is relevant, if circumstantial, evidence. Actual depth is an obstruction to viewing when an essentially frontal concept is presented to spectators "in the round."

Most representations of theatrical or near-theatrical spectacles agree in that their architectural frame is in some sense manneristic. This is a dangerous and subjective term, but the aspects that concern us—false perspectives, oblique angles, broken pediments, overpiled and perversely varied classical elements, and in the north, strapwork and such things that give the lie to the solid assumptions of classical architecture—have a very long life. They form the antiarchitecture of the world of pageantry and they cohabit with architecture, true and solid, almost from the morning of the Renaissance. Around 1600 they were apparently on the retreat, but they were not dead. Inigo Jones, a prophet of "true" architecture, knew their place and used them where they belonged, in masques.[29] My contention is that mannerism is the stuff of dreams and would be in place on the façade of the tiring-house, in costumes and around the stage, and in the insubstantial painted decoration, while the solid carpentry of the galleried circle would partake, where it could, of "true" and solid classical idioms. Hence the eclectic framing of the 1580s, a countrified vehicle for mannerism, would be out of place in the theatre proper, while the more urbane mannerism of broken rooflines, conceited parapets, jeweled and strapped enrichments to arcades, which flourished about the same date and was resuscitated, almost as a deliberate romanticism, a generation later by Jones and his companions while they were mastering the pure message of Palladio, would have been no less in place in the second Globe than the first, on and around the stage, and banished, as utterly as with Jones, from the architecture proper.

There is no direct and positive evidence about the façade of the tiring-house and the encompassing of the stage in either Globe. Its visual qualities satisfied a London audience, at least some of whom were not architecturally blind or illiterate; it was solid enough not to appear obviously tired and *démodé* within decades, yet enough, in the last days of the first Globe, to be invested with the visionary splendor that surrounds the masque in the *Tempest*. Those who sense this assume, probably rightly, that it was a creditable example of the fairly stabilized manneristic idiom still acceptable to wealthy clients in the screenwork and joinery of Hatfield or Audley End, both ca. 1610–15 and both completely metropolitan. Such a conjunction with the second Globe would suggest that it, too, may have shared the same slightly staid grandeur. Architectural adventurousness has been rare and suspect at most periods in England, London included. We have no reason to impute it to Robert Cecil—or to Shakespeare. Certainly the triumphal apparatus for King James in 1604 was conservative enough.[30] On the other hand, a theatre, with its built-in frame of fantasy, can sometimes, in its less structural parts, be a vehicle for fashions that its builders may think ephemeral, but not actually unsafe. In these parts the second Globe may have been shaped by a newer sensibility, a cautious touch of baroque rotundity, such as can be seen in the façade (preserved in the Victoria and Albert Museum) of the Paul Pinder House from Bishopsgate, (fig. VI-7), whose recorded interiors were still in the mannerist idiom.[31] It would be rash to attempt to reconstruct it, but it would have been more thoroughly of the seventeenth century and in spirit with the mainland. We dare not guess its details but may assume that it was up to date and pan-European.

This lighter spirit, less solidly classical and more tolerant of the Gothic heritage, appears in a small way and with private patronage in ecclesiastical fittings, flowing on the Laudian tide, dangerously near to Popery and its suspected mask of theatre. Such may be seen at Passenham, in north Buckinghamshire, and above all in the nonparochial chapel at Rycote, near Oxford, whose devices include private pews, one with an ogee cupola, as at the apex of the second Globe, covering a blue "heaven," with stars cut out of playing cards. More general in English churches, more obstinately private and less amenable to regulation is the vast and costly variety of the theatre of death—the last refuge of the procession that had for centuries grown less liturgical; in its tombs almost the only field for compact architecture in an established church overprovided with covered buildings. Despite nearly two centuries of keen ecclesiology, it has been left to the last two generations, tutored by Sir Nikolaus Pevsner, to treat these tombs not as fodder for genealogists but as grand architecture writ

Fig. VI–7. Sir Paul Pinder's house, Bishopsgate, London, early seventeenth century. (Courtesy Victoria and Albert Museum; photo ca. 1885.)

small, provincial, but trying hard to be metropolitan, occasionally successfully cosmopolitan. The subject is too large for easy generalization: suffice it to say that there is often a niched and tiered reredos, like a tiring-house façade; a tester or "heaven," flat or arched, borne on ornate columns with a grossly wide intercolumniation; allegories may inhabit the niches, and the principals, grandly tired, often not even playing at death, kneel or recline or even stand upon their little stage.[32]

Tombs are stages of silence, and they are narrow, but their colors surely ring true. The other ecclesiastical stage was the pulpit. Inhibited by strict licensing and almost silenced in the established church—save for printed homilies not unlike departmental handouts—in Shakespeare's maturity it was gradually recovering its confidence and its rhetoric (John Donne was less than ten years Shakespeare's junior), the humanistic, rather than legalistic, heritage of the Reformation, and the Counterreformation. The theatre played a part in this recovery, at least by providing continuity of the architectural expression that suited it most, however little that expression was used in the established churches. The secret of the completeness and finality with which the theatre, as a structure, sprang fully armed upon Elizabethan London surely lies in the unanimity of reforming spirits concerning what was needed for an auditorium, religious or secular. Such unanimity is more comprehensible when we see that men like George Buchanan and Agrippa d'Aubigné, however Calvinistic, had no objection to drama as literary form rather than as an "ungodly spectacle." Whatever had yet been built for the public stage, the French Huguenots were quick to erect new "temples" for their conventicles in the 1560s, and when these were torn down, to build anew in the same manner after the Edict of Nantes. The first one well recorded, the Paradis of Lyon,[33] was a theatre-like rotunda, with a "pit" and two tiers of surrounding seats, while the famous temple of Charenton,[34] though rectangular, had three stages of seating. The galleries of the former were held behind barnlike posts; the latter, as late as 1623 and considered the pattern for Protestant preaching-houses for centuries to come, had elegant giant columns. When it became possible to build undisguised meetinghouses, in England from the 1690s but in New England rather earlier, consciously or unconsciously the Charenton model was followed, though less monumentally and usually with two tiers of seating and with tiers of columns rather than a giant order. The continuity of concept is unbroken and includes the only surviving seventeenth-century building in England that calls itself a theatre, the Sheldonian at Oxford, built for a conservative prelate of the Restoration. It is secular, intended for rhetoric rather than preaching or spectacle, and with its polygonal façade limited to one half only (for it is a true theatre, whereas the Globe was externally an amphitheatre) it preserves a feature belonging to most Elizabethan playhouses but not to Antiquity. It is stone walled, and some of the finer English meetinghouses have brick or stone shells, but their inner supports, and the overwhelming majority of them in their entirety, are or were timber-framed.

It is above all the scale of the stage that distinguishes the playhouses. Indeed, were it not for the Fortune indenture, we would hardly have guessed that the stages were so large. Even so, the stage can be seen as a magnified rostrum, its conventional rhetorical postures not differing in kind from those proper to a pulpit, its ceiled "heavens" a tester, or sounding board, raised to the height of the upper gallery. Even the great ogee-crowned cupola that seems to have broken through the boards of "heaven" to provide its light-well has parallels in other seat-encircled auditoria, including the Sheldonian

133

Fig. VI–8. Sparrowe's House, Ipswich, Suffolk, ca. 1660, showing elaborate plasterwork and ground-floor timber pilasters in the pre-Civil War metropolitan idiom. (Courtesy National Monuments Record, England; lithograph of 1851 by F. Russel.)

and many recorded early meetinghouses, particularly in New England.[35] The almost baroque profile of that on the second Globe, matched on the elegant and near contemporaneous monuments of Augsburg, may indeed be the one visible witness of a like modernity in the works about the stage. There is no cause to think it a subsequent modification.

Had the second Globe survived the Civil Wars, the men of the Restoration might not have felt ashamed of it. The well-spaced if slightly provincial decor of Sparrowe's house at Ipswich (fig. VI-8) is of that date, but

134

in the mode of prewar London, and in its carpentry, perhaps, the nearest we can come to the Globe.

A number of buildings remain in the towns of eastern England from Canterbury to Norwich, rendered all over, many with plastic decor in deep relief, if seldom as elegant as Sparrowe's House, or, like the Samson and Hercules House in Norwich, with three-dimensional sculpture, but more often plain. In the early nineteenth century many more remained even in London, outside the area of the great fire. The applied decor was sometimes genuinely baroque and the usage increased as the seventeenth century advanced, so the second Globe came fairly early in the series. Nevertheless, its visual impact was surely as solid as that of any building. If, like many buildings for spectacle, it might have needed a "face-lift" in a generation or so, the carpentry beneath its skin could be assumed to be reliable and did not need to display its means of strength.

VII. *The Stage and Its Surroundings*

GLYNNE WICKHAM

Of all the aspects of both the first and the second Globes, that which we know least about from a strictly factual point of view is the stage and its surroundings. This is the genuinely "missing" part of the missing monument. No pictures have survived, no ground plans, no elevations—not even a detailed description in a diary or a letter. What, then, do we know—know as fact, and for certain? I do not see how I can honestly say more than I committed to print some seven years ago in volume 2, part 2, of *Early English Stages;* with your indulgence I will quote from those pages in which I discussed the Globe.

> The first Globe was the first playhouse built in England exclusively by professional actors and for their own exclusive use: to that extent, we are right to credit it as being a major advance on any of its predecessors, and indeed Ben Jonson tells us as much when describing it as "the glory of the Bank." For all that, its basic shape was still that of the traditional game-house, warranting description by Shakespeare as a cockpit (*Henry V*, Prologue) and lacking such relatively simple refinements as the tiled roof and cantilevered "heavens" of the later Hope playhouse.
>
> The ridge of the thatched roof was "as round as a tailor's clew" (ball). When this caught fire during a performance of *Henry VIII*, and the "wooden O" disintegrated in flames, the audience escaped unscathed through "two narrow doors."
>
> This brief recital covers the sum total of factual knowledge that has come down to us about the (internal) appearance of this theatre (as seen by a spectator in the yard, standing or sitting).
>
> Nor has the second Globe fared any better. We know that it was built on the same site: we know that it was roofed with tiles instead of thatch and we possess a reliable picture of its external appearance in Hollar's View of London once we have reversed the labels placed in the engraving above the Hope and the Globe. We know how the building of it was financed and that it cost £1,400, nearly three times as much, that is, as the first Fortune (£520) and £400 more than the sum initially raised

to build the second Fortune (£1,000). And that is all we know. Everything else that we *think* we know is speculation (pp. 116–17).

As I said, this is the really missing part of the missing monument. I wish I could say that I am now in a position to retract this statement, thanks either to someone else's sparkling findings in the past seven years or, to my own. Alas, on the latter count I cannot.[1] So there, of course, my paper on the stage and its surroundings ought to end. However, I was not invited to participate in this symposium to deliver myself of so brief and negative a communication. I therefore asked myself what reasonable alternative was open to me. Happily, I have found an escape clause in the final word of the passage that I quoted to you: "speculation." So take courage; for it is along that route (in the light of the warning I have already given) that I intend to proceed.

Let us start with the sine qua non of any play: the actor, the stage, and the audience. Here I am, as it were, the actor; there you are, the audience; and this orator's platform, for better or worse, is my stage. Let us try to translate this into Elizabethan terms of reference and see what happens. I will start with the stage, since what the actor stands on is really the most important thing for him; because if he is firm and comfortable on his feet he can be confident, and with confidence he has some hope of being able to act. If he lacks confidence, he cannot act; I believe that to have been as true in Shakespeare's time as it is today.

The Elizabethan actor expected to find wooden boards under his feet, boards raised up off the ground, laid on trestles, on large hogshead barrels, or set on fixed posts. The boards must, therefore, have responded noisily to his feet. They were to that end covered with rushes to dampen the sound. So here I am, as it were, walking like an Elizabethan actor on the freshly cut rushes thickly strewn (to simulate a deep-pile carpet) on the planks, and raised up some four to five feet from the ground on the trestles, or posts, beneath these boards. So far, so good.

My next question as an actor is, How far am I allowed to move? Well, I am allowed to move approximately ten feet to my left and approximately another ten feet to my right—not very far by way of straying from the center-stage position. That is because of those cursed culture-vultures who insist on chatting up the actors and even sitting on the stage on stools to the left and right of me. They hand over good money for the privilege, so they must be tolerated. But clearly it cramps the actor's style. All in all, then, I have some twenty feet of stage distance in the lateral plane. I have much the same in front and behind. If I walk any further than ten feet downstage from the center-stage position I shall fall flat on my face off the stage and into the yard. Ideally, as an actor, I would like a rail for protection and sometimes, no doubt, the Elizabethan actor got a rail. I was a little distressed to see, earlier in the symposium, when Walter Hodges was talking about the Swan playhouse, that, having shown us the de Witt drawing (fig. VII-1) which has no rail round the stage, he then showed us his own reconstruction of the Swan with a rail. This, it seems to me, is just the sort of way in which we begin to impose upon the evidence those items that we would like to have been there and which we come to take for granted because we have put them there ourselves. Clearly, actors would like the protection that such a rail gives, and indeed, if the actors had a rail it would be very restful and convenient to sit on from time to time, more especially when one has to deliver asides (and sometimes soliloquies) and has not been supplied by the director with any other stage furniture. Such a rail makes a frontier, a convenient frontier between the world of the play, marking the boundary where it begins and ends, and that of real life—or as Elizabethans would have phrased it, between "game" and "earnest." Yet for all that, we only have two references to rails on the stage in all the plays known to me. There is a stage direction in the final scene of *The Hector of Germany,* performed at the Red Bull in approximately 1614, a stage direction that reads "sits on the rail." And Shakespeare himself turns this possibility to dramatic effect in *Henry VIII* when the porter somewhat briskly—as the christening procession is approaching—says, "You i' the camlet, get up o' the rail: I'll peck you o'er the pales else" (5.4). I suppose there could be some other way of explaining the word *rail* in those circumstances, but I doubt it. More especially, it would seem to me perverse to try and deny the possibility of its existence when we know that a rail certainly existed in the *Messalina* and *Roxana* vignettes and in the much later Inigo Jones drawings for the Cockpit-in-Court.

That observation, however, prompts me to pick up one other point that has been made here. I have every sympathy with the member of the audience who asked Professor Hosley whether it is in fact legitimate to use the other Inigo Jones drawing of the unknown theatre (Worcester College, Oxford, Nos. 7B and C) as evidence in the context of the Globe, since the drawing of the unknown theatre—whether it be the Phoenix, the Salisbury Court, or any other theatre actually built—cannot be dated before 1617 or 1618 and was thus drawn long after the second Globe had been built.

Next, can we take it as fact that the stage was raised? I know of very few references to stages that were not raised from 1540 onward, and it does seem that it was relatively rare for stages in England to be raised before 1540 other than at court. The idea clearly comes from Italian example and from attempts to revive the plays of the Latin playwrights. It reached the court early in the century; but we also find raised stages asked for in Norwich in the 1540s, and references to them become steadily more frequent after that. I do not think there can be any doubt, therefore, that the raised stage was the norm by the time professional actors were able to raise enough capital to pay for the erection of permanent playhouses for themselves and their colleagues.

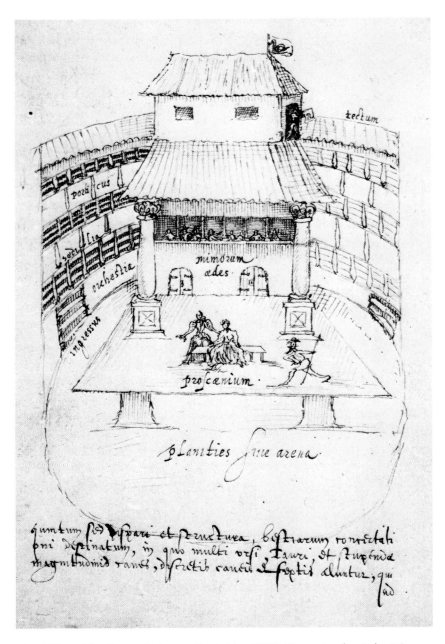

Fig. VII–1. The Swan playhouse, Bankside, 1596. (From the sketch by Johannes de Witt.)

139

One effect of a raised stage was to provide cellarage space. This space would have been dark and awkward in any event, but it must also have been damp, since the playhouse was sited on a marsh. Some scholars have suggested that de Witt, in depicting those strange, dark patches at the front of the stage and immediately below it in his sketch of the Swan, was trying to draw windows that allowed light into the room below; but, as most of us now accept that it was habitual to drape the front of the stage with colored cloths to indicate the type of play to be performed (in the manner that for centuries pageant-wagons had been draped with pageant-cloths), these cloths would have effectively blacked out the windows and thus made their presence there virtually irrelevant from the start. This reasoning leads me to the conclusion that we must accept a rather dark and awkward area under the stage which nevertheless possessed at least one great virtue for playmakers and actors: it provided a strange acoustic. A useful place, in other words, not only for ghosts who would appear to inhabit a hell that was literally below the stage—below the earth—just as the "heavens" were directly above it, but also a place that, in terms of the drama, could be used to create extremely powerful theatrical effects. From a stage manager's more mundane viewpoint it also provided a useful furniture store. That the Globe was provided with such cellarage and with such an acoustic would seem to be certain in terms of what we know of *Hamlet* and the prince's first encounter with the "old mole" who works in the earth so fast (1.5).

But granted a cellarage, how do we reach it? Are there stairs down to it? Is the only access through traps, as is often the case in English inns built in the sixteenth or seventeenth centuries, where one can still see landlords having to lift traps in their floor in order to fetch beer from the cellar? Adams, of course, postulated the existence of five, possibly even six, traps in the floor of the first Globe. I think we must admit to the certainty of one to account for Ophelia's grave if for no other reason. Both stage directions and text of *Macbeth* confirm the existence of one and suggest the possibility of more, but to proliferate the number of traps seems to me to be impermissible in light of such factual knowledge as we possess.

Nor must we even generalize, I think, about the existence of stage traps. Consider the Boar's Head Playhouse when it was refurbished in 1599 and the stage was moved; the problem then was clearing away the rubbish that had accumulated underneath it. How did the rubbish get there? Was it rubbish in the sense of stage properties and the like which had been stored there, fallen out of use, and were no longer wanted? Or was it the sweepings from the yard? It is difficult for us to establish which of these two possibilities accounts for its existence in such quantity. But I would ask you to remember the Boar's Head and the moving of the stage and the rubbish under it for another very important reason. The Boar's Head stage of 1598 was free-standing; it was not even adjacent to, let alone directly incorporated into, the tiring-house. We have to ask ourselves—and this, therefore, is the next question I would like to ask of this imaginary Elizabethan actor on his stage—how he regarded his dressing room. Before doing so I should perhaps just note in passing that Leslie Hotson went so far as to postulate that the tiring-house was in the cellarage under the stage, hence the "windows" I referred to earlier. Before moving to the tiring-house, however, I think it would be convenient to dispose of the actor's relationship to the auditorium.

Where the Globe is concerned—and here I go back to the first of my remarks that we know to be a fact—the first Globe was also the first playhouse that a company of actors could regard as wholly its own, tailored, as it were, to meet its own specifications. This is a very important fact because, from the actors' point of view, controlled entry must have been the most important single aspect of the auditorium. This ensured that those who came to see the play first paid to see it. This question immediately generates two more: how many people in Elizabethan London wanted to see a play? And how many people who would in fact pay could be attracted to come and see it? Third, again within this economic context, there was the all-important matter of potential spectators' capacity to pay. How were the seats to be priced? So three of the most important factors governing the actors' attitudes toward their auditorium were ultimately controlled by the economic circumstances of their profession. These were the primary controls over the design and construction of the frame: making it large enough to contain the anticipated maximum capacity; making it safe enough to control entry to it and extract from the patrons the vital admission fees; and so arranging and distributing the areas within that frame that all who wished to come and see the play could come and would not be debarred through inability to pay. The actual range of the prices is, to that extent, important and suffices to explain the sacrifice the actors made of their own stage, however large, in order to allow spectators to sit on it and to be seen and to make the nuisance of themselves that we know from Ben Jonson, Thomas Dekker, and other writers that they did make.

What other considerations operated on the actors with respect to the frame, the auditorium? Clearly, sightlines; the fact that people had paid to enter the playhouse to attend a performance. I think it is important, however, that we readjust our sights and recall that patrons then as often came to *hear* a play as to *see* it. Certainly, in most documents of the period 1576–1642 relating to visiting playhouses the phrase that is chosen to describe this activity is to "hear the play," rather than "to see the play." This suggests to me that sightlines were perhaps not the problem to an Elizabethan acting company, to Shakespeare's acting company, that they are to us. If people wanted a good view, it was recognized that they must reach the theatre early enough to ensure that they got it. If they chose to take a chance and arrived shortly before the advertised starting time, it was in the knowledge that many of the seats (if there were any) had very bad sightlines. If they then got a place with a bad sightline and asked for a refund, the actors could, and probably did, respond by saying, "No. Get here earlier next time."

In short, I would argue that the controls operating on the frame—on its layout, design, amenities, and facilities—were primarily economic and not esthetic. The tiring-house is another matter. Any actor must have three essential commodities: a stage on which to act, an auditorium to contain the spectators who come to see his performance, and a changing room. *Tiring-house* is the word we use in talking of the changing rooms in the Elizabethan theatre. The first question we must ask about its design and appearance is whether it was integrated with the stage or not. As I have already said, at the Boar's Head, before 1599, it clearly was not. Where, then, did the actors change? Only one answer presents itself; they must have been able to get off the stage and cross the yard to one of the rooms in the inn especially reserved for them as a changing room. I say "one of the rooms": but is it not extremely awkward, supposing your exit is downstage left and your next entrance is upstage right, to have to "tour the yard," as it were, in the course of your journey to and from your dressing room? I would assume that two tiring-houses in this instance was the norm. We know that two tiring-houses was the norm in at least some Oxford and Cambridge colleges—tiring-houses especially constructed on either side of the stage. In public play-houses, however, we must assume (if only for lack of any better evidence) that de Witt's drawing of the Swan more nearly represents the norm by the time the first Globe came to be built. In this drawing, as you will recall, the tiring-house lies immediately behind the stage and is integrated with the stage by the two great doors to left and right, through which the actors made their entrances and exits. Now the tiring-house, relative to the stage and its surroundings, is a very large area, so I think it would be wise to approach discussion of it level by level.

Let us take the stage level first. Were there in the first Globe or in the second Globe two doors or three? The Swan shows us two; the Red Bull had three; the Phoenix had three; the Cockpit-in-Court had five; initially, the Boar's Head had none. What, then, do we make of the situation at the Globe, *since we have to guess?* Let us start with the first Globe; did it have two or three? Perhaps that is beside the point, since we are thinking of reconstructing the second Globe, but it helps to reassure us in opting for the solution that we would ourselves instinctively prefer, if we possess an answer to that question. The balance of probability is three. Now, having opted for that solution with some degree of confidence, many of you will doubtless be wondering what happens in consequence to the so-called inner stage. In other words, was there, in addition to the two great doors of the Swan, a third and larger door, a door not unlike the central door of five in the Inigo Jones's *frons scenae* for his remodeled Cockpit-in-Court (see fig. VII-2), or was there an inner stage? Clearly, the Swan did not possess an inner stage. Just as clearly, Inigo Jones's Cockpit-in-Court of 1630 did not possess an inner stage. So the two drawings of actual stages that we possess agree in denying the existence of an inner stage, yet the idea that there was one dies very hard. All I think we can do here is to arrive, again, at a tentative judgment; the probability is that neither the first nor the second Globe had an inner stage. If either of them did have an inner stage, if the inner stage was as essential as its champions proclaim, then surely it is astonishing that the Swan should not have had one and still more astonishing that the Cockpit-in-Court should not have had one. This is absolutely vital information, because it is not just historical data of interest to antiquarians and teachers; it is information that actually controls the production of plays. It is thus very dangerous, in my view, for an assembly of scholars to supply the wrong answer in the definitive form of an actual building; for if it transpires that we have made the wrong choice, then that decision must serve to distort, in action, reconstruction of every play performed on that stage. It will give to positive error the validity of supposed truth. So much, then, for the inner stage. All that I wish to say at this juncture is that this is an area of the stage and its surroundings that we must approach with maximum caution.

If we now move to the upper levels of the tiring-house, we have to ask ourselves questions about galleries and windows, since both have been placed there in earlier models authorized by scholars and constructed by architects. First, did galleries or windows exist in either Globe? And if so, what purpose—what dramatic purpose—did they serve? The Swan shows us a single gallery at first-floor level, but no windows. In 1598 the Boar's Head had galleries, but as I have said, they were in no way integrated with the stage; the stage was moved closer to the great west gallery in 1599, but we have no information about it being actually integrated with the gallery in terms of an architectural *frons scenae* and so on. About the Phoenix it is difficult to tell. We have the *Roxana* and the *Messalina* drawings, (fig. VII-3), and we have the unassigned Inigo Jones drawing on the note paper with the 1617 watermark to suggest ideas. The former pair show a stage thrusting forward in the form of an inverted V instead of a rectangle like all those other stages we have so far discussed as models for the Globe, and the latter depicts the usual rectangle. The *Roxana* and *Messalina* drawings depict windows but no doors; the Jones drawing incorporates an arch at the center, but no windows or doors. To assume the existence of a gallery at first-floor level in the second Globe seems safe; to claim the existence of doors and windows seems rash.

The only safe course of action appears, therefore, to be to postulate the existence of a gallery that could do double duty as an extension either of

Fig. VII–2. Royal Cockpit, Whitehall, as converted into a theatre by Inigo Jones in 1630. (Drawing from the Jones/Webb Collection, Worcester College Library, reproduced by permission of the Provost and Fellows of Worcester College, Oxford.)

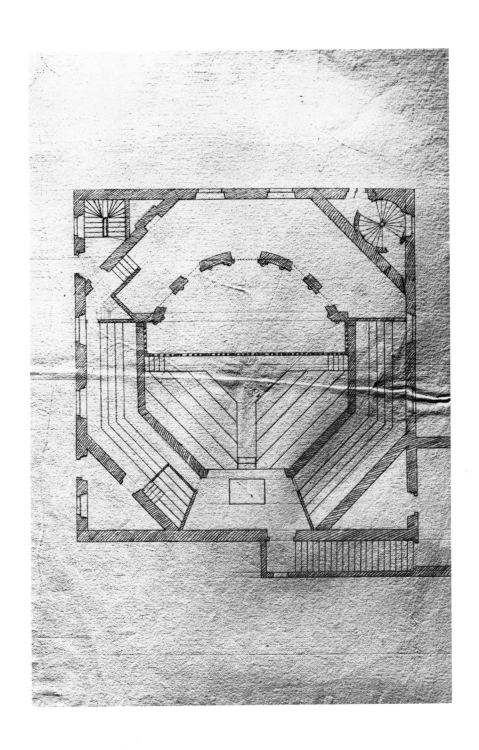

the stage or of the auditorium, according to the requirements of particular plays. By 1630, at the Cockpit-in-Court, we have one central opening above the great central arch and no more; no gallery, but one window. Again, however, both these features—the gallery and the window(s)—have a vital bearing on production, and when preparing a brief for an architect today we need to employ the same caveat that I have urged with respect to the existence or nonexistence of an inner stage. On the evidence of the Boar's Head and the Swan, provided you accept de Witt's drawing as depicting a rehearsal rather than a performance, it would appear that the gallery could be used as the actors wanted it used: either in a play that demanded an upper level as an acting area or, if the play did not demand an upper level, as additional seating space to earn more money. A third possibility is that "house seats" were provided there (i.e., free seats reserved for the manager's and the actors' personal friends). However, the sightlines again come into question, since it is scarcely possible to imagine worse sightlines than those that would be provided by seeing the whole production, as it were, inside out and back to front. Anyone who has sung in a choir or attended an orchestral concert in a concert hall where there are seats between the organ and the orchestra or just above the tubas and the kettle drums will know exactly what I mean. J. C. Adams in his reconstruction of the first Globe postulated a third gallery at the level of the top gallery in the auditorium for regular use by musicians and for occasional use by actors. Suffice it to say that none of the surviving pictures shows any such gallery. Only in the triumphal arches of the street pageants do figures appear simultaneously on three levels in the vertical plane.

Thus far we have spoken of the actor on his stage; of his contact and his relationship with his auditorium; of his contact and his relationship with his changing room; and of the possibility that, in addition to the strictly necessary exits and entrances, features of the back wall—where a back wall existed—were turned to dramatic and theatrical use. We have yet to consider what lay above the actor's head: the "heavens" and those pillars that cause such concern in scholarly discussions. In an essay of mine referred to by Herbert Berry in his book *The First Public Playhouse* I have argued that there were neither "heavens" nor pillars in the Theatre, the Curtain, or at Newington Butts. The first playhouse to contain them was the Rose. They appear to have been added to the Rose in 1590–91, when very expensive alterations were undertaken in the area of the tiring-house. They must have been completed and ready when Lord Strange's company moved in to start the remarkably successful season of 1591–2; but even then, if Henslowe's *Diary* is to be believed, these "heavens" did not contain a throne and attendant machinery. We must, I think, envisage the existence of "heavens" and pillars to support those "heavens" at the Rose from 1591 onward. But it is in 1595 that Henslowe expends yet more money on incorporating his "throne" into those "heavens."

Fig. VII–3. The stage for *Messalina* by N. Richards and the stage for *Roxana* by William Alabaster. These two small pictures of English stages backed by curtains probably represent private (perhaps the same) playhouse conditions for college performances at a university. (Details from book title pages of the mid-seventeenth century. Photos Harvard Theatre Collection.)

The Swan was built a year after Henslowe incorporated the throne into his "heavens." Given the amount of money that Langley poured into the Swan, and given its reputation for smartness, it would have been surprising if it did not contain "heavens," and, sure enough, this item appears in the de Witt drawing, together with marble-painted pillars crowned by Corinthian capitals. It is an obvious temptation to assume that from that moment onward "heavens" and pillars must have been an invariable feature of every playhouse and, thus, an integral part of both the first and the second Globe. But temptations exist to be resisted. Neither in the 1598 nor in the 1599 Boar's Head were there any "heavens." Provision is made in 1599 for a roof but not for "heavens": it cannot therefore have been regarded as essential at the time the first Globe was built. And even in 1613, more or less simultaneously with the building of the second Globe, Henslowe specifically eliminates stage pillars from his building contract at the Hope while retaining "heavens," and, as Richard Southern has proved, these must have been cantilevered.

Let me synthesize the several lines of argument that I have sketched thus far. If I have disappointed anyone by the caution of my approach to my topic, that is because the facts (more precisely the lack of facts) allowed me no alternative compatible with honesty. No matter how passionately and convincingly Walter Hodges, Richard Hosley, and John Orrell have argued the case for accepting Hollar's drawings of the *exterior* of the second Globe playhouse as being so accurate in every detail as to warrant immediate rebuilding of the monument deemed hitherto to be missing, an accurate pictorial record of the *interior* remains as notably missing today as it has been since the death of the longest-lived spectator to see a play acted on its stage.

Reconstructed models come and go, and if our desire were to build yet another model—the Detroit model—I would not feel obliged to be so cautious. But that is not our purpose. We have joined forces to prepare a collective brief for an architect, for carpenters, for masons, for painters, and doubtless for something unknown to Shakespeare and the Burbage brothers—electricians. We are also seeking to persuade other people to commit several millions of dollars to finance these craftsmen in their work. What they design and build on the strength of our brief—if the building is not simply to exist as a spectacle for tourists to gape at—will then invite actual use by actors and directors. Furthermore, I fancy that if those actors and directors are professionals they will insist on modifying the architects' plans in directions they assume to be vital for securing regular audiences of upward of two thousand paying patrons at each performance. This action, where actor-audience relationships are concerned, will of itself alter a genuine reconstruction of Shakespeare's Globe out of all recognition in the interest of patrons' comfort and expectancies. If the actors and directors are not professionals, then they are likely to be staff and students of college English and Theatre departments whose use of the building in the name of research will serve to solidify in the minds of future generations all those errors that we have guessed into the building as images of truth, for no better reason than that we lacked adequate factual information to avoid making such mistakes.

If, therefore, sufficient goodwill is forthcoming to raise the large funds needed to carry the imaginative initiative of this symposium into practice, we must somehow find equivalent means to dissipate the euphoria that encourages us to suppose that we can wholly re-create Shakespeare's Globe playhouse as he knew it; we must, in other words, separate fact from fiction in a recognizable manner. To this end I suggest that where the *frame* of the building (to use the Elizabethan term) is concerned, we boldly brief the architects to build in solid timber, stone, plaster, and tiles, but that where the *interior* is concerned we insist upon the use of moveable materials and that we label all work done on, above, below, and around the stage as frankly hypothetical and experimental. Granted such flexible treatment of the interior—especially the stage itself and the tiring-house façade—the same scene can be played on stages three feet or five feet high, with or without stools for spectators on the stage, with one trap or four, with or without pillars, and last but not least, with or without an inner stage and with or without scenic emblems to identify locality of the sort listed in the inventory of the Lord Admiral's Men at the Rose in 1598. I refer, of course, to trees, tombs, "cities," and so on; in short, all the emblematic scenic devices inherited from Tudor and medieval theatre practice of which we possess many pictorial examples, supplemented by details of materials and costs to help us reconstruct them.

There is one scenic item about which I must say something, since it is likely to figure in the brief for the building supplied to the architect. This is the "throne" situated in the "heavens." Is it not curious that the throne appears to have been the only scenic object that needed to be hoisted up into the loft space above the "heavens," and that was winched down with much creaking when it was needed? Rather might we have expected, granted storage space in the loft, that this would have been the natural way of getting all stage properties—cities, arbors, tombs, battlements, and so on—onto the stage and off again in the order provided for by the stage directions and with each change of location. In fact, if we are to believe the evidence, only the throne, characters like Ariel or gods and goddesses, and birds like Jove's eagle actually came out of the "heavens" trap and descended to the stage. I am sure there must be a logical explanation for this phenomenon. My own strictly speculative answer is that use of a throne on any Elizabethan or Jacobean stage at once served to set the scene of the stage action as passing in an audience chamber or a court of law: a throne is a throne and not just any old chair. It is a chair set on a small base, or dais, approached by a step or two, and surmounted by a cloth of estate. It is a large and clumsy object to handle, and if we place it in the very center of our acting area, which measures not much more than twenty feet by twenty feet, it becomes a damnable nuisance to the actors. It must not be there when not wanted to identify the locality of the scene since it denies the actors the crucial center-stage position. If it cannot stay *in situ,* it must be moved, so it is hoisted up and down. The same logic, it seems to me, governs the equally large and cumbersome four-poster bed with its curtains. This, as we all know, was just as regularly "thrust out" onto the stage at the start of a scene (often with its occupant already in it) and then "thrust in" when the scene ended. The only difference is that the bed problem was resolved in the horizontal plane while that of the throne was solved in the vertical plane. I leave all questions relating to the setting and striking of other scenic properties, together with details of their appearance, to Bernard Beckerman (see Chapter VIII) and return now to the larger problem of how to reconstruct the interior of the building, the stage and its surroundings.

If it proves possible to preserve flexibility in both the design and materials used, then even if we cannot be sure whether we are witnessing a peformance that Jacobeans, miraculously resurrected to see it, would instantly recognize as occurring in the Globe they knew, we will certainly learn more about the sightlines, acoustics, and acting techniques they accepted as normal than we have the means to do now. Only if we deceive ourselves into supposing that any experiment undertaken in such an environment can ever *define* the conditions of performance that originally accompanied any particular scene in any particular play will we be disappointed. To this end, if we remind ourselves every time we put a scene into rehearsal of the simple fact that Shakespeare is not known to have written any play for first performance in the second Globe, and that every play he wrote for the first Globe must have had to be trimmed in one way or another to fit its successor, that thought of itself should prove a helpful corrective and open a path toward uninhibited, imaginative experiment.

VIII. *The Use and Management of the Elizabethan Stage*

BERNARD BECKERMAN

ovies about life in the theatre frequently have an obligatory night-before-opening scene. The house is dark. The stage is lit by a naked lamp. It throws a harsh glare on the cavernous set. The heroine—for it usually is a heroine—stands in the shadows, her eyes gleaming with tears, gazing at the dim seats soon to be filled, inhaling the aroma of an expected triumph. Yet despite this overblown atmosphere of tremor and hope, not everything in the scene need be false. Often the moment captures a truthful echo of that mystic sensation actors feel for the boards of a stage.

The potency of that sensation cannot be discounted. It stimulates histrionic endeavors mere wood and canvas cannot arouse. It transforms cramped wings into palatial antechambers. The performing space of a stage, while it has all the usual dimensions of height, width, and depth, also has for the actor a fourth dimension, a dimension of imaginative possibilities that transcends limitations of a mortal kind.

If I stress the emotional attachment of the actor to the stage, it is not because I underestimate the importance of a theatre's physical structure. Just as much as it is a threshold for dreams, a theatre is a manufacturing plant that turns out products of the imagination. The construction of the plant together with its efficiency has much to do with the results that actors, playwrights, and designers achieve. In New York, at the Vivian Beaumont Theatre of Lincoln Center, we have the sad case of a manufacturing plant whose physical layout has so far defeated most efforts to use it effectively. But even though we cannot and should not ignore the physical use and management of the stage, we must not, at the same time, overlook the imaginative and esthetic tie between stage space and the performer.

But how are we to gain insight into what that imaginative and esthetic tie was in Shakespeare's day? Stage documents of the time hardly help us. Yet perhaps we cannot start with the past but must first understand how contemporary actors use and manage contemporary stages.

151

Through a perspective on the present, we may be able to appreciate the past more acutely.

Stage usage, past as well as present, has a dual character. The stage is first of all a geographical space, a physical entity of a certain size and conformation, equipped in a certain way, and connected with the audience area in a defined manner. As geographical space, it can or cannot accommodate certain kinds of scenery, and it encourages or inhibits certain types of stage business. It also has specific acoustical properties. Most significantly, the geographical space either has a fixed architectural character or, as is common at present, approximates virtual neutrality, and thus invites transformation through scenery, costume, and lighting.

Depending partly on its geographical character and partly on its societal function, a stage is also a behavioral space; that is, the space is endowed with an imaginative dimension that facilitates the display of particular kinds of behavior. It may represent a street in a Greek city, as in Roman comedy, or it may house an endless variety of domestic interiors, as in turn-of-the-century European and American plays. However it evolves, the kind of behavioral space a period utilizes reveals its conviction about where significant human action occurs. For example, one of the prevailing assumptions in the contemporary theatre—one so deeply ingrained that we may not realize it is an assumption—is that the neutral stage area must be individualized for each play. With few exceptions, actors and directors expect to turn the stage area into an idiosyncratic world that can house the events of the play in question. The world may be one of physical appearance, or it may represent a psychic landscape. No matter. Somehow the stage is to be altered to suit the play at hand and *only* the play at hand. We scorn using the scenery of one production for another. This practice is the result of our prevailing belief in environment as a crucial force affecting human behavior.

But not only does contemporary use and management of the stage demand the change of the geographical space into a unique behavioral space, it also insists that the resulting scene reflect some truth about the physical and psychic world. Sheer fancy is not entirely excluded, especially in ballet and musical comedy. But our bias is toward a behavioral space that is an analogue for an existing or previously existent world. A concomitant of this bias is that we want the stage to convey not only the appearance but also the feel, the mood of that world. For that reason the stage encloses, embalms, the actor. In many cases its behavioral character is extended beyond the stage to embrace the audience. These features of stage use that I have described are as much a part of the latest experiment by someone like Robert Wilson or Richard Foreman as they are of the most recent realistic production.

As geographical space, the stage is designed to facilitate the creation of a behavioral space. The contemporary stage does this largely through scenic and technological means. It uses scenery to enclose the stage area and give it identity; it uses stage lighting to provide finish and styling of the spectacle. In short, the contemporary theatre relies upon the designer and his construction to create the behavioral space within which the actor can operate. This is true even when the actor speaks directly to the audience. Only rarely, and usually in revivals of earlier plays, is this dominance of scenic technology relinquished.

Out of the interaction between the physical stage and its acting conventions emerges a ruling esthetic. How a stage is glamorized, how it organizes its visual elements, and how it achieves surprise—all esthetic matters—are determined by how geographical space relates to behavioral space. The matter of surprise illustrates, for example, the delicate balance among these factors. Until recently, one element of visual surprise depended upon the presence of stage curtains. The audience came to a shrouded wall. Not until the lights went out and the curtain rose was the audience transported into a hidden land. Now, however, influenced by the open stage, many if not most plays dispense with the curtain. On entering the theatre, the audience sees the setting at once, often in a softened light. Then the house lights and the wash of light over the setting go out. There is darkness. The stage lights come up, illuminating the set magically. Stage art is thus emphasized. But it is not realized completely, for the magic is marred. In the few moments after the house lights go down, we dimly see and hear the actors furtively getting into position onstage. In this change of physical means, the stage is caught between the old habit of the designer creating the behavioral environment and newer efforts to have the actor transform the geographical space into a world of imaginative action.

These three uses of the contemporary stage, as geographical space, as behavioral space, and as esthetic space, can now be compared to the uses of the Shakespearean stage. Such a comparison will throw into relief, I believe, the principal ways in which the Elizabethan player treated his playhouse. To begin with, let us consider whether the central assumption of modern staging had any place in Elizabethan practice. To what extent, if any, did the Elizabethan player expect to alter his stage to accommodate individual plays? Given the rapid change of bill, the circumscribed list of properties in Henslowe's inventory, and the great number of scenes in a play, we are safe in supposing, as most scholars do, that the Elizabethans did very little to alter the stage for each play. Yet they did introduce some changes. For tragedies, we are told, they may have draped their stages in black. For new plays they frequently ordered special clothes and other stage items. According to some scholars, they may even have changed hangings or used set pieces as mansions.

On the whole, we can be confident that the Elizabethan players did not try to create an entirely new environment, as we do now and as the court designer Inigo Jones did then. However, there is sufficient evidence that they were prepared to make minor modifications in the

153

stage. The questions we need to answer are: how extensive were such modifications? and then, what were the principles, if any, that guided these modifications?

The evidence for answering these questions is slight and inconclusive. Study of stage requirements as specified by the dialogue or the stage directions of playscripts can be tricky. It is not always certain that a scenic element mentioned in the text, such as Pompey's statue in *Julius Caesar,* ever actually appeared on stage. Nevertheless, scripts taken as a whole tend to support the conclusion that stage properties were few and stage scenery extremely rare. Graphic evidence, the little there is, seconds this conclusion. The stage of the Swan, as depicted by Johannes de Witt, holds a bench, and one of the actors carries a staff.

The most concrete evidence for stage equipment and furnishings lies in the property list once attached to Philip Henslowe's papers. Although the list has long since disappeared, scholars accept the authenticity of the copy published by Edmund Malone in 1790. Headed by the statement "The Enventary tacken of all the properties for my Lord Admeralles men, the 10 of Marche 1598," the list was one of several lists of apparel and playbooks dated either the same day or within a week, one way or the other, of the property list.[1]

If the heading of the property list is to be accepted at face value, the list represents "*all* the properties" (emphasis mine) owned by the Lord Admirals' Men as of the date specified. Yet this seems unlikely. A bridle is listed for *Tamburlaine.* But what about Tamburlaine's "chaire" (4.2)? Also, the only furniture specified is a bedstead. Yet stools and seats of various kinds must have been in use. Stage furniture constituted the largest category of properties required by the plays of the period. Could such furniture have belonged to Henslowe and so have been the property of the playhouse rather than of the company? Elsewhere Henslowe records payment to carpenters for making the throne in the "heavens."[2] If my conjecture about furniture is correct, the property list must then represent those distinctive properties built for a particular play and intended to produce an unusual theatrical effect.

The list contains 35 items encompassing 139 properties. For the most part we can separate these objects into set props and hand props, that is, properties large enough to be placed on stage for sitting, climbing, or manipulating, and properties worn or carried on stage by the actors. A small number of properties is difficult to catalog. What exactly was Belin Dun's stable: a painted cloth or a structure like the arbor in *The Spanish Tragedy?* The same uncertainty exists concerning the "city of Rome." If, however, we assume that these two items were painted cloths, then we find three cloths or hangings in the Lord Admiral's inventory.

Allowing for the possibility that all the doubtful cases in the list were set properties, we arrive at a total of 23 set properties in the total number of 139. If indeed this is the complete list of set props in the possession of the players, then the inventory is quite small. Bear in mind that the accounts from Henslowe's *Diary* indicate that the Lord Admiral's Men were performing about fifty different plays a year.[3] In addition, some plays were carried over from the preceding years. The inventory, for example, includes a cauldron for *A Jew of Malta,* the longest running play in the *Diary* accounts and one that had been in the repertory since 1592. On the basis of these accounts it is reasonable to assume that seventy-five plays or thereabouts were actively maintained in the Lord Admiral's repertory. From this figure we can calculate that on the average there was one set prop for every three plays.

So limited a pool of properties and painted cloths confirms the view that there was little alteration in the stage itself from play to play. Even were a number of properties used repeatedly in different plays, the total number available would not appreciably affect the physical appearance of the stage façade. Consequently, we have to conclude that insofar as individualizing a play was concerned, modification of the stage played little or no part.

But before we drop our examination of the inventory, we might do well to look at the kinds of properties listed. Three, or four if we include the sign for Mother Redcap, were painted cloths or boards. In addition to the painted cloths and the one bedstead I have already mentioned, the properties fall into one of several categories. There are three tombs. There are also three trees. Most numerous are properties upon which actors can rest or climb, of which we find four to seven examples: stairs for Phaeton, two moss banks, a frame for a beheading, possibly another frame for climbing upon during the siege of London. A rock and an altar may also satisfy that purpose. The remaining five properties consist of a cage, a Hell mouth, a chariot, a cauldron, and a canopy.

As I review this list, I cannot help but wonder why, with so few properties, there were three tombs? Why three trees? Why two moss banks? It would be understandable if, say, the trees were all needed in the same play. Of the three trees, one is the tree with the golden apples, another Tantalus' tree, the third a bay tree. Could they all have appeared in Heywood's plays of the Silver and Brazen Ages? Possibly. But then the three tombs could hardly have been for a single play. One was for Dido, another for Guido. What seems plausible is that certain kinds of properties—trees and tombs seem to belong to this small group—were used for spectacular or even symbolic effect. In addition, another group of properties was practicable: these were almost invariably stairs and scaffolds. In fact, in the *Diary* accounts, Henslowe advanced money to the players for set properties only twice: on October 2 or 3, 1602, he paid for a scaffold and bar for the play *Berowne* and within a week afterward, for poles from which to hang Absalom.[4] The use of such elevations in a naive and literal way is indicated by the stairs for Phaeton, probably to stage his fall from the heavens.

Tentative as our conclusions must then be, we can reply to the question of how the stage was altered for production by stating, first, that insofar as the evidence shows, modification to the stage was slight. This point applies to the use of hangings as well as set properties. We know there were hangings behind which Polonius could hide. We have no indication, however, that the players had a supply of these for different plays. Three for seventy-five plays hardly count. Second, plays required very few set properties, and very few were used. When they were used, they were intended to promote a single, self-contained spectacular effect or to serve the physical need of raising an actor off the stage floor. Furniture properties, on the other hand, may have been a standard part of a playhouse supply, and seldom built for a specific production. Third, in comparison to properties, the players maintained a large wardrobe to which they were continually adding. For example, in the two-year period from October of 1597 to October of 1599 Henslowe made thirty-five payments for costumes for the Lord Admiral's Men.[5] He also laid out twenty payments for "divers things." While the "divers things" might have included some properties, we know that they definitely did embrace costumes since some of the payments were made to tailors.[6] During the same period there is not one documented instance of Henslowe laying out money for a stage property. We can thus see the relative importance of costumes to properties. Furthermore, while it is chancy to draw too many conclusions from the apparel list, the repeated identification of garments by color, such as "1 peche coller satten doublett" or "1 read scarllet clocke with sylver buttons," suggests that the costumes lent an astonishing brilliance to the stage. The implication for a Globe reconstruction is that a substantial budget—perhaps even an endowment—might be needed to support the building of a wardrobe.

If, as I have shown, there was little physical transformation of the stage from play to play, can we say that the stage and its façade had any behavioral character at all? Did the occasional set property, when placed against the fixed façade of the tiring-house, change the behavioral association of the stage? Or did the fixed façade embody a continuing significance that was constant throughout every play? Put another way, did the single property or the stage as a whole serve as a powerful and resonant emblem? Neither the set properties listed in the Lord Admiral's inventory nor the list scholars have drawn from stage directions and texts encourage a positive reply. While castles and gardens, to name two frequently cited emblems, may be part of the medieval and chivalric emblem tradition, representations of such emblems do not appear onstage often enough to affect Elizabethan principles of staging. Recently I had occasion to investigate closely all the extant plays written between 1564 and 1590. Since these years embrace a substantial number of moral interludes, we should expect that among them, if anywhere, a tradition of emblematic staging could be found. The most likely focus of such staging would be the abstract personifications. It would have been quite possible to use a system of conventional costuming in order to identify virtues and vices and evoke established patterns of resonance. Yet among the 213 personifications in these plays, there is no certain instance of symbolic or emblematic staging. With very few exceptions all the characters are named, either by themselves or by someone else on stage, as soon as they enter. The players do not depend upon the audience's recognizing a conventional type merely by appearance or dress. In a few instances, in fact, a character dares the spectators to identify him. In *The Trial of Treasure,* Vice teases them by saying,

> I perceive by your lookes my name ye would knowe,
> Why you are not ignoraunt of that I dare saye.
>
> (B 1ʳ 17–18)

But then rather quickly he supplies his own name, Inclination. In *Liberality and Prodigality,* the first player on stage points to the feathers he is wearing and states that they show his name as "cannot be in words more plaine." Still, he too has to inform the audience,

> And so I am to put you out of doubt,
> Even Vanitie wholly, within, without.
>
> (A 4ʳ 5, 14–15)

What we find in these scenes is a pattern of dramatic illustration that relies on oral narration. Of the existence of pervasive symbols that define the visual impact of the stage there is little evidence.

I now turn to my second question: did the stage and its façade represent a constant symbolic world? Other writers besides myself have been impressed enough by the designation of the trap area as hell and the shadow cover over the stage as heaven to assume that the stage as a whole presented a type of the universe. There is probably something in this notion, but how actively the stage-as-universe occupied the audience's consciousness is problematical. While the topos of theatre-of-the-world was too widely known and too often cited to be dismissed entirely, we should not take the occasional description of "All the world's a stage" as an assurance that the playhouse was unrelievedly seen as an earthly microcosm. In all likelihood this image was part of the background tradition that could always be evoked by a dramatist when he wished, even though most of the time it remained dormant.

If the stage-as-world had a continuing significance, that significance may have been essentially negative. Why, we have to ask ourselves, did the players continue to use a persistently nonscenic stage for over sixty-five years? Economy and tradition may have played some part in this. But from the mid-sixteenth century onward, Elizabethan taste seemed sat-

157

isfied with an open, undefined playing area. This acceptance may be understandable during the early years of touring players. But why did the London audiences continue to accept this style of staging when, after 1576 and
especially after 1609, the players had the means and the example for
enriching and varying their presentations? I suspect that the isolation of
actors in space, particularly when they play against the sumptuous façade
with its echo of the medieval universe, heightened the free-wheeling, ad-
venturesome tone of Elizabethan life. In a world where courtiers depended
not only on land but perhaps more on favors and monopolies, place lost
some of its intrinsic sanctity. Men sold their lands in order to dress finely
and flamboyantly, as has long been noted. No wonder the stage reflects the
detachment of the person from his environment. Seen in this light, the
player performs in the behavioral space of an ambivalent universe where
hell and heaven may—or may not—be operative.

My inevitable conclusion, then, is that whatever sense of locale a
play or scene showed was derived from what the actors brought on stage.
Doors, posts, and walls did not convey information about locale indepen-
dently. Quite the reverse. The players projected an identity upon the
individual part of the stage by calling, for instance, the upper level the
walls of Corioli or one of the doors Brabantio's house. Furthermore, the
environment that the players projected onto the façade or about the platform needed to be only as detailed as the narrative required for the moment. On occasion the fictive space was localized—the Jerusalem chamber
in Henry IV's palace is one example (2 *Henry IV* 4.4). Usually, however,
the locale remained generalized: the city of Rome, the forest of Arden, or
the blasted heath as a whole, not any particular part of it. Thus, the
behavioral space was not naturalistic in our sense of the term, but idealistic
in the sense that the players located themselves in an idea of a place. That
idea, being fundamentally abstract, could have been embodied in a symbolic form, as production at court may have done. But this was not the
practice in the public playhouse. Instead, the idea of a behavioral space was
conveyed by the players on a nonscenic level through the dialogue and to a
lesser extent through dress.

The use of the stage as physical space could not be affected by this
handling of behavioral space. It meant that the stage never consistently
represented a fictional locale. From this we can assume that, one, the players'
continuing relation to the stage as a whole was in terms of its geographical or
presentational character, and two, the players used the physical parts of the
stage only intermittently. The validity and hence the implications of these
assumptions are evident in four ways: (1) in the players' physical orientation
to the audience; (2) in the staging of spectacle; (3) in the pattern of entrances
and exits; and (4) in the use of the stage platform.

Consider the players' orientation to the audience. Thomas Platter
assures us that everyone could see well at the Globe.[7] What we know of the

size and shape of public playhouses seems to confirm his observation, up to a point. But we need to qualify his remark and understand it in Elizabethan, not modern, terms. Two matters deserve examination. First, public plays were performed in daylight. Audiences partially or perhaps in some productions wholly surrounded the playing area. To make himself felt, the player could not wait for stage lights to pick him out of the dark; he had to assert himself vigorously to command attention. Dressed for the most part in the style of the day, he had to rely on the authority of his presence to take and hold the stage, a challenge that the contemporary actor does not quite face. I had a glimmer of how different the effect could be when I saw the Italian production of *Orlando Furioso*. It was acted on platforms thrust among the audience, and the actors on those platforms had to fight for attention.

Secondly, although Platter wrote of seeing well in the playhouse, what that "well" means depends upon one's expectations. Our criteria for seeing well, for instance, has been changing. Those of us who grew up with the proscenium stage theatre expect to see everything pertinent that the actor does, even though we might miss details if we are in the balcony. By contrast, during the last two decades we have learned from performances in the round and on open stages that we must be content to have important bits of business hidden from us, in exchange for which we enjoy an unaccustomed intimacy. In effect, we may have come closer to Elizabethan conditions. Yet we cannot be sure. We know very little about Elizabethan playhouse sightlines. One of the great contributions the projected reconstruction can make is to enable us individually to test the sightlines. What will it be like to stand where groundlings stood and see the actors loom above us? Or how will it affect our response to sit in one of the better places of the gallery watching the players strut past the heads of the groundlings? Until we live those moments, we cannot know how they might alter our feeling for Shakespearean performance. Again I advert to *Orlando Furioso*. At the performance in New York there were bleachers on either side of the playing area. One could choose to sit at the side or join the standees near the platforms. The two different positions aroused quite different sensations.

Point two pertains to the staging of spectacle. Unlike ourselves, the Elizabethans could not rely on illusion achieved through the control of light. Nor could they depend on visual composition of groups of people, the kind of visual composition that characterizes the informal design of a Chekhovian play or the geometrical patterns of *A Chorus Line*. Nor, given the distribution of the audience on three sides of the stage, could they rely on scenic spectacle. What they did use were three other types of spectacle: processions, striking entrances, and shows of horror. Processions and striking entrances included entrances of groups through one door and exits at another as well as entries of chariots. Most striking were descents from above or the raising of figures or objects from below. Both involved stage machinery. One of the puzzling things about Elizabethan stage usage is the role of the flying machinery. Flying machinery for descents required a stage house, quite an elaborate one as reconstructed by Walter Hodges. Yet flying, insofar as the plays indicate, was infrequent. What is one to make of the relatively heavy investment for so little use? While I do not doubt that flying machinery existed in some playhouses at least, I wonder whether it was present in all.

The third and most widespread type of spectacle was much less dependent on physical features of the stage. Horror could be invoked by bringing in a bloody head on a pike or by revealing the dead in grisly form as in *The Revenger's Tragedy*. Such displays, as in *The Duchess of Malfi,* seem to require a discovery-space, but some of the most violent demonstrations of horror, as in *Titus Andronicus* and *The Spanish Tragedy,* depended wholly upon the actors.

The third use of the stage—and the most important for us to consider—concerns the handling of entrances and exits. This usage is one of the most controversial in Elizabethan stage scholarship, and it is intimately connected with the question of the now abandoned "inner stage" or the so-called discovery-space. Most of us will concede, I believe, that there is no independent playing area built into the stage façade. What is at issue is the number of entries, their form, and how they relate to spaces that permit discovery.

While, as I say, there is controversy on these matters, there is at the same time collegial recognition that the evidence is inconclusive and even contradictory. We might not always agree, but for the most part we disagree cordially. For instance, Richard Hosley and I, using much the same textual evidence, have reviewed the stage requirement for the first Globe playhouse. On many points we come to similar conclusions. But on the number of entries, we disagree. Professor Hosley argues that there were only two.[8] I am inclined to think there were three. But the real significance of the matter is not which of us, if either, is right, but how the issue of two or three entries affects staging.

Is it indeed important to theatrical production to determine whether there are two or three entrances? Would a performance be much affected by whether it used two or three doors? The modern theatre is not of much help in answering these questions. Virtually all the open stages constructed under the influence of the Elizabethan revival have multiplied the number of possible entrances. Either the entire area surrounding the stage is left free, as in the Central Park stage of the New York Shakespeare Festival, or multiple entrances are laid out not only on the stage proper but also in the auditorium itself through vomitoria, as in Stratford, Ontario. Confinement to two or three entries, as practiced in the Shakespearean theatre, is thus quite at odds with present taste.

In Elizabethan and Jacobean drama, many if not most scenes end with all the players on stage leaving through one door and all the players in the next scene entering at another. Were such a sequence the only type of movement from scene to scene, we would have no trouble in agreeing upon two entries. But there are other types of transitions that suggest the need of a third entry. In some cases a character exits in one direction, a second character exits in another direction, and for the next scene a new character enters immediately. The reverse also occurs. One character exits, and then two characters enter from separate points. To illustrate: in a total of twenty-three scene transitions, *Lear* has eight of the sort I have just described. For example, at the end of act 1, scene 5, the distraught Lear, a Gentleman, and the Fool depart, heading for Regan's castle. We can assume that they all leave through one door. The next scene (2.1) starts with the stage direction "Enter Bastard and Curan severally," as in the Folio, or "meeting," as in the Quarto of 1608. If we assume that the stage has only two doors, then either Edmund or Curan must enter at the door through which Lear and the Fool have just left. There is nothing impossible in that, but it does affect the rhythm of presentation and especially our tendency, influenced by the cinema, it is true, to overlap scenes in performance.

More problematic is the type of transition that occurs between the first and second scene in act 3. In the first scene, Kent and a Gentleman are searching for Lear in the storm. At the end of the scene Kent tells the Gentleman:

> Few words but to effect more than all yet:
> That when we have found the King.
> Ile this way, you that, he that first lights
> On him, hollow the other.   *Exeunt.*
> (Q1608)

Unquestionably, they go out at separate doors. The next stage direction reads "Enter Lear and Foole." The opening line is "Blow wind & cracke your cheekes, rage, blow." Are we to suppose that Lear enters immediately through one of the doors used either by Kent or the Gentleman? Or should his frenzied entrance be delayed a beat? Or does he come through a third entry?

Logic and verisimilitude are not justification enough to argue for a third entry. But we do have some corroboratory evidence. The clearest case for a third entry at the Globe appears in *The Devil's Charter*. In one scene (4.2) Alexander, the Borgia pope, is discovered in some recessed enclosure. He then "commeth upon the Stage out of his study." Later in the same scene, while the study is still open to view, he sees the apparition of his son Caesar pursuing the ghost of his second son across the stage. The directions specify that they enter at one door and "vanish in at another doore." This explicit instance is backed by other more circumstantial examples in many plays. They argue for a third entry, at some theatres if not at all, and

161

encourage further study of the relationship between the rhythm and style of staging and the number of entrances.

It is in respect to such study that the proposed reconstruction can be extremely helpful. The stage façade should be so designed that it could be outfitted with two, three, perhaps even five entrances. The central entrance should also be large enough to serve as a place for discovery as well as concealment. The variant faces should be so devised that they do not appear to be what we call stage plugs but seem fully architectural.

Last of the ways that the physical stage affects usage involves the platform itself. One of the arguments for the efficacy of the platform stage is that it permits the actor to move close to the audience for intimate moments, such as soliloquies. Yet moving to the front of the platform, if envisaged in a complete playhouse, does not necessarily lead to intimacy, except for the groundlings in the immediate vicinity of the actor. Actually, when the player moves to the front of the stage, he is in less close contact with the audience on either side of him, including the audience in the gentlemen's rooms. Even the notion of intimacy as connected to the soliloquy is a misconception since psychological privacy may be important to some soliloquies, those of *Hamlet,* for example, but less so for others, such as those of *King John*. Indeed, the historical trend after 1576 was toward a reduction in the number and length of soliloquies in the drama.

This point about the soliloquy applies fairly broadly to most scenes. The stage platform had no fixed associations for the players. Large and neutral, the platform served more as a *platea* than a *locus*. It accommodated whatever tonality the players imparted to it. Only its size was distinctive. Considering that so many scenes involved only two or three people, we see again how the platform demanded that the actors play audaciously.

In imagining its use, furthermore, we should keep in mind that most members of the audience saw the action from an elevated position. Such a vantage point facilitates appreciation of physical relationships *between* players rather than physical display *within* a scenic environment. Again, this point is relevant to the proposed reconstruction. Unless the majority of the audience is placed in the galleries, the theatrical effect will be false.

From these various observations, I should like to draw some conclusions about the esthetics of the Elizabethan stage. The physical façade seems to have served as a glamorous frame for a performance. It was impressive in and of itself. To excite and thrill the audience the players would not depend on scenic means. Instead, they would rely partly on pageantry and surprise through physical movement. Oddly enough, the fewer the doors, the more concentrated the impact produced by an entrance. Shakespeare in particular found ways of stimulating excitement by giving performers vigorous verbal and situational impulses to contrast with the rigidity of the stage façade.

Perhaps the players used the façade and platform most of all as a great sounding board against which to bounce their voices. One of the important things for us to examine is the way structure can affect sound. The wood flooring of the platform, built over an open area beneath, must have provided a giant reverberator. Since we do not have a gallery-type theatre in operation now, we do not know how it might affect the voice. Care should be taken in the choice of materials and the preservation of reverberant spaces. We want to go beyond the mere attainment of audibility, and assure richness of sound. A wood and plaster building shaped like the Globe must have produced both clarity of expression and fullness of tone. To have this in a building accomodating twenty-five hundred to three thousand people is a wonder indeed.

To my comments on sound, I would like to add some observations on the contrast between artificial and natural light. This subject affects staging markedly, as I found in directing plays on a Shakespearean replica. The Elizabethan stage, most of us would grant, was colorful. Playing on a colorful stage, however, is one thing in artificial light, another in natural light. Actors lit by artificial light, when playing against a colorful façade that is either lit directly or that receives considerable spill light, tend to get lost. The background color acts on the actor's profile, simulating an effect akin to those charts that test for color blindness. By comparison, in natural light the background color is softer and does not interfere with a clear perception of the actor. If at all possible, then, the playhouse should have a dome that would permit us to see scenes in natural illumination as well as in stage light.

Finally, in developing such a project as a new Globe playhouse, we might bear in mind that while we cannot re-create the experience of Shakespeare's day itself, we can create an approximation of the instrument that Shakespeare used. But it must be the entire instrument, in all its complexity. I think of the task as analogous to the rediscovery and employment of Renaissance musical instruments. The object is to draw from the instrument a living sound, and the living sound we might draw from a reconstruction will be our sound, not that of olden days. Nevertheless, by erecting the instrument that once housed the original music, we can hope to discover something fresh about the nuances of actor and text, actor and actor, and actor and audience. What they shall be, we will not know until we hear and see Shakespeare at the wooden O.

IX. *Types and Methods of the Dutch Rhetoricians' Theatre*

W. M. H. HUMMELEN

Translated by H. S. Lake

*I*n 1944 George Kernodle published in *From Art to Theatre* what he called, with fitting pride, "the first account in English of the plays and stages of the Societies of Rhetoric and the first account in any language of how these stages were related to the tableau tradition and to the other theatres of the time,"[1] I suppose that outside Holland, and especially in English-speaking countries, knowledge of the rhetoricians' theatre is founded chiefly on Kernodle's study of it, which has until now been the most recent and the most easily accessible. For this reason it would seem practical for me to start with this work. I shall have to be critical of it in parts, but it is not my intention thereby to detract from its great merits as a pioneering work. The basis of my reasoning is research that I have carried out over the past ten years, some of which I have already published,[2] some of which I hope to publish in the foreseeable future. In order to provide the greatest amount of information there will often be a strong emphasis on the conclusions I have arrived at, but I hope all the same to be able to give a sufficiently clear picture of the manner in which I reached them.

For his analysis of the link between the staging of the *rederijkers'*, or rhetoricians', plays, and the *tableaux vivants* as used for the joyous entries of royal personages, Kernodle had access to about one-third of the nearly six hundred surviving dramatic texts, because he drew exclusively on printed sources. These are for the greater part contemporary editions of the plays, as there is a regrettable lack of modern editions, especially of the many plays that survived only in manuscript form.[3] One third of six hundred seems a considerable number, but, although Kernodle himself expressly pointed out that the major part of his material consisted of plays written for various dramatic contests in the northern and southern Netherlands, I do not believe he was aware that limiting himself to printed sources might affect the validity of his conclusions. On the contrary, in an article of slightly more recent date he tends to reduce all the rhetoricians' activities to what happened at contests.[4]

The rhetoricians' plays were only printed if there was a special reason, the most common reason being that they had been performed at a contest that in some way or other had acquired a certain fame. Competition plays of this kind constitute a special category. They were all structured by the need to provide an answer to a question formulated by the organizers, such as *Welc den mensche stervende meesten troost es?* ("What gives the greatest comfort to every dying man?") The rules of the contest also lay down certain conditions with regard to the length of the plays.[5]

It was only because he was using this relatively homogeneous material that Kernodle was able to formulate his theory of the development of the rhetoricians' plays out of the *tableaux vivants* of the Joyous Entries. The same material also led him to conclude that the inner stage was used chiefly for displaying *tableaux vivants* and that its use for other purposes, in particular for interior scenes,[6] was only a more or less sporadic occurrence. In reality, however, this kind of use of the inner stage was far more varied and common than appears from the limited number of instances adduced by Kernodle. This can be demonstrated—I shall do so shortly—by reference to biblical plays, of which many more have survived than Kernodle supposed.[7] Most of them, unfortunately, are still only to be seen in manuscript form.

Kernodle's ideas on the use of the inner stage appear to be supported by the long-familiar pictures of stage performances by rhetoricians in that none of them shows the curtains of the stage façade drawn back. In the work of the engraver Crispijn de Passe, however, I have found two illustrations of a stage façade with the curtains open. The more important of the two appears in the Melpomene engraving (ca. 1605–10) (fig. IX-1). The scene is the tragic climax of a Pyramus and Thisbe play.[8] The figure on the right, on the side stage, can be identified as a *sinneken,* a character comparable with Vice in English plays. The trumpeter up above the corner of the stage between two torches is presumably the watchman who, according to Ovid, saw Thisbe leaving the town and took her to be a goddess.[9]

The curtains next to the fountain would not have been open, at least not as far as they are, simply to allow the figures who are seen watching from the inner stage (the other actors? members of the chamber?) to look out onto the stage. Therefore, the opened curtains must surely have something to do with revealing the fountain. The fountain's position is shown rather ambiguously in this engraving, but we may hardly suppose that it stood in front of the curtains from the beginning of the play; that would be an extremely impractical arrangement, since it would mean that one of the stage entrances would be blocked throughout, while to judge from the engraving there are already only two or three entrances available in the stage façade. For this reason, we must surely interpret the engraving as showing a fountain placed directly behind the curtains. The opening of the curtains means that the nocturnal meeting place on the forestage is identified by means of a property on the inner stage.

Fig. IX–1. Detail of the Melpomene engraving, ca. 1605–10, by Crispijn de Passe. (Copyright Rijksmuseum, Amsterdam.)

It is not absolutely clear from this Melpomene engraving how broad the whole stage is. But a façade with three stage entrances, the middle one of which can function as an inner stage, is repeatedly referred to by Jacob Duym in the stage directions for his plays (published in 1600 and 1606) as "according to the old custom." Because, as in the Melpomene engraving, for example, the stage entrances on the extreme left and right are not so narrow that they cannot give access to an inner stage, we might here talk of a façade with three compartments. It is the basic stage façade, as used by Hodges for his "basic platform stage" (fig. IX-2).[10]

For his drawing, Hodges was evidently inspired by an illustration of a façade with three compartments used at Louvain in 1594 for a performance of *The Judgement of Solomon* (fig. IX-3). By making the forestage so much larger, however, he departs from his model not merely in the matter of a subordinate detail; he is saying, in effect, that the space behind the façade does not count as part of the acting area. In my opinion, this is a mistaken view.

Fig. IX–2. Basic stage façade used for basic platform stage. (C. Walter Hodges, "Unworthy Scaffolds: A Theory for the Reconstruction of Elizabethan Playhouses," *Shakespeare Survey* 3 [1950]:86.)

Fig. IX–3. Performance of *The Judgement of Solomon* at Louvain, 1594. (From M. A. P. C. Poelhekke, C. G. N. De Vooys and G. Brom, *Platenatlas bij de Nederlandsche literatuurgeschiedenis* [Groningen: Wolters, 1934], fig. 26.)

It is true that the performance of 1594 took place after a procession, but as we can see from the blazon on the frieze, it was organized by a chamber of rhetoric, probably the Daisy of Louvain. What we are looking at, therefore, is presumably not a stage specially built for this occasion, but staging owned by the chamber. In that case it is mere coincidence that on this occasion the space behind the curtains was left unused. The absence of partitions must not be interpreted as evidence that acting took place only on the forestage. As an indication of the compartments, the caryatids are paramount. Partitions can easily be erected if there is a real need for them.

I can illustrate this observation with a picture of a street theatre erected for the entry of the duke of Anjou into Antwerp in 1582 (fig. IX-4). In the left compartment Samuel cuts off a piece of Saul's robe as a sign of his loss of sovereignty over Israel. In the middle, surrounded by the sons of Jesse, Samuel chooses David to be Saul's successor, and in the right-hand compartment we see David triumphant over Goliath. There are no partitions to separate these scenes from each other; the caryatids are both sufficient and at the same time indispensable.

Here again we are dealing with staging used for stage performances on other occasions by the Marigold chamber of rhetoric. This chamber and the other two had been engaged by the city authorities, because the authorities had insufficient time and money to see to all the decoration of the city themselves.[11] The employment perforce of (as the account of the entry words it) "whatever came to hand, whatever was ready and available" also explains the presence of the cell door, behind which we see Discord, in the understructure of the stage.[12] Evidently the Marigold did not wish to miss this chance of brightening up its performance with this asset, even if it had to be positioned somewhat unusually and inappositely. To judge by the stages of the Gillyflowers and the Olive Branch, the two middle caryatids, or pillars, were not load-bearing and could therefore be removed for occasions such as this. The same applies to the forestage, indispensable for the performance of plays (figs. IX-5 and IX-6). These chambers, too, draw express attention to their identity by incorporating their blazon into the decorations of their theatres.

Twelve years later the Antwerp chambers of rhetoric, partly as a result of the emigration of many of their members to the Protestant North, were as good as defunct. But the example set by their scaffolds seem to have been so strong that when *tableaux vivants* had to be put on for the entry of Archduke Ernest of Austria, no better idea was forthcoming than that of simply imitating the rhetoricians' stages, outmoded caryatids and all. This is why it is important for us to know the dimensions of these scaffolds of 1594. In some cases, the contracts for their erection have been preserved. They were all between seven and nine feet deep, and the stages (referred to in the Latin as *proscenium*) were seven feet high. This is slightly higher than Hodges' "reasonable guess," which "would put the normal stage height for a street theatre playing to standing spectators as something between 5 feet 6 inches and 6 feet above the ground."[13] The stages on the Driehoek, in the Lange Nieuwstraat, and on the Grote Markt were 30, 25, and 40 feet wide, respectively. In the case of the last of these (fig. IX-7), however, it should be borne in mind that it was placed in front of the town hall and should therefore be *loco suo non indignum* ("not unworthy of its place"). The traditionalism with which the work was approached is evidenced by the presence of the two caryatids in the middle, which could easily have been left out, as far as the character of the *tableau vivant* behind them is concerned.

The stage directions for so many of the rhetoricians' plays take it for granted that it will be possible to show God on his throne "above," so the extension of a stage like those of Louvain or Antwerp, with a fourth compartment on top, must have been extremely common. An illustration of such a stage has been preserved in the printed version of the plays performed in a contest in Haarlem in 1606 (fig. IX-8). A similar construction was used in 1565 for the performance, in a small village on one of the islands of Zeeland, of a play of the Assumption of Our Lady.

The manuscript in which the play is preserved, and which also contains two other plays by the same author, Job Gommersz, is an autograph. This, together with the fact that Gommersz had no previous experience as a writer for the stage, may explain why there are so many stage directions in the text and why they are so detailed. The opening or closing of the curtains is expressly indicated no fewer than thirteen times, for example. An important aid to our interpretation of the *mise en scène* is the stage direction *pausa,* common in rhetoricians' plays (including this one), which indicates a break in the action during which music may be played, for example, but which also means that there is no one on stage. Many authors, furthermore, employ special meters and verse forms to indicate moments when the stage is empty (what I call metascene boundaries) and to differentiate them from scene boundaries. The *mise en scène* envisaged by the author of *Our Lady's Assumption* may be reconstructed as follows.

The central compartment acts as the Valley of Jehoshaphat, where Mary is buried; Heaven is in the compartment above this. One of the side compartments—let us assume the right-hand one—is Mary's house at the foot of Mount Sion, and in the other stands the bed of a sixteenth-century character, who under the influence of Protestant heresy no longer knows what to believe about St. Mary and to whom the events of Mary's Assumption are revealed in a vision. The action around this person is, so to speak, the frame surrounding the play. The first scene of the action, which is performed on the forestage, ends with this person retiring to bed.

Fig. IX–4. Entry of François, duke of Anjou, into Antwerp, 1582. Stage of the Marigold. (From *La joyeuse et magnifique entrée de monseigneur François, fils de France,* etc. [Antwerp, 1582], fig. IV.)

Fig. IX–5. Entry of François, duke of Anjou, into Antwerp, 1582. Stage of the Gillyflowers. (From *La joyeuse et magnifique entrée,* fig. VII.)

Fig. IX–6. Entry of François, duke of Anjou, into Antwerp, 1582. Stage of the Olive Branch. (From *La joyeuse et magnifique entrée*, fig. IX.)

Fig. IX–7. Entry of Ernest, archduke of Austria, into Antwerp, 1594. Stage of the Grote Markt. (From Joannes Bochius, *Descriptio publicae gratulationis*, etc. [Antwerp, 1595], p. 111.)

Fig. IX–8. Stage of the contest of Haarlem, 1606. (From *Const-thoonende Ivweel*, etc. [Zwolle, 1607].)

This is followed in the right-hand compartment by a meeting between Mary and Jesus during which Mary is prepared for her death. The action then returns momentarily to the frame: two Vices on the left of the stage try to persuade the man in bed to ignore the vision, but in vain. There then follows a series of metascenes in the house of Mary, each of which is concluded by the closing of the curtains. First we see Mary alone, meditating on what Jesus has said to her. Next we see her with an angel bringing her a palm branch and a shroud as protection against the onslaughts by devils on her deathbed, a trial she fears greatly. Then St. John arrives on the forestage, and as the house of Mary opens to receive him we see that she is now in the company of Joseph of Arimathaea and the three maidens who are to lay out her corpse. This is followed directly by the arrival of the other apostles, for which the house of Mary is again opened, so that they can all stand round her while she intones the Magnificat. The hour of her death is now at hand. Behind the closed curtains of the façade we hear Jesus, singing and accompanied by angels, move across to the compartment representing Mary's house. The curtains open, and Mary dies in Jesus' arms. Jesus departs, again behind closed curtains, and the prayer that John then intones by Mary's body is treated as a separate metascene. Behind the curtains Mary is now placed on a bier, and after her house has been opened again the assembled company moves off in procession, singing the funeral psalm, to the Valley of Jehoshaphat in the middle compartment.

There, without further interruption, we see the episode of the abortive attempt by the Jews to take possession of the body. When the Jews have left the stage the curtains of the Valley of Jehoshaphat are closed, not to be opened again until we have heard the apostles answer Jesus' question of how they want him to pay tribute to his mother. As the curtains open, Jesus, who is standing by the grave, calls to Mary to ascend to Heaven. The actor playing Jesus must now run quickly round behind the group of apostles standing by the grave in order to go upstairs by steps at the back of the compartment. In the meantime Mary, kneeling, is lifted on a little platform straight up until she is in the upper compartment, which has opened to receive her, precisely between God the Father and God the Son, who, with their right and left hands, respectively, hold the crown that they then place on Mary's head. An uncertain number of small angels and numerous Old Testament prophets are also present in Heaven for Mary's arrival. After she has been welcomed, the curtains of the upper compartment are closed again, and the play is concluded downstairs with a scene centered on the man lying in bed in the left-hand compartment, who now reappears there.

Thus a large part of the action, and not just the occasional scene, as in Kernodle's examples, takes place in one of the compartments. Notwithstanding this, using the stage in this way is still entirely within the possibilities of the "first stage façade" as Kernodle describes it. At the same time it is easy to see that the possibilities of such a stage are relatively limited. What is to be done, for example, when the action of a play demands far more than three separate compartments? New elements must then be added, either to the way in which the stage is used or to the staging itself. I will consider both solutions.

The first can be demonstrated by reference to a play in three parts based on chapters 16–28 of the Acts of the Apostles. The author is Willem van Haecht, the *factor,* or professional poet, to the Gillyflowers, the Antwerp chamber of rhetoric to which I have already referred. The first and second parts were performed in 1563 and 1564; the third was completed in 1564 and was doubtless intended for production in the following year. Not only these dates but also the many similarities between the three parts make it probable that they were all written for the same sort of stage. True, the manuscript is not an autograph, but it is nonetheless very close to the original. It contains numerous stage directions.

To stage the play, the chamber needed a stage façade with three compartments downstairs and at least one upstairs, or perhaps with *three* compartments upstairs, as in the contest organized by Willem van Haecht and his Gillyflowers at Antwerp in 1561 (fig. IX-9).[14] The compartments in the middle, upstairs and downstairs are used as inner stages. The upstairs compartment, of course, is used chiefly for the appearances by Christ but also, as I shall explain in a moment, for other scenes.

St. Paul's life, as described in the part of the Acts of the Apostles with which we are concerned here, took him to scores of places. To show this on so small a stage as I have just outlined would be impossible without making the same stage entrances and inner stages represent different scenes of action during the course of the performance. Now the meaning of an inner stage can be changed by closing the curtains and replacing those properties whose chief function is to indicate the scene of action with new ones. A second and less common device used here is to invest a previously neutral entrance with a special meaning simply by showing a screen, placed behind the entrance curtains, painted to show castle gates or the door of a prison cell. Obviously the author attempts to keep the stage entrances as neutral as possible for as long as possible in each episode. Much less often than in the plays of Jacob Duym, for example, the characters exit into their own houses; here they simply leave the stage "to go home." In this way several people can use the same stage entrance to go to different houses.

The most radical change of meaning, of course, occurs when the action shifts over a greater distance. Traveling as such is not shown. When St. Paul's arrival in Rome following his departure from Malta has to be portrayed, the stage direction read: "Malta in. Rome out, with the three Taverns." Clearly the author regards Tres Tabernae as the place where Paul stayed in Rome. These stage directions indicate that—probably by removing one placard from the façade and replacing it with another—the meaning of the entire façade is changed. At such moments, too, the stage entrances with castle gates or cell door screens could be returned to their neutral state by closing the curtains.

Van Haecht's way of depicting the shipwreck on the coast of Malta is very revealing. The ship itself is placed in the compartment upstairs, otherwise used to represent Heaven. At the beginning of this metascene the angel who resides there by virtue of his office is employed by the author to push the curtains aside; understandably, it would have presented problems to have the castaways do it themselves. The events on board are dramatized faithfully according to the description in the Bible, except that they are punctuated by shouts from the lighthouse keepers (to left and right of the shipwreck compartment) and inhabitants of Malta (on the forestage) who witness the wreck from the shore. Finally those aboard leave the ship by the back of the façade and so return downstairs into the compartment below the ship. At the beginning of the Malta episode this is fitted out with trees (the leaves of which serve as food for the shipwrecked mariners), firewood

Fig. IX–9. Stage of the contest at Antwerp, 1561. (From *Spelen van sinne . . . Ghespeelt . . . binnen der stadt van Andtwerpen,* etc. [Antwerp, 1561].)

(concealing a snake that is later to bite Paul on the hand), fire to light the wood, and water to put the fire out at the end of the metascene that follows. The islanders leave the scene momentarily in order to fetch food. When they return they are accompanied by Publius, the Roman governor of the island, who invites Paul to go with him to his house. The stage is cleared, the fire extinguished, and the inner stage closed. When it opens again we see the interior of Publius' house with a bed on which lies Publius' sick father, who is later healed by Paul.

So much for the first solution. What the second solution, the addition of new elements to the basic stage façade, entailed is illustrated by a sketch of a stage façade used for a performance of *De Stathouwer* (fig. IX-10). The sketch is contained in a manuscript of 1709 that is a copy of a manuscript dating from 1619.[15] At either side it shows a *sinnepoort* (gate for the Vices), and between them, from left to right, the *gevangenisen* (the prison), the *houdeensij camer* (the duke's presence chamber), the *stathouwers camer* (the stadtholder's chamber), a neutral stage entrance, and the *herberge* (inn) with its sign inscribed *trouwe* ("fidelity").

Since the frieze with its architectural decorations does not continue over the *sinnepoorten,* and since they are shown as narrower than the five stage entrances in the middle, I suspect that the artist was unfamiliar with the theory of perspective but wanted to indicate that these gates should be understood to be at the sides of the stage. From the text of the play it is clear that only the duke's presence chamber and the prison are used as inner stages. Strictly speaking, the neutral stage entrance is super-fluous. The equal dimensions of the various different stage entrances suggest that they could all be used as inner stages if need be so we can speak of five compartments. It therefore appears as if the stage entrances and inner stages called for by *De Stathouwer* have been distributed over an existing façade. By the expansion of the number of compartments from the usual three to five, this façade was designed to obviate the need for compartments to double.

This is certainly precisely what Jacob Duym had in mind when for some of his plays he asked for a façade divided into five parts instead of three, even though he only used at the most two or three stage entrances as inner stages (he calls them *open camers,* "open chambers"). He needed the other stage entrances because he was at pains to provide each group of characters with its own "house" or "chamber" or stage entrance.

This desire to provide each group with its own location is observable not only in the plays of Jacob Duym but also in the work of some other playwrights of the time. It is difficult to explain as a development from the use of the stage as we see it in Willem van Haecht's apostle play. Conceivably there is some influence here of school drama, which presupposes a *mise en scène* with stage entrances having fixed meanings. We need think only of the compartmented stage-house shown in the illustrations to the Lyons *Terence* of 1493, in which each stage entrance seems to be coupled to a particular character by means of a superscription. There are other aspects of the work of the last years of the sixteenth century and the beginning of the seventeenth, when Duym was writing his plays, that also show signs of the direct or indirect influence of Terence.

In this connection we may wonder how we should interpret the stage façade found by Kernodle among the illustrations of the show architecture used for the entry of Archduke Ernest of Austria into Brussels in 1594 (fig. IX-11). Ever since Kernodle first published this "combination of throne pavilion with an arcade and a forestage [that] provided an important

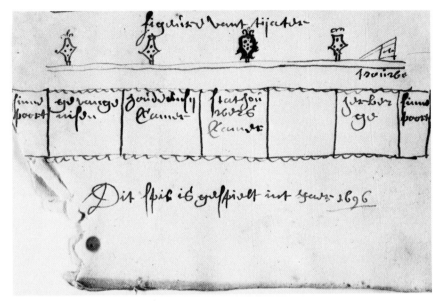

Fig. IX–10. Sketch of the stage of *De Stathouwer*, 1619. (From a 1709 manuscript copy of a 1619 manuscript, University Library, Nijmegen.)

Fig. IX–11. Entry of Ernest, archduke of Austria, into Brussels, 1594. Stage of St. Mary's Garland. (From *Descriptio et explicatio pegmatum*, etc. [Brussels, 1594].)

pattern for the Elizabethan stage,"[16] it has been reappearing in studies of the Elizabethan playhouse.[17] But it is impossible to talk of an important pattern being provided by this façade without also referring to the way it was used.

Was it actually used for dramatic performances? Or was it merely a street theatre erected especially for this entrance and for this *tableau vivant?* If that be the case, then it is a more or less arbitrary choice to pick out this particular construction from the fifteen as being an important pattern.

In the end, however, it turns out that Kernodle has picked the right construction for precisely this stage—see the blazon at the top in the middle—proves to belong to the St. Mary's Garland, one of the three Brussels chambers of rhetoric to provide a stage. Both the discrepancy between *tableau* and stage (and the unusual form of the latter) and the financial arrangements agreed to with the city authorities concerning the chambers' contribution to joyous entries make it likely that in this case, too, we are dealing not with a piece of ephemeral show architecture but with the chamber's own stage, on which performances are also given on other occasions.

But how? Has the stage only two inner stages, one upstairs and one down? In the light of what we know about the use of inner stages in this period this seems unlikely. We may suppose that the two stage entrances to right and left of the throne pavilion can also be used as inner stages, albeit of secondary status. Such a difference in status is also found in earlier stage façades, such as those used for the contests in Antwerp (1561) and Haarlem (1606) (see figs. IX-9 and IX-8).

Inexplicable, at least in terms of surviving texts of the rhetoricians' plays, is the gallery in the upper storey. Its origins may lie in the architectural need to fill the space between the side walls on the upstairs floor as well as downstairs. But are they the side walls of the framework in which the stage façade was erected in 1594? I doubt it, since the framework looks as if it is more likely to be secondary to the façade. The poles or pillars that bear the roof at the front are not even decorated. Perhaps they were originally the side walls of the St. Mary's Garland's meeting-place—their chamber—which this façade was built to fit. However, we have no evidence as to how the chamber was arranged, or how performances in it were organized, to support this supposition.

For the sake of completeness I must also point out that there was a greatly different *mise en scène* in five of Jacob Duym's twelve plays. Briefly, this may be described as being *à la Valenciennes*, and it was largely dictated by the subject matter of the plays concerned. Three of them, for example, are about sieges. Duym served in the army of the Prince of Orange and was imprisoned by the Spaniards before he emigrated to the Protestant North, so he naturally was particularly interested in this subject. I do not think there is any need for me to go into further detail on this point here. The remarkable thing is that this type of staging—and Kernodle has demonstrated precisely how it could be superseded by the stage façade—should at such a late period turn up almost literally alongside the stage façade.

As far as I know, Duym's plays saw the end of this kind of *mise en scène* in the Low Countries. The stage façade, on the other hand, survived for many more years, albeit with a mixture of multiple and sequential *mise en scènes*. Even in the sixteenth century this mixture would not have been unknown, however, and if it could have been avoided, it would only have been by the grace of the modest demands of the play to be performed. Even in those plays that are based on narrative material, after all, the localization (as Beckerman would term it) is only partially specific, the rest being general or neutral.

Both Van Haecht's *Dwerck der Apostelen* and Duym's plays with their strict coupling of particular compartments to particular characters are, in the end, rather special. Van Haecht's drastic changes in the meaning of the façade are closely tied in to the special nature of the content of his play. And in his stage directions Duym gives an unequivocal outline of what seems to him to be the ideal situation. This does not, however, mean that the work of Duym and Van Haecht is any the less representative of what can perhaps be described as two trends in *mise en scène* tradition. And that these trends can be discerned at all is due to a special characteristic that Duym and Van Haecht share: they are both exceptions to the rule that stage directions are given sparingly.

In Van Haecht's work, in particular, it is clear how much the façade actually *is* a façade. There is no fixed conception whatsoever of the space behind it. At one moment the upper and lower compartments are separated by a watertight floor, at the next they form a continuous whole.[18] Here what Kernodle says of the 1561 Antwerp stage applies: it is "little more than a Renaissance frame for six tableau openings"[19]—though in this case rather more is shown in them than tableaux. But to what extent can we apply Kernodle's words to this façade of the apostle play when he says of the one at Antwerp that it "kept in symbolic form the power to represent the scenic devices from which it was derived"?[20] In the Van Haecht play the façade is no more a ship than the façade in the Melpomene engraving is actually a fountain. Yet it is conspicuous that it is precisely these two scenic devices that can be proved to have been capable of being enclosed by the façade. Moreover, the absence of any extensive aids to accentuate the meanings of the tower and city walls, both in Van Haecht and in the Melpomene engraving, points to those meanings indeed being kept in symbolic form in the façade.

Gommersz, Van Haecht, Duym: there is no difference, in principle, among the possibilities of the inner stage. I go no further into its use for interior scenes, any more than I need go into the use of the upper compartment for both heavenly scenes and scenes for which there is no room below. It is worth noting, however, that the stage directions for Mary's ascension into Heaven are unique in sixteenth-century theatrical literature in the Low Countries. But given the frequent use of the inner stage and the convention of placing Heaven in a compartment in an upper storey, the solution to the technical problem of such an ascension is actually fairly obvious. In the theatre that Jacob van Campen built in Amsterdam in 1637 (the Schouwburg) there was still a lift similar to the one that must have been used for *Our Lady's Assumption*.[21] The placing of the Valley of Jehoshaphat in a compartment, and not on the forestage, was doubtless connected with the engineering of the lift. But that does not alter the fact that there was evidently no insuperable objection to placing an exterior scene on an inner stage.

It should also be noted that Gommersz uses the curtains to divide the action. He places the individual images next to each other, and if possible in opposition to each other, quite in line with rhetoricians' dramatic techniques. This is diametrically opposed to the emphasis on the use of exit lines that Beckerman observes in the Globe plays. As he says, exit lines "clearly demonstrate that it was the physical departure of the actors which gave fluency to the action."[22]

The separate presentation of each event, of course, reminds one of the *tableaux vivants,* and undoubtedly the example of the tableaux was of crucial significance for the use of the inner stage. The connection that Kernodle sees between the two may be debatable as far as English plays are concerned, but when it comes to the Low Countries there is no lack of evidence.[23] At the same time it is possible to detect in the rhetoricians' plays the influence of quite a different tradition, in which all the action takes place on the forestage. Sometimes, indeed, it looks as if both traditions are at work side by side in one and the same play. The play *De Stathouwer,* to which I have referred, is an example of this, when the possibility of using the tavern and the stadtholder's chamber as inner stage is expressly rejected. The absence of an inner stage is a particular characteristic of what Southern has called the booth stage.[24] This is the form of stage that is most often depicted in paintings of carnivals and fairs at which dramatic performances are being given, and it is evidently well suited for farces. As I said, the effects of this tradition are also felt in other types of play. But in plays requiring a more complicated stage than that for a farce, it is nonetheless fairly difficult to find clear-cut examples of, for instance, interior scenes being performed exclusively on the forestage, complete with all the usual props for an interior.

Although the differences between the situations on either side of the English Channel are relative rather than absolute, they are still marked. This will become apparent when I compare what we know about the Netherlandish theatre with the description that Beckerman gives of the use of props and of the "enclosure" in the Globe. It is characteristic of the rhetoricians' plays that no large properties are moved about; there is never any question of a bed being "thrust out," for example, or being carried off the stage. Even tables used in interior scenes on the forestage are present throughout, so that they have only to be laid for food and drink to be placed upon them. The other side of the coin, of course, is also the opposite of the situation in the Globe; the enclosure, by contrast, is used here precisely for the setting of furniture, or of properties such as the fountain in the Melpomene engraving.

It is not (as in the Globe) only sleeping, studying, or foregathering characters who may be revealed to the public by drawing the curtains of the discovery-space aside. In this respect the possibilities of the façade in Dutch plays appear to be endless. They range from a neighbor sitting at her spinning wheel in her room, giving advice, which she could just as well have given on the forestage, to Susanna bathing in her orchard (this, incidentally, is an example of a façade enclosing a garden). Undoubtedly the discovery-space may be termed an inner stage. Both in the case of Mary's house and in that of the Valley of Jehoshaphat, the façade has room for Mary, Jesus and his accompanying angels, eleven apostles, Joseph of Arimathaea, and three virgins. Mary's singing of the Magnificat is expressly directed to take place inside, with Mary surrounded by all the other characters except Jesus and the angels.

The inner stage, then, is clearly also an area in which acting takes place.[25] This is not to say, however, that at the same time the forestage cannot be used during scenes being played principally in the inner stage. The attack by the Jews on Mary's funeral cortège, which is planned on the forestage while the procession itself is already going on in the inner stage, is an example of this. I assume that all those who have to reach the compartments by way of the forestage enter through the side stage. Various illustrations of dramatic performances show this to be possible.

So far I have confined myself almost exclusively to performances in the open air. Apart from performances during meals (for which there is little need for much in the way of decoration), very little acting took place indoors during the sixteenth century, and that was the occasional performance in the rhetoricians' chamber. Nothing is known about the arrangement of the stage on such occasions.

In the second decade of the seventeenth century, however, at least in Amsterdam, the bulk of performances moved indoors. This goes hand in hand with the fact that by charging for admission the rhetoricians were able to provide considerable financial support for charitable institutions, such as the orphanage and homes for old men and women. At the same time this development was a stimulus for the writing and printing of plays.

In 1615 the art dealer Abraham de Koning became the first person to put an illustration on the title page of a play, *Iephthah*, which he had written himself and which was printed at his expense. From then on, such engravings constituted an important new source of information about the arrangement of the stage.

The engraving on the title page of *Iephthah* (fig. IX-12) exhibits three peculiarities that give grounds for supposing that it is more than simply an illustration of the well-known biblical story. To start with there is a departure from the iconographic tradition of showing Jephthah's daughter emerging from his house. Jephthah, it will be recalled, had sworn an oath that he would sacrifice the first person he should meet coming out of his house on his return from his victory over the Ammonites. In the second place the floor of the gateway is raised in a way not seen in the actual gates of castles or cities. Third, between the tower on the left and the crenellated wall in the middle a piece of architectural decoration that could not have appeared on or between real defensive structures is just visible.

These peculiarities can be explained if we assume that the engraving is meant to reflect something of the arrangement of the stage used for the performance of de Koning's play. Jephthah's daughter may be standing to one side in order that the engraving can provide a clear picture of the central element of the stage, the façade with an inner stage whose floor is raised to increase the visibility of the characters to the audience. Below the architectural decorations to the right of the round tower we can just see the top of an arch, possibly the upper part of an arch-shaped opening in a screen, which might be the entrance to an inner stage. This would mean a combination of utility and show architecture, which is also found in the work of Jacob Duym, who, in one of his plays, calls on the one hand for "the form of a city" and on the other hand for "an open chamber."

For the performance of de Koning's play a tower is completely superfluous, whereas the Arcadian surroundings in which the last act is supposed to take place are quite absent. This means that what we see in the engraving is certainly not a stage set designed especially for *Iephthah;* at best, it must be a stage intended for the performance of several different plays. And the angle formed by the back and side walls cannot be explained in terms of open-air structure, so that we have to regard this as some kind of indoor stage.

Abraham de Koning was a member of the chamber of rhetoric called the White Lavender, most of whose membership was drawn from immigrants from Brabant. According to the preface, *Iephthah* was performed by this chamber. If the engraving refers to performances indoors, they must have been in the White Lavender's chamber, which was on an attic floor of the Marienkerk, and later over the Regulierspoort, one of the gates of Amsterdam. From the texts of other plays that were performed there it may be deduced that there was certainly at least one upper compartment, above the most central and most easily seen compartment below.[26] All the Brabant plays also allow for the possibility of playing scenes whose action takes place in the open. Perhaps the properties needed for this are hidden by Jephthah's army in the engraving.

Because I had absolutely nothing to go on when considering what this part of the stage may have looked like, I decided to omit it altogether from a reconstruction (fig. IX-13) that I drew ten years ago. I attribute the form of the central gateway in front of the inner stage, with a Tudor arch, unlikely in Holland, to the way in which the curtains in front of the opening hang. In my view there can be little doubt that the tower on the left had a gate, since otherwise it would be necessary to use the compartment next to it as the entrance to the tower. To be honest, however, I am rather less sure of the gate in the tower on the right, though given the width of this façade a third stage entrance would be perfectly possible.

The first building in Holland not merely to be adapted for stage performances but to be actually designed as a theatre was the Neder-duytsche Academie. The Academie was founded in 1617 by Samuel Coster, who together with a number of others, including two of the most important playwrights of the period, left the Eglantine chamber of rhetoric for this purpose. This enterprise, one of whose aims was to provide higher education in the vernacular, foundered within five years, and in 1622 the theatre was sold to the Amsterdam city orphanage, the Burgerweeshuis, which thereafter loaned it to the White Lavender in return for part of their proceeds.[27] Research into the stage of the Nederduytsche Academie (about which I hope soon to publish a more detailed account) has led to the following conclusions.

The dimensions of the floor of the hall were about twenty meters by sixteen. The stage was at one end, against the wall. An inventory drawn up for the sale in 1622 refers to the presence of *omdraeyende doecken*, or turning cloths. From those plays with stage directions that refer to turning and reversing it emerges that these "turning cloths" were screens painted on both sides. When they all faced one way they represented a landscape, and when turned round they showed a building. The building side of these screens could be used either as a background for an exterior scene or as décor for an interior scene. Because of that, little more can have been shown of the building than a wall with architectural decorations, windows, and the like.

The space in front of the screens can be closed off with curtains, which are also mentioned in the inventory and in stage directions, forming an inner stage. This was used not only for exterior and interior scenes but also for *tableaux vivants*.

There are two illustrations of plays that are connected with the Academie through their authors and performers and whose curious features cannot be explained on pictorial grounds but point to the stage set in the Academie. From an illustration in Jacob Struys' *Ontschakingh van Proserpina*

Fig. IX–12. Title page engraving of Abraham de Koning's *Iephthah*, 1615.

Fig. IX–13. Reconstruction of the stage of the White Lavender at Amsterdam.

(1634, fig. IX-14) and from the title page engraving for his *Romeo en Juliette* (1634, fig. IX-15) it can be deduced that the central inner stage is flanked by doors. The engravings show us a side compartment next to one of the doors just mentioned, at an angle to the rear wall.

This side compartment could also be used for a bed, as we see in the title page engraving for Jacob Jansz. Colevelt's *Hartoginne van Savoyen* (1634, fig. IX-16). And in the title page engraving for Meindert Pietersz. Voskuyl's *Kuyssche Roelandyne* (1636, fig. IX-17) and a painting by Jan Miense Molenaar executed in 1636, of a scene from Gerbrand Adriaenszoon Bredero's *Lucelle* (probably performed at the Academie in 1632) (fig. IX-18), we see the inner stage being used respectively as a church and as the interior of a dwelling-house.

In 1618 Claes Jansz. de Visscher did an engraving (fig. IX-19) that depicts a scene from a short occasional play performed to mark the first anniversary of the Nederduytsche Academie. The two doors flanking the inner stage are masked here by a cabin (left) and a cave (right, a servant with food just emerging from it). Half of the space between the cabin and the cave is occupied by a row of seven Muses. If one assumes that they each need at least half a meter in this position, the inner stage must be about seven meters wide.

Analysis of Willem Dircksz. Hooft's play *Hedendaegsche Verlooren Soon* (1628, 1630) reveals that apart from the inner stage flanked by door-ways and the side compartments to right and left of it, there were two other stage entrances, for which there can only be room at the extreme left and right. Figure IX-20 shows my reconstruction of the ground plan of the Academie. The heaven is not, as in the rhetoricians' plays of the preceding period, a compartment in which scenes can be played, but a vehicle with which a limited number of characters can descend or ascend. It is true that from some plays dealing with sieges it appears that it was possible to have characters acting "on the walls" of a city, but how this worked in practice is not clear. What does seem certain is that in comparison with the stage of the White Lavender, various changes have taken place in the upper storey of the stage in the Academie that resulted on the one hand in more spectacular motion of the heaven as a vehicle, but on the other hand, and possibly as a consequence, did not make acting "upstairs" any simpler. Clearly, acting on two levels was less popular in the Academie than in the White Lavender.

One of the consequences of erecting a stage in a hall is that the central compartment becomes the focus of attention, since the side compartments, if they are to be used as inner stages, are placed less advantageously from the audience's point of view. One might say that in the Nederdeuytsche Academie they drew their conclusions from this, in the sense that there is a greater disparity of dimensions between the central and side compartments there than in the White Lavender stage. The unique position

Fig. IX–14. Illustration from Jacob Struys's *Ontschakingh van Proserpina*, 1631.

Fig. IX–15. Title page engraving of Jacob Struys's *Romeo en Juliette*, 1634.

Fig. IX–16. Title page engraving of Jacob Jansz. Colevelt's *Hartoginne van Savoyen*, 1634.

Fig. IX–17. Title page engraving of Meindert Pietersz. Voskuyl's *Kuyssche Roelandyne*, 1636.

Fig. IX–18. Jan Miense Molenaar's painting of a scene from Gerbrand Adriaensz. Bredero's *Lucelle*, 1636. (Muiderslot, Muiden.)

Fig. IX–19. Engraving by Claes Jansz. de Visscher, *Ghezelschap der Goden op de Bruyloft van Apollo met de Academie*, 1618. (University Library, Leiden.)

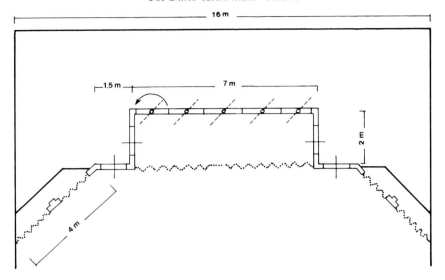

Fig. IX–20. Reconstruction of the ground plan of the stage in the Neder-duytsche Academie.

of the central compartment then means that any need to change the meaning of a compartment will be concentrated on this one. In the Neder-duytsche Academie this need is met by the reversible screens. On the other hand, the Academie appears to have had more stage entrances than the White Lavender. This might be seen as an accommodation of the trend toward creating the firmest possible mental connection between characters and stage entrances. The result is the mixed form of multiple and sequential *mise en scènes* to which I have referred.[28]

In the context of the main theme of this symposium, however, what seems to me to be most important is that the tradition of the inner stage is maintained so strongly both in the Chamber of the White Lavender and in the Nederduytsche Academie. Any influence on the English theatre from that of the Low Countries ought to be apparent, if anywhere, in the use of the inner stage. Because in this respect, at least, the paths on either side of the Channel are so diverse, it is largely only in a differential diagnostic sense that what I have said can be regarded as a positive contribution to answering the questions we are asking here.

X. Decorative and Mechanical Effects Relevant to the Theatre of Shakespeare

JOHN RONAYNE

Decorative Effects

Style

What did the Globe look like inside? Highly decorative, I think, to make a dramatic contrast with the plain exterior.

This is what the "architectural" cabinets produced in the sixteenth and seventeenth centuries are like. They are plain on the outside, but when the doors are opened the carved, sparkling interiors take away the onlooker's breath; who expects such riches to be concealed within such humble exteriors? Hints of classicism are detectable in their style, but the predominant feeling is exuberant and grotesque.

There are other examples of this stylistic tension between classical and grotesque. One is the early seventeenth-century library of Langley Marish church in Buckinghamshire (fig. X-1).[1] The mantelpiece carries two sober Tuscan columns, yet the walls are ablaze with colored cartouches of strapwork, a spiky, flamboyant motif said to have come from the Low Countries, where engravers like Vredeman de Vries used it as a border decoration around maps and prints.

Pattern books were produced containing elaborations of this style to suit all purposes. The painted staircase at Knole House in Kent is one of the best examples of this bravura decoration (fig. X-2). It was derived from designs by Martin de Vos and has remained untouched since 1605. It is a reasonable bet that this was the basis of the style used inside the Globe. However, the Globe playhouse was open to the air. This dictated a more robust treatment, rather like that of the traditional street fountains that still stand in many German and Swiss towns. Their style is reminiscent of the fairground, with bright, lustrous colors, often varnished against the weather.

So much for style. A review of the carpentry and the painting and decorating techniques of the period will make our mental picture of the Globe's interior more specific.

Three-dimensional decorative elements

How were the gallery fronts and the tiring-house wall constructed? The walls of the houses at the Teatro Olimpico in Vicenza (1585) are constructed from flat vertical planks butted together and battened across at the rear. Contemporary illustrations survive to show both vertical and horizontal boarding for theatre and scaffold walls.[2] The masking rooms erected in the 1630s are described in the accounts as being "bourded with slit dealebourds, the inside with whole dealebourds battend."[3]

Sabbattini, writing in 1638, preferred boards to canvas for his scenic houses.[4] Furttenbach used thin boards for his proscenium arch and made his parapet at the front of boards 3 inches thick.[5]

Sawn woodwork

Flat planks can be sawn into decorative shapes. We see this today in Swiss and Tyrolean country chalets and in the flat sawn balusters of the eighteenth-century court theatre at Bayreuth.[6] These examples carry on the sixteenth-century tradition of Serlio, who specified that the rooftops and statues of his tragic scene should be cutouts.[7] The cutout arches at the back of the Olimpico vistas are left square-cut. The best "profiling" work would be "feathered," or beveled back to hide the edge. Domestic dummy board figures, popular from about 1600, are good examples of this technique.

The characteristic Elizabethan ogee finials and newel posts—those, for example, on the staircase at Harvington Hall, Worcestershire—were produced simply by sawing the same shape on all four sides of a timber. There is no reason why the Globe should have departed from this fashion.

Turned woodwork

The balusters of the Knole staircase were produced on a lathe, as were heavier balusters at the Farnese Theatre in Parma (1619) and the little court theatre at Sabbioneta (1588). The contract for the Hope Theatre, 1613,[8] calls for "turned cullumes vppon and over the stage," but since it specifies that the "heavens" should have no support from the stage, these must have been balusters for a stage rail and perhaps a stage balcony.

It was feasible to turn longer pillars, but the lathe itself would have had to be specially extended and the treadle drive exchanged for a great wheel-and-belt of the type illustrated by Moxon in 1680.[9] Very large pillars were usually shaped by eye with an adze.

Wood carving

Hardwick House in Oxfordshire has a room full of exuberant carving, with typical terminal figures adorning the doorcase (fig. X-3). Sir Nikolaus Pevsner, in *The Buildings of England—Oxfordshire* (p. 840), calls this room "a tour-de-force of affluent late Elizabethan decoration. . . . the chief aim was richness of effect."

191

Fig. X–1. Library, St. Mary's Church, Langley Marish, Buckinghamshire, 1620s. (Courtesy National Monuments Record, England.)

Fig. X–2. Arcading of great staircase, Knole House, Sevenoaks, Kent, 1605. (Courtesy National Monuments Record, England.)

Fig. X–3. Doorcase, Hardwick House, Oxfordshire, ca. 1600. (Photo author.)

The square posts at the Fortune Theatre were carved "palasterwise" with satyrs.[10] The celebrated Bed of Ware, mentioned in *Twelfth Night* and now in the Victoria and Albert Museum (V&A), has terminal figures, carved and painted, on its headboard.

Plaster modeling

The statues on the Olimpico houses are made of plaster. Sticks of wood, split to size and snapped off to length, act as armatures. Each figure was roughly shaped from rags drenched in heavy plaster, and the modeling was then built up with finer plaster (less sand, more lime and water, with hair acting as a bond).

Plasterwork, like the hunting frieze at Hardwick Hall in Derbyshire, was often painted. In 1601 the Painter-Stainers Company complained that plasterers were "usurping" their work and leaving them nothing to do.[11]

Fig. X–4. Painters at work, 1689. (From E. Porcellius, *Curioser Spiegel* [1689], pl. XXII.)

Plaster stamping

For repetitive motifs, plaster can be stamped in molds. Vasari, writing in 1550, describes how the wooden mold is carved and powdered with marble dust. The plaster, "not actually hard nor really soft," is pushed into the mold, and the two are separated by tapping with a hammer.[12]

Paper molding

Papier-mâché as a cheap method of molding repetitive shapes was described by Sir Hugh Platt in *The Jewel House of Art and Nature* (1594). He specified "the pap of common paper, being well wrought with the hand of a workman." He recognized the need of a bonding medium (fish glue) and hardeners (sand, sawdust, and mineral powders) but admitted that papier-mâché "would endure no weather."

The Greenwich Palace Banquet House accounts of 1527 mention "linen cloth for lining knots (ornaments) cast in paper, brown and white paper to make knots with, sponges, oil, pork grease, flour for paste, . . . shavings of white paper to make lions etc. . . ."[13]

195

Painted decoration

I have relied heavily on John Smith's *Art of Painting*,[14] which describes in detail the tools, materials, and style of seventeenth-century trade painting, as opposed to the techniques of fine art painting. More sophisticated treatises of earlier date are available, and I will make use of them here, but they deal with limning (manuscript illumination), easel-painting, and other indoor, small-scale, studio arts.

Painters

Painting, like all other trades, was well organized in London. John Smith recognized the metropolitan nature of skilled trades when he wrote of "great Cities where painters usually reside," of "Colour shops," of books of gold leaf from the "Gold Beaters," and of hints on glue-making for those "not willing to send to London." The Painter-Stainers Company demanded a seven-year apprenticeship, most of which was spent grinding colors.

The most common job was painting the exterior woodwork of houses and shops. Protection from the weather was as much in the customer's mind as was decoration. William Sutherland, an administrator at the Royal Dockyards at Portsmouth, wrote in *Britain's Glory: or, Shipbuilding Unvail'd* (1717) of the value of paint, as well as pitch and varnish, in the protection of ship's timber—"undeniably," he says, "a very good preservative if rightly applied."

Painting has always been an uncomfortable trade, often being performed on a scaffold and in all weathers (fig. X-4). Sutherland records that "rather than the Painter would lose the Painting of a ship he would actually paint the work when it rained upon the part that his brush mov'd on" (p. 191). He tried to formalize contracts for his painters that would avoid such dilemmas. In a contract of 1695 he devised elaborate distinctions between plain work and "flourish'd work."

Plain painting

Even for plain timber painting, the preparation was long and tedious. First, any cracks in the wood had to be filled with putty, for, according to Smith, "if these are not secured the wet will insinuate itself into those defects, and make the quicker despatch in roting the whole Work." Then followed a thin wash of boiled linseed oil and Spanish Brown, a cheap and plentiful earth color, which acted as a sealer. After two days this layer would be dry to the touch, although linseed oil actually stays soft for years underneath its surface. Another sealing wash might be applied before two or even three priming coats of thick white lead. Before the color was applied, this priming could be sanded with "sharp stone or emery."

196

White lead was the one really opaque pigment. However, working with lead was one of the direst hazards of the painter's job. Raising the lead fumes by sanding was a prime cause of "painter's colic." It was the painting trade that introduced "wet and dry" sanding.

Stone, lead, and wood colors

Smith tells us that "Pales and Posts are sometimes laid over only with White which they call a Stone Colour." In 1630, Matthew Goodricke was noted as "payntinge stone Cullor in oyle dyvers Cornishes pendaunts and mouldings" at the Cockpit-in-Court.[15] The 1637 Works Accounts for the Banqueting House at Whitehall mention "painting the ceeling(e)s and windowes with walnuttree collo(u)r in oyle."[16] Smith gives recipes for the colors of "new oak" and "Olive Wood." Lead color was achieved by mixing indigo and white.

Decorative painting

Working with simple, formalized motifs is essential in trade decoration, where everything must be reduced to a system so that it can be tackled by a team, without individual style.

A late sixteenth-century balustrade in the lecture hall of the Hôtel de Lamoignon is painted in a system of light, middle, and dark tones.[17] Beautifully modulated shadows do not always "register" from a distance. A sixteenth-century door in the V&A collection is decorated with a sort of informal, high-speed strapwork (fig. X-5). The mural (ca. 1575) in the parlor at Little Moreton Hall in Cheshire is boldly shadowed in imitation of paneling. Much of the 1620s painting on the walls and ceilings at Bolsover Castle in Derbyshire is sytematically shadowed and stenciled.

Sutherland required his painters to specify "what the colour shall be and whether shadow'd or Carved frieze." Smith explains how to mix the "shadows" of various colors.

Drawing and stenciling

For transferring the design itself to the work, pouncing (dusting charcoal through lines of pin holes in a paper drawing) and templates were traditional. Richard Tothill, in his treatise of 1573,[18] suggested a sort of homemade carbon paper. Smith tells us that lead pencils could be bought, but "made up so deceitfully" that he recommends the reader to buy lead in the lump, and to glue cuttings of it into a quill. He goes on to list squares, rulers, and brass compasses "for setting out and proportioning your work."

Stencils were used as a quick way of painting repetitive motifs. A fifteenth-century stenciled panel from West Stow Church, Suffolk, is pre-

Fig. X–5. Detail of painted oak and pine door, English, sixteenth century. (Crown copyright, Victoria and Albert Museum, W37, 1913; photo author.)

served in the V&A, as are the seventeenth-century Hill Hall murals, which include stenciled borders. Stenciled strapwork appears on the beams of Little Moreton Hall chapel, ca. 1560.

Marbling

De Witt tells us that the wooden pillars at the Swan Theatre were painted to imitate marble so as to "deceive even the most prying."[19] The original marbling on the houses at the Teatro Olimpico can still be seen. Illustrated books were produced to record the magnificence of sixteenth-century triumphal arches with their marbled pillars and panels. The account of an entry into Pesaro in 1621 mentions "the wonderful imitation of valuable marbles and precious stone . . . paragone . . . lapis lazuli . . . and oriental granite."[20] Vasari lists the imitation of porphyry, serpentine, and red and gray granites on the walls of houses and palaces.[21] The pillars of the Knole staircase are painted to resemble granite.

The tools for marbling are simple—a rag for dabbing and flogging, a brush handle for scoring in the veins, and a feather for fine blending—but to paint convincing marble requires years of practice. As Smith says, the skill "must be attained by ocular inspection, it being impossible to deliver the manner of the Operation by Precept without Example."

Woodgraining

Smith makes reference to woodgraining in his discussion of walnut tree color, which was made up from burnt umber plus white and could be "veined with Burnt Umber alone, and in the deepest places with Black." The V&A and its outstation at Ham House, Surrey, both contain examples of seventeenth-century woodgraining. Wren's Sheldonian Theatre in Oxford is grained like cedar and the gallery columns are marbled.

Sparkle finishes

Among the "items for colors" in the Greenwich accounts of 1527 is mentioned "½ lb of ground glass," which was perhaps used in the French way, to add a sparkle to varnish. In an anonymous pamphlet of 1685,[22] directions are given how "to lay on your Mettle Speckles: First wet your work with Varnish, with a soft brush, then while 'tis wet dust your speckles upon it thro' a piece of Tiffany, and then Varnish it twice, to keep 'em from rubbing off, 'tis enough." The same pamphlet obscurely described tortoise-shell finishes done by "clouding" the paint, and "red work with Black Speckles," produced by flicking paint from the brush.

Masonry patterns

Triumphal arches, and doubtless theatres, were often decorated with masonry simulated in paint. The shadows of stone blocks and lines of mortar could be made quite convincing. In 1501, when Catherine of Aragon was received into London, one of the pageant arches was "empeynted like frestone and whight lyme, so that the semys of the stone were perceyved like as mortur or sement had been between."[23]

In 1581, the canvas-covered walls of the Westminster Banqueting House were painted "most artificiallie with a worke called rustike much like to stone."[24]

One of the most spectacular rustications was known as diamond point. It was used on one of the triumphal arches that welcomed Louis XIII into Paris in 1629, and it can still be seen on the trumpeters' box in the 1748 Margrave's Theatre at Bayreuth.[25] According to Macci's account, Sabbattini used diamond point ("finta di macigno a punta di diamante") on one of the monuments for the Pesaro triumph of 1621, and he includes it in his illustration of designs for the stage parapet (bk. 2, chap. 31). He also shows a plainer rustication, with borders drawn inside each block (fig. X-6). This motif turns up in Hans Eworth's painting *Elizabeth and the Three Goddesses.*[26] The queen is standing under an arch that looks curiously insubstantial, as though it were made of canvas. Its painted stonework looks flat; it has been reduced to a conventional cipher, presumably accepted by Elizabethans as being simply the way that stone was represented.

Plain rustication, with its chamfered joints highlighted and shadowed, is still popular in Italy, where it is commonly painted on the plain walls of houses (fig. X-7). For the walls of Robert Fludd's *Theatrum Orbi* (1619), the engraver used the same pattern. He embellished it with what looks like vermiculated rustication, which was supposed to give an antique, worm-eaten appearance to stonework.[27] A vermiculated finish appears on one of the Antwerp arches illustrated in Scribonius' album of 1550. Plain brickwork is indicated on the upper wall in Fludd's illustration. Brick patterns are painted on the Olimpico houses. Furttenbach specifies that his *periaktoi* houses should be painted with "big red stone blocks and white lines."[28] John Smith gives his recipe for brick color as red lead mixed with a little white and yellow ocher.

Painted illusions of reality

The steps leading from the stage to the floor of the hall were sometimes only painted on the flat parapet.[29] In Elizabethan England it was conventional to paint duplicate banisters on the blind wall of a staircase. Examples of this illusion survive at Knole, Aston Hall, Mapledurham House, and Harvington Hall. The engraving in Turberville's *Noble Art of Venerie* (1576) shows flat palings painted as spindly, round balusters.[30] The same effect can be seen on many vernacular buildings, for example, the eighteenth-century mill at Bachmühle, Switzerland.

I would suppose that many of the figures, niches, and decoration shown in illustrations of triumphal arches were painted rather than modeled. This is suggested by several details on the engravings of King James I's entry into London in 1604. Willem Kip's engravings of the triumphal arches built by Stephen Harrison for this occasion are reproduced in Hodges' *Globe Restored*. A good example to illustrate my idea here is *Arch of the New World* (fig. X-8). The two belvedere towers at the sides are drawn exactly as though they were closed in with canvas. The central panel between them might as well have been painted; by Harrison's scale it was 40 feet above the ground. The niches that contain the Four Kingdoms and the Four Virtues measure only 4 feet in height. Even if they were intended to accommodate children, the drawing of those niches positioned on the round towers suggest that they were two dimensional; they curve with the

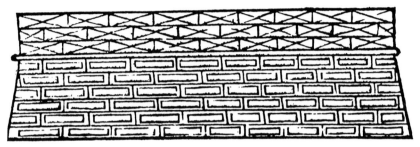

Fig. X–6. Nicola Sabbattini's designs for a stage parapet. (Sabbattini, *Practica* [Rome, 1638]; reproduced in *The Renaissance Stage,* ed. Bernard Hewitt and trans. Allardyce Nicoll, John D. McDowell, and George R. Kernodle [Coral Gables: University of Miami Press, 1958], figs. 33–34.)

Fig. X–7. Wall painted in plain rustication, Nervi, Italy, 1976. (Photo author.)

walls instead of showing any depth. The two niches at the extreme sides are drawn in an impossible perspective.

Painted heavens

Clouds were painted on the curved soffits of Harrisons' *Flemish Arch* and his *Arch of London*. The so-called *English Wagner Book* of 1594 describes the ceiling of an Elizabethan stage: "Now above all was there the gay Clowdes . . . adorned with the heavenly firmament, and often spotted with golden teares which men callen Stars. There was lively portrayed the whole Imperiall Army of the faire heavenly inhabitaunts. . . ."[31] The Greenwich accounts of 1527 speak of lead stars that were gilded and pinned up. Stars were also cut out of paper. A century later, at Rycote Chapel near Oxford, the stars decorating the vault were cut from old playing cards and gilded (fig. X-9). The Star Chamber at Bolsover also had playing-card stars.

The gallery and pew ceilings at Rycote are painted with simple, brave clouds with no shaded tones. The Rycote treatment may be seen at Cullen House in Scotland,[32] where the painted-heavens ceiling is inhabited by the usual allegorical figures. These images were propagated by Continental engravings, for example, those by Virgil Solis of Nuremburg. The V&A has a series of English plaster panels painted in about 1600 that are based firmly upon Solis (fig. X-10). They show Jupiter, Mercury, Venus, and Cupid in heavenly surroundings, and even reproduce Solis's characteristically intestinal clouds.

The zodiac was a popular motif; it adorned the ceiling of the Enchanted Chamber at Binche in 1549, and Irwin Smith has prescribed it for the first Globe's ceiling.[33]

Gold

In Elizabethan times gold leaf was sold in books of 24 three-inch-square leaves; it is still sold in this form. The leaves are extremely thin and have to be transferred delicately from the book to the work. Smith recommends "Cane Plyers," or a cloth "Pallat" moistened with the breath, or a foxtail, as mentioned in the Greenwich accounts, which would be stroked on the cheek to create static electricity. He suggest that gold, once burnished down, can be shadowed with a transparent solution of burnt umber. Substitutes for pure gold included "party gold," a sandwich of silver and gold; "green gold," an alloy of silver and gold; and "orsedye," an alloy of copper and zinc. Gold paint (that is, powdered metal in suspension) was mentioned as early as the twelfth century by Theophilus, but was rarely used for large-scale work.

The most common dodge, especially outdoors, was to lay a silver or even a tin foil and color it gold "with a Lacker-Varnish made of Gum-Lake dissolved in Spirit of Wine." Models for admiralty ships were lavishly gilded, for example, that of *The Prince* (1670), preserved in the Science Museum, London. In practice, however, the gilding was simply represented by yellow paint.[34] An order of 1715 refers to "the usual colour yellow."[35]

Pigments

Mixing colors with the unrefined pigments of the seventeenth century was haphazard, although ready-ground and mixed oil paint, tied up in skin bladders, was beginning to be sold.

Pigment names were often generic and unspecific. Sometimes they referred to different treatments of the same material. A few examples of pigments will show the vast range of their sources and the difficulty of their production.

White lead was made, notably in Venice, by corroding sheets of lead over vinegar. Ceruse was the name given to the purest type, sometimes called Vennis Cerius. Yellow monoxide of lead was called Masticot. Another mineral pigment, orpiment, was known as Yellow Arsenick, and John Smith warns to "take care that the fumes of it don't offend the Brain in the time of grinding." Red lead was unpredictable; burning it at different rates produced different colors—more orangey or more purplish. Byze, or bice, was known in a blue and green form, as was verditer, a nitrate of copper mixed with whiting. Tothill mentions that green byze was often mixed with sand by the apothecaries, "to multiply it to their gain" (fol. vi). The word for indigo was notoriously corrupted. Tothill lists it as "Indebaudias"; the Greenwich Palace accounts speak of "ynde bavedens." All writers on pigments praise the color vermilion, obtained from quicksilver and brimstone, but Tothill recommends that the painter "put into it three chyves of Saffron" to "take away the evil sente" (fol. v).

A less spectacular red was made from "Brasill," or Brazil wood, an ingredient mentioned in many English accounts. In 1634 John Bate *(The Mysteryes of Nature and Art)* explained that the color was produced by boiling shavings of the wood in vinegar and small beer. Smith records that yellow ocher could be dug out of the Shotover Hills near Oxford. Ultramarine, "so vastly dear," was derived from lapis lazuli. Lamp black, as the name suggests, was lamp soot. Large quantities were obtained by burning sappy fir trees. Smith indicates that Norway and Sweden were the main producers, and says that "this colour is usually made up in small Boxes and Barrels of Deal, of several sizes, and so brought over to us." The ivory fragments that were burned to make ivory black were the raspings of the comb-maker. Lake pigments, such as crimson and madder, were liquid

Fig. X–8. *Arch of the New World,* triumphal arch for King James I's entry into London, 1604. (From the engraving by W. Kip. Crown copyright, Victoria and Albert Museum, Prints and Drawings, no E.O. 83.)

before being mixed with a medium. Dry pigments had to be ground with a "muller," or pebble, on a marble grindstone, using a "voider," or spatula, of "lanthorn horn" to keep the powder from dispersing.

The oils and mediums were as hard to obtain as were the pigments. Sir Hugh Platt shows a press for extracting oil from herbs (fig. X-11) and the apparatus for distilling spirits from oils.

Brushes

In the seventeenth century the term *brushes* referred only to the large, coarse type. Smaller ones were called, confusingly, *pencils.*

Fig. X–9. Detail of gallery ceiling, Rycote Chapel, Oxfordshire, early seventeenth century, showing stars cut from playing cards and gilded. (Photo author.)

Fig. X–10. Painted plaster panels, Stodmarsh Court, near Canterbury, ca. 1600, showing Jupiter, Mercury, Venus, and Cupid in heavenly surroundings. (Crown copyright, Victoria and Albert Museum, W28, 1913; photo Victoria and Albert Museum.)

Fig. X–11. Herb press. (From Sir Hugh Platt, *The Jewel House of Art and Nature* [London, 1594].)

Fig. X–12. Three cranes. (From Claes Jansz. de Visscher's panorama of London, 1616.)

Brushes were always made of bristles, usually hog bristles. They were mostly round, up to 2 inches in diameter, although flat ones were known, being used for drawing lines and wood-graining. Round brushes were normally held in split wooden handles lashed round with cord. When buying brushes John Smith was wary of "hairs that sprawl about," and if the hairs were loose he recommended "driving in thin Wooden Wedges between the Thread with which they are bound round." Metal stocks were known, being made of tin. The stocks, or "tails," for pencils were the quills of feathers. Their sizes were referred to by the kind of quills used, from the smallest, those of the duck, right up to those of the goose and the swan. The quills of waterfowl were preferred for their natural resistance to moisture. The feather end of the quill was cut off and replaced by a wooden handle. Both brushes bound with cord and pencils in quills are still made.

The hair used for soft brushes was taken from the tails of squirrels; from ermine, which is slightly more resilient for fine work; and possibly from red sable. The first specific mention of sable brushes was in the eighteenth century, but sable was certainly available in the seventeenth.

Hops were recommended as a moth deterrent for soft brushes.

Mechanical Effects

Mechanical effects were clearly as popular in the Elizabethan theatre as they had been on the medieval stage. The two principal devices were the trap door and the flying chair. Ben Jonson derided the popularity of flying effects; he looked forward to plays "where neither Chorus wafts you ore the seas; Nor creaking throne comes downe, the boyes to please."[36] The Prologue to *All Fools,* first acted at the Rose Theatre, mentions that "none knows The hidden causes of those strange effects, That rise from this hell, or fall from this heaven."[37] Today we know even less about their hidden causes. However, we are not quite at a loss in reconstructing the machines. Contemporary descriptions and the general technology of the time may be combined into reasonable inferences.

Cranes

The three cranes opposite Bankside, shown on the maps and views of Elizabethan London, are of a common medieval type with a single fixed boom. Power was provided by a treadwheel normally contained in a housing. Visscher's view of 1616 shows one of the cranes swiveling like a windmill on a central pivoting post (fig. X-12). The crane of 1667, which is preserved on the seafront at Harwich, has a fixed wheelhouse and a movable boom.[38] Crane booms were not made to lever upward. The rope passed over a pulley, just like the simple hoists that

207

had been used for centuries to haul up goods and furniture to the lofts of houses and corn halls.

Sheerlegs

Daniel Barbaro, writing in the 1550s, illustrates a lifting machine with four stout posts joined at the apex, whereas Robert Fludd's version has a sturdy tripod (both illustrated in Yates, *Theatre of the World*). A fifteenth-century drawing of a cannon hoist shows two sheerlegs with a crossbeam between them.[39] Single sheerlegs of two poles were useful on building sites, for example, to erect the prefabricated sections of timber houses, and in dockyards for the masting of ships.

If the flying throne at the Globe had needed a crane device to project it forward, sheerlegs would have provided the simplest and most stable method.

Block and tackle

Most Renaissance engineers were fascinated by the complexity of pulley trains. Sabbattini recommends the book *Mechaniche,* written by his mentor, Ubaldus, for the further study of the relationship between effort and load which changes with the multiplication of pullies. In practice, however, Sabbattini only resorts to block and tackle once, in the case of a cloud machine that had to be operated in the small space between the back shutter and the wall of the hall. I think a complex of pullies would have been unnecessary at the Globe, although descriptions by diplomats and courtiers suggest their use in performances at court.

Counterweights

A counterweight is used to decrease the effort needed to drive a machine, or to bring the machine into a finer balance so that it can be manipulated forward and in reverse.

Sabbattini says that little bags of sand are suitable (bk. 1, chap. 37). Their weight can be finely adjusted, and they make no noise. Sand-bags are clearly shown in the drawings of seventeenth-century Venetian machinery that are kept in Parma[40] and are still in use at the eighteenth-century theatre at Drottningholm, Stockholm.

The weights mentioned by Furttenbach are of lead and oak. He arranged for one of his back shutters to be "so fastened to a counterweight that it comes apart by the force of a blow."[41]

Georgius Agricola shows a lever for lifting a furnace door with a rock lashed on to it as a counterweight.[42] Agostino Ramelli shows a complicated project for a bucket winch with a refined counterweight of metal made in the shape of a ball, squashed so as to maximize its fall in a limited space.[43]

Levers

The counterweighted lever is controllable and strong. Zeising shows a pile-driving lever resting on a kind of rope hammock, which would have allowed great flexibility of movement.[44] Sabbattini's most ambitious lever device is a 25-foot beam that lowers a cloud throne forward onto the stage (fig. X-13). The beam rests on a fulcrum of iron and was presumably visible to the audience during the descent, even though Sabbattini says that it would be masked by the cloud hanging in front of it. The operator of this machine had to be attentive. Sabbattini notes that once the cloud had reached the stage and the actor had disembarked, the cloud might "ascend of itself on account of the greater contrary weight" (bk. 2, chap. 45).

A lever cloud of this type may have been used in England in 1606. An account of the masque *Hymenaei* describes ladies sitting in clouds that "descended upon the stage not after the stale, downright perpendicular fashion, like a bucket into a well, but came gently sloping down."[45] This might be taken to imply that the usual descent was perpendicular.

Furttenbach used levers for both of his cloud machines (fig. X-14). His floor-mounted device had little engineering elegance: it comprised a 16-foot boom with a 2-foot wrought iron hook, from which hung a 9-foot cloud with half a hundredweight of lead screwed to it to make it hang straight. His other cloud lever was pivoted on the roof beams "like a cannon" and was designed to dip only a few feet below the level of the sky borders. Both devices had the advantage of being operated directly, by men lifting and depressing the weighted ends.

Treadwheels

Several Elizabethan treadwheels have survived. Perhaps the finest is at Grey's Court in Oxfordshire. This has the same construction as the Catherington donkey wheel (fig. X-15), which is preserved at the Open Air Museum at Singleton, Sussex. The spokes are set through the axle, halved together inside and wedged. The rim is made up from sections of wood sawn into curves. Guard pegs stop the rope from wandering along the axle.

The 1587 donkey wheel at Carisbrooke Castle on the Isle of Wight has a "clasp-arm" construction, in which the spokes grip the outside of the axle. This arrangement is not as strong as that in which spokes pierce the axle because the clasp-arm spokes have a tendency to burst outward. However, Agricola illustrates it, and clasp-arm became the usual method.

Bearings

The Singleton wheel also provides an example of a typical bearing. The end of the axle shaft is rounded and a metal hoop hammered on to stop it splitting. A piece of iron called a wing gudgeon was hammered into the end with its protruding pin, about 2 inches in diameter, resting in a hole in the support post.

Bearings were usually lubricated with animal fat. Sometimes animals in mills were tethered with their hindquarters positioned over the bearings to provide natural lubrication.

Agricola shows an ingenious idea for a frictionless bearing. The axle tip or gudgeon pin rests on a little wheel that can itself revolve. Ramelli elaborates this idea by showing two little wheels for the axle to rest on. Such wheels would have been made of hard wood, such as lignum vitae, with wrought iron spindles (fig. X-16).

Windlasses

Treadwheels are large and exert great power. Where a smaller machine is necessary and some loss of power is acceptable, a windlass may be used. It is an axle shaft operated by pulling on handles rather than by climbing. The distance between the handles is dictated by the distance a man's arm can reach. Where, to obtain a greater gearing ratio, the arc described by the handle grips is large, many handles must be provided. The thirteenth-century portcullis winch in the Byward Tower, London, has a wheel with sixteen handles. The 1644 Swan windmill at Lienden in Holland has an eight-handled windlass.

Smaller windlasses can be driven by four handles. Two bars are driven directly through the axle at right angles. The simplest way of fitting both handles is to offset them; this arrangement appears in the Parma drawings, in Sabbattini, and in Agricola. Long axle shafts were provided with two or even three sets of handles (fig. X-17).

Capstans had offset handles as well as the more sophisticated arrangement of removable handles that fitted into mortices cut into the shaft.

Crank handles

Agricola shows a windlass with cross-handles at one end and a crank handle at the other end (fig. X-18). This is a two-speed version: the cross-handles can turn the shaft slowly and accurately while the crank is capable of much quicker revolutions, in this case to speed the descent of a bucket. A flywheel provides momentum.

From early illustrations of crank handles, it is difficult to see how the handle is secured to the shaft. Sabbattini's always look as though the

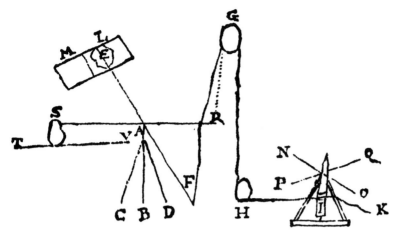

Fig. X–13. Sabbattini's lever device to lower a cloud throne. (From *Practica*, bk. 2, chap. 45, first method.)

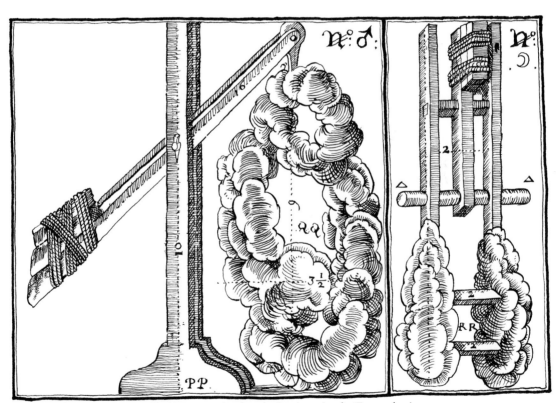

Fig. X–14. Joseph Furttenbach's crane cloud and pivoting cloud. (Furttenbach, *Mannhafter Künstspiegel* [1663].)

Fig. X–15. Catherington donkey wheel, ca. 1600. (Open Air Museum, Singleton, Sussex; photo author.)

handle is forged out of a single piece of iron hammered into the end of the wooden shaft. Perhaps the pointed end of the handle was beaten flat to make it grip the wood inside. A sixteenth-century drawing of mining machinery shows the shaft spindle passing through the handle;[46] a cotter pin might have been passed through both handle and spindle (fig. X-19). One of Agricola's spindles appears to terminate in a square section over which a wooden handle is morticed.

Gearing

The larger the shaft diameter, the harder the work will become, but the quicker the rope will be paid out. The Elizabethan donkey wheel at Berden Priory in Essex has its shaft diameter increased by means of a cage of wooden laths mounted all the way round it. The sack hoist at the Beaulieu mill in Hampshire has a similar cage of wooden rods. These examples are lighter than those produced by the usual method of nailing straight pieces of wood all round the shaft (for example, the Carisbrooke wheel).

Fig. X–16. Frictionless bearings. (From Georgius Agricola, *De re metallica* [Basel, 1556]; Agostino Ramelli, *Le Diverse et Artificiose Machine* [Paris, 1588].)

Fig. X–17. Windlasses with double offset handles. (From Agricola, *De re metallica*.)

Fig. X–18. Windlass with crank and offset handles. (From Agricola, *De re metallica*.)

Fig. X–19. Cranked windlass. (Redrawn from H. Grosse, in Bertrand Gille, *The Renaissance Engineers* [London: Lund Humphries, 1966], p. 193.)

Brakes

Machines that were powered by animal or natural force, such as wagons, donkey wheels, windmills, and watermills, often had devices to control the speed and lock the machine once it had come to rest. On English wagons, roller-scotches or drag-shoes were crudely interposed between the wheel and the road. Some donkey wheels were braked by a friction rope taken right round the outside of the wheel. At Marston Hall in Kent a lever attached to the end of the rope could be locked in place by a peg. Windmills are slowed down by a great curved shoe of wood strapped round the circumference of the windshaft's "brake wheel." A windlass has no need of a brake since its control, as well as its power, is determined by its operator.

Rope

Hemp, cotton, and flax for making rope were all available in the seventeenth century. Ordinary untarred hemp is strong: a rope of 1¼ inches in circumference has a breaking load of just under two tons.[47] Sutherland, in eulogizing rope for "Mechanical Operations," recognized that it stretches in use (p. 264). When a rope is required to have an accurate length—for example, one carrying a counterweight that must not reach the ground too soon—it must be prestretched by being hung up in as long a continuous piece as possible with weights attached.[48] Sabbattini mentions that treating cords with soap improves their running (bk. 2, chap. 46).

Thrones

The flying thrones depicted in the Parma drawings are built out of boards (fig. X-20). They were usually decorated with clouds to signify divinity. These were made flat, with profiled edges. Sabbattini specifies a cloth-covered framework (bk. 2, chap. 43), while Furttenbach calls for his clouds to be built out of solid boards.[49] If the flying throne at the Globe also served as the "state" chair, being merely set on stage by the winch apparatus,[50] then cloudings would have been inappropriate. They may have been detachable.

An entry in the accounts for the Cockpit-in-Court seems to imply a throne with clouds made of cloth which fold up as it passes through an opening in the cloth ceiling.[51] One hundred shillings were paid to "John Walker Property maker viz for hanging the Throne and Chaire in the Cockpit with cloth bound about with whalebone packthred and wyer for the better foulding of the same to come downe from the Cloudes to the stage." I think this could be read to mean not a folding cloud throne but a fixed one, the "foulding" referring to the ceiling cloth, which opened like a

Fig. X–20. Flying throne. (From the Parma drawings.)

concertina, the whalebone keeping the folds straight and tidy. If, however, John Walker's throne clouds did fold he would be approaching the ingenuity of the Italians. The Parma drawings show several cloud cradles that could articulate by means of jointed levers.

For less spectacular descents, Sabbattini describes a lightweight saddle-and-stirrup frame made of iron that allowed a dancer to descend to the stage and begin his dance immediately (bk. 2, chap. 50). A similar effect could be achieved if the actor's foot rested in a loop at the end of a rope. Agricola shows a man being winched down a mine shaft seated on a simple wooden bar tied to the end of the rope.

Reconstructing the flying effect at the Globe

What were the characteristics of the winch gear at the Globe? I think it would have been under direct manual control rather than freewheeling under a brake. Jonson's description of a "creaking" throne suggests a heavy, gentle descent under drive.

216

Describing a cloud descent at court in 1613, the agent of Savoy likened the noise to that of the raising and lowering of the mast of a ship.[52] The descent should be stately. For a fast descent, such as would be in character for Ariel in *The Tempest*, the actor could slide down a fixed rope in the way circus performers do.

I think that a counterweight would have been used to relieve some of the effort and to assist control. It could have been arranged to reach its rest at the same time as the throne reached the stage. The weight could be adjusted to the point where the operator's only opponent was friction.

The speed of descent depends on the relationship of the diameters of drive-wheel and axle-shaft (the gearing ratio) and on how fast the operator can place hand over hand. To estimate a reasonable working speed for a man pulling the winch, let us suppose a wheel-and-axle machine with the "wheel"—in this case probably cross-handles—measuring 3 feet in diameter and the axle 9 inches, a gearing ratio of 1:4 (3 feet is a comfortable distance for a man to stretch his arm). Reaching for a handle, gripping it, and pulling it down can be comfortably done twice in a second. Thus the operator would complete one revolution every 2 seconds. An axle diameter of 9 inches means a circumference of 28 inches. If we accept Walter Hodges' notion that the drop from the "heavens" to the stage at the Globe was about 26 feet,[53] then paying out 26 feet of rope would require 11 revolutions of the axle. This would mean a descent time of 22 seconds. If the total load of actor plus chair came to 250 pounds, the effort would be about 60 pounds before counterweighting. By increasing the axle diameter to 12 inches, the descent would take 16½ seconds with an effort of 83 lbs.

Sliding traps

For the best dramatic effect, a trap door should open surreptitiously. Thomas Dekker described the device as "a false Trappe."[54] Some sort of slider would be best, especially since it would interfere little with the space under the stage. Furthermore, vertical sliding devices were quite common in contemporary carpentry. The fifteenth-century house at Singleton has a sliding window shutter. Agricola recorded the sliding doors of furnaces. Sluice gates slide up and down. The shutters on the court stage were opened and closed by sliding.

However, when a horizontal door like a stage trap is to slide, several problems arise. The runners must be made strong enough to withstand the weight of actors, yet narrow, to minimize friction. The trap section must be made flush with the stage surface; this implies a need for a retaining slot, which may jam. The operation of pulling the trap must be perfectly even and straight, or it will have to be returned and pulled again.

In all the arrangements for trap doors that Sabbattini describes, he never suggests a sliding trap. Perhaps he avoided it because he knew the

217

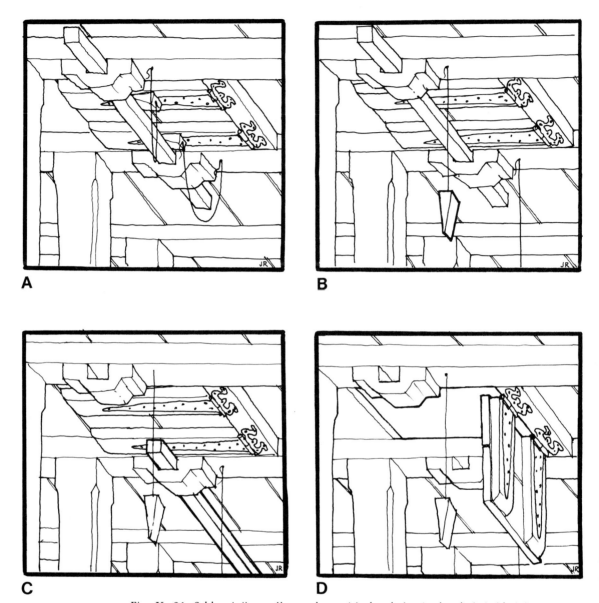

Fig. X–21. Sabbattini's small trap door with drawbolt: A, drawbolt held tight by wedges; B, wedges removed; C, drawbolt pulled out; D, door swings down. (Reconstruction by author.)

Fig. X–22. Sabbattini's larger trap door. (Reconstruction by author.)

general problems of sliding. He explains that the grooves of back shutters "must be well polished, smoothed and soaped, and nailed to the stage floor in such a manner that the nails do not offer any impediment to the free running of the shutter" (bk. 2, chap. 13). Later he finds it necessary to experiment with little wheels (bk. 2, chap. 15).

Hinged traps

Sabbattini shows all his trap doors as hinged. Hinged traps are traditional in the floors of windmills, in castle turrets, and in cellars. As stage traps, they require a lot of space to swing down but are swift and silent in operation and can be fitted flush to the stage without trouble.

For his small trap (bk. 2, chap. 17, pt. 1), Sabbattini supports the door from beneath with a sliding drawbolt, held tight by wedges (fig. X-21 *top left*). When the operator removed the wedges, the door would drop a tiny distance onto the drawbolt (fig. X-21 *top right*). This might in practice have served as a useful warning to any performer who forgot that the trap was about to open. The drawbolt was then pulled out to one side (fig. X-21 *bottom left*), allowing the door to swing down (fig. X-21 *bottom right*). For a larger trap Sabbattini stipulates that the door should be sup-

219

Fig. X–23. First method for climbing out Sabbattini's trap door. (Reconstruction by author.)

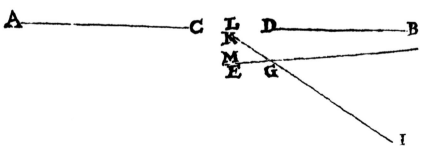

Fig. X–24. See-saw method for raising a performer through Sabbattini's trap door. (Reconstruction by author.)

ported by three props hinged to it and jammed against the floor of the hall (bk. 2, chap. 17, pt. 2) (fig. X-22). They were pulled away by three men. The operation sounds hazardous even without the complication of getting groups of actors up and down—a problem that Sabbattini does not discuss.

Three methods for getting a single performer up and through the small trap are discussed. The first method (bk. 2, chap. 18) employs a fixed ladder for the actor to climb once the door is open. The obvious difficulty here is that the actor on the ladder must not obstruct the door; but this can be arranged if he leans sideways, as Sabbattini suggests (fig. X-23). Sabbattini's second method (bk. 2, chap. 19) is nothing mechanical. The actor climbs onto a flat wooden stretcher and is simply heaved up to the level of the stage by two men. The third way is to raise him on a see-saw to a height where he can step out onto the stage (fig. X-24).

The difficulty of trap-door operations would have been increased by the actor's own encumbrances. In the *Arraignment of Paris,* Pluto is said to ascend from below in his chair.[55] In *Messalina* a trap is required to swallow three murderers "by degrees" and six lines later be ready to accept two more characters.[56]

Many stage directions refer to hellfire, flames, and smoke issuing from traps. These effects were achieved by igniting powdered resin (as illustrated by Sabbattini in bk. 2, chap. 23) and must have made the space under the stage a veritable "hell" for the stagehands.

All in all, trap work would seem to be troublesome and dangerous. As Glynne Wickham points out,[57] not one of Marlowe's stage directions actually demands a trap in the stage floor; perhaps trap work was avoided whenever possible.

Should, then, a trap be included in our reconstructed Globe? I think so. The third Globe should provide as many technical options as possible. We hope to learn much from the practical experience of using it.

* For their help in my research I wish to thank Mr. Ian Bristow, Miss Jo Darrer of the Victoria and Albert Museum Conservation Department, Dr. Rosamund Harley of Gateshead Technical College, and Mr. Michael Wright of the Science Museum, London.

Appendix A. *Extracts from the Discussions*

The discussions at the symposium, which covered a wide range of detail and opinion, were recorded on tape. However, since it might here prove more confusing than useful, besides being very lengthy, to print the tape transcript in full, the following extracts have been made; we hope they give a fair account of the points raised. The extracts follow the general order of the proceedings, but for easier reference they are grouped under new headings of their own.

Speakers from the platform are identified with their answers. Speakers from the body of the hall are identified with their questions and are listed at the end of this section.

Uses and Activities of a Reconstruction

Q. *Louis Marder:* Is it possible that a play performed in this beautiful Globe, which we will eventually have, will not work well because there are other factors involved that we don't know about? Is it possible to think that the Elizabethans, and Shakespeare, might have said, "Oh, if only we had a really good stage to do these things on!" and might have wanted a stage such as we have today at the British National Theatre and elsewhere?

A. *John Russell Brown:* I think the answer to that is very straightforward. One of the great things about the Elizabethan theatre is that it toured. It seemed to the Elizabethan actors that they were always on the move—from plague or the risk of plague or because of various other problems. They were used to many different kinds of stages; quite as many different kinds of stages as our young actors have today, who go around the cellars and attics and converted pubs of our present "fringe" or "alternative" theatres. And when they came to build the second Globe, they had the experience of two permanent theatres behind them—and they built the same again, on the same foundation. The King's Men had experienced many other models while they were using the Globe, and yet they developed a second Globe. So the odds are that they were pretty content.

Q. *Margaret Smith:* Would the actors be performing in the afternoon, as Shakespeare's company did?

A. *Brown:* I believe it is very important to act in the afternoon wherever possible, because there is an enormously different quality of performance in such circumstances. Sit the audience in the same light as you place the actors in and a kind of contact happens—I don't think necessarily through the ears or the eyes but almost, as it were, through the pores of the skin. I do believe that if the audience is close enough, surrounded enough, mobile enough, given enough life of their own to sustain themselves if they get bored, to enable them to comment easily on what is happening, then the audience-stage relationship is something of a totally different kind.

Q. *M. C. Bradbrook:* Other things happened at the Globe besides the play, did they not? They had fencing matches and sometimes debates. Don't you think it might be exciting if the local community did some of its local things there? If you had, for instance, a good revivalist preacher? (Laughter).

A. *Brown:* Yes, indeed. I think one of the main difficulties of reconstructing the Globe is to make it a place the people will go to for a huge variety of reasons. "A place of resort" is a marvelous Elizabethan phrase. A theatre should be a place of resort, and whatever will do that for the community seems to me to be well worth exploring.

Q. *John Wilders:* I should like to know how Professor Brown would avoid a certain kind of risk, which is the hardening of conjecture into fact. He's mentioned quite a lot about the behavior of the audience in the Globe Theatre, and indeed, the behavior of the audience at that time is documented more fully than the nature of the building. But as scholars warn us, most of the evidence is subjective. A great deal of it was written by opponents who have their best interest in attacking the theatre, and I wonder (a) whether we can reliably reconstruct how the Globe audience behaved, and (b) if we acted on these conjectures—because that's what they are, conjectures—how would we avoid creating the impression that because it's being done in the reconstructed Globe, that's how it was done in the original?

A. *Brown:* I don't think anything ought to be done only one way in the new Globe. Of course, there's a great deal of biased evidence about audience behavior in Shakespeare's day; but there are some facts about audience handling—the kind of entrance they made, the fact that they arrived in the afternoon, and so on. Let us try to apply certain things we know for sure, and see what happens. The world lies all before us and I think it's extremely unlikely that we shall find a place of rest for at least twenty years, by which time let us hope there will be twenty Globe theatres, all with their own individual places of rest. The mind is a fertile thing. What we've been stuck at is the obstacle that we haven't yet got this place to work in. For God's sake, let's get it, and get on with lots of different kinds of activity in it.

The Globe Property on Bankside

Q. *Bradbrook, following a question about tenancies:* Do we know anything further about the tenants? I mean, is there any suggestion that these houses clustered around were full of respectable people? What were they?

A. *Herbert Berry:* Well, in Renaissance times, you just can't tell. For example, there's George Archer, who called himself a porter. Now, one would have thought he was a working man if ever there was one. In fact, he was a rent gatherer for forty years and a highly literate man; he signed his name in a very literate sort of way. And there are various other people of that sort. Their professions were given as working men, but some of them were called gentlemen as well. All one can say is that this looked very much like a slice of London life. But, curiously in the London of that time, the distinction we make now between "good" and "bad" districts simply was not so marked. You'd find check by jowl cottages and palaces and hovels, and in the city there were literally thousands and thousands of "residences" that were no more than twelve feet square, twelve by ten— that sort of thing. And, presumably, generation after generation of people brought up families in those residences. The concept of living space in those days was very different from what it is today. You just can't make this sort of comparison. You can't say, Well, because it's got the brothels it's necessarily a bad district. It wasn't—the Bishop of Winchester lived on Bankside, too, and he owned the "stews."

The Stage Superstructure and the Question of Pillars

Q. *Arthur Beer:* Dr. Hodges, I find the idea of the open roof, which you show in your drawing, very seductive. I'm only curious to know how you explain the appearance in the late plays of so many gods and things like that descending from the heavens—whether it would be manageable within this framework.

A. *C. Walter Hodges:* In my reconstruction drawing I do show a machine that would serve the purpose. It is a crane machine that comes forward from a space at the back—the sort of crane we are told they had in the ancient Greek playhouses.

Q. *David George:* In a recent drawing you show two stage posts supporting the superstructure. Previously you had done away with these. Do you have to restore the posts to support a fresh weight that you have now, perhaps because of the replacement of a ceiling? Because if the ceiling is there, then you have terrible problems explaining that lantern structure in the roof as a light for the stage. Once you put that solid ceiling back in, the lantern has no function. I took an elementary precaution a few years ago, after your book had come out, and made a list of all the stage directions in plays that were or may have been performed at the second Globe. Three of them showed a need for posts or an aperture in a wooden ceiling. So I began to think, How would Mr. Hodges explain what to do with that lantern if he were forced to put back the solid ceiling?

A. *Hodges:* First, if there is a solid ceiling there, then one must certainly assume that there cannot be a lantern. But, what can it possibly be if it isn't a lantern? It can't be for decorative purposes because it's not in a position that requires or can display decoration. It is also quite an expensive piece of carpentry, so evidently it wasn't put there for nothing. It's not a chimney or a louvre to let smoke out. So if it wasn't a lantern I don't know what else it might have been, and if it *was* a lantern it must surely have been intended to light the space below. It is possible there *was* a sort of *partial* ceiling surrounding an open space, rather like a fly floor in a modern proscenium theatre. These are all things we will have to work out, and once we get going we will see.

Brown: It does seem to me that in most theatres I've worked in—and I think I could without exaggeration say *all* theatres I've worked in—what people in the theatre always ask for is more storage space. And when one looks at the large structure over the stage, the availability of that for storing things like costumes is very suggestive. I think one of the most remarkable things about every model of the Globe playhouse that I have seen is the restricted space for the tiring-house. There is no place to store anything or for the actors to get themselves ready in, to marshal all those extra things they need to use. But to be able to put precious things (and remember that one cloak for a play could cost as much money as the entire afternoon taking of a theatre crowded with people) up there in that loft, where no thief could get to them, would be an extremely useful addition;

and that has always been my simplistic, nonarchitectural, but surely rather practical thought: more space for storage, storage for things that were incredibly valuable. We are, as you yourself constantly remind us, sir, in the realm of the speculative. I am approaching it from what I know to be a theatrical need.

Q. *Orville Larson:* I have another suggestion about the so-called lantern. If you insist that there were cloud machines in Elizabethan theatres, then I suggest that this round area was a spot where the horizontal capstan that moved the clouds up and down might have been operable. It is a round building, and your stagehands at the capstan are moving in a circle.

A. *Hodges:* I think it doesn't have enough room for that. As I show it, it is only eight feet in diameter.

Q. *Roger Gross:* Can we say how wide the stage pillars would have to be?

A. *Hodges:* Given the scale that I show in my drawing I would say they would have to be a good foot or, say, fifteen inches in diameter.

Q. *Gross:* I wouldn't assume too quickly, then, that a theatre person would want to be rid of them. I speak as a director of Shakespeare who has often called for the designer to put in pillars that were not needed, because those pillars are tremendously valuable stage tools. I would think that the staging value of having the pillars, to stand behind or to climb up or whatever, would be much greater than the drawback about sightlines.

A. *Hodges:* That drawing of the stage printed in the brochure, showing those pillars—would that have been acceptable, do you suppose, to the Jacobean actor? What sort of a theatre would it make? Would it have been a good thing to have? Do you like it?

Q. *Gross:* The pillars in your drawing struck me as being too big. And also, for what it's worth—though this has no historical value at all—in staging problems, anyone who gets into using pillars for their staging values finds that he wants benches around them. You want something that you can put your foot up on, stand on. You would want something at the base of that pillar.

A. *Hodges:* But that is not in Elizabethan stagecraft. It is the feeling of *modern* actors and directors, working together, in which they are giving certain visual effects—that there must be structures to sit on or to put one's foot on—without which we feel uncomfortable. That is a modern type of thinking, is it not?

Q. *Gross:* Yes, I'm sure it is, but just from my experience I would say that the fifteen-inch pillar at the base would certainly not be a problem. If it were two feet wide it could get to be a problem.

A. *Bernard Beckerman:* I would agree with the last speaker that if you are a director and you have the posts, you are inclined to want benches around them. But I agree completely, also, that it is a modern theory. Again, I think it's going to be very hard to answer the question about the posts unless it is possible to have a Globe with and without posts, because, since we don't have them at present in any of our replicas, we really don't know how much the posts might get in the way. And I think it would be most desirable to have the opportunity to do it both ways.

Q. *Richard Hosley:* I was just going to suggest that one of Walter Hodges' basic assumptions in working up this theory is that the posts were bothersome, that they were objectionable. They *seem* objectionable to us at first glance. I think that's a very modern notion, just as modern as the notion that it's useful to have a little seat around the base of them.

A. *Hodges:* In support of that I would say that when Elizabethan people went to church, if they came late and weren't lucky enough to get a good place there, they might have had to take a place behind one of the pillars where they couldn't see the preacher. That might not have mattered very much: they went to *hear* him rather than *see* him. But do we think that this would have been acceptable in a theatre? What I'm hoping will come out of this symposium is a general feeling as to what we should do about such things as this.

Audience on the Stage, Actors in the Yard

Q. *Beckerman:* The only question I have is concerned with the audience sitting on the stage and the consequent crowding of the platform. I think that it did happen but that it happened later, and the question is, How much we should allow for that?

A. *Glynne Wickham:* I come back on the word *later*. I agree that in the public playhouses before the end of the sixteenth century I know of no evidence of the audience sitting on the stage. But it was already a habit at St. Paul's Playhouse by the time Jonson's *Cynthia's Revels* was written, and if Jonson could bother to write such a long prologue, which is wholly based on parodying the abominable behavior of the audience who do sit on the stage there and go out of their way to annoy and abuse the actors, this seems to me to lose all point or force if it wasn't recognizable, if it was something quite new. My only further point would be that when Dekker came to write the famous passage in *The Gull's Horn Book* he did begin—I think I'm right in saying—four separate indented sentences by use of the words "when sitting on the stage," as though this were something habitual, something that everybody knew about. Again, it loses its point if it's a novelty and nobody knows about it. So I think, certainly, when it comes to rebuilding the second Globe, if we're talking about 1612–13 whether in the private playhouses or in the public playhouses, it has become a problem that the actors are denied a substantial area of a large stage.

Beckerman: I would make these comments. In 1604, when we have the production of Marston's *The Malcontent,* which is taken over by the King's Men in reprisal for the children's company taking over one of their plays, Webster writes an induction specifically for their performance, and in the action of that induction there is the removal by the King's Men actors— Burbage is one of them—of a fool who wants to sit on the stage. He is severely mocked and is finally persuaded to leave. With regard to Dekker: remember he is writing *The Gull's Horn Book,* and he is *in that context* advising the gull to get up on the stage (I think of a private playhouse) and then mocking him for doing so. I would agree with you that by the time the second Globe was in operation there probably was considerable sitting on the stage and it was beginning to become aggravating. The problem we will have, of course, is that while we will have the second Globe, we will be presenting the plays from the first Globe on that second Globe stage; so how shall we create the right staging conditions? Here's another case where we can do both; we can have scenes with people sitting on the stage and scenes without.

Q. *Paul Mulholland:* I'd like to hear either of the speakers on the question which was once raised by Allardyce Nicoll which he called "passing over the stage." I think Nicoll suggests the possibility of stairs at the downstage corners of the stage.

A. *Wickham:* That is a question I myself wanted to ask, about entrances through the auditorium. For example, Dunsinane. I do not see how Birnham Wood could come to Dunsinane, given the order of the scenes in the closing act of *Macbeth,* unless the English army comes in through the auditorium. Again, ship scenes; is there any reason why—granted that the audiences at court will accept ships on wheels in the banquet hall—is there any reason why they shouldn't accept ships on wheels in the yard? As far as I know the problem has not been tackled in a systematic and scholarly way at all, in terms of how they came into the building other than through the public entrance doors, and still less the questions of horses, chariots, and ships (unless they are already there). Certainly they come into court theatres through the ordinary doors. It's always dangerous to take foreign material, but there's a splendid picture of a tournament in Florence in the late sixteenth century with scenic machines outside the arena clearly ready to go in. I cannot, therefore, eliminate the possibility, but I can't tell you how they came in. Professor Hosley may well be able to do so.

Hosley: I find myself skeptical about this business of entering the stage from the yard. The reason I do is that there is no evidence for it in any of the plays. You go through 650 or 720 Elizabethan plays and you never find any stage directions that can be interpreted in this way. Where is the evidence? It is in that enigmatic, ambiguous phrase that Allardyce Nicoll picked up: "passing over the stage." I think that means just to enter at one door; and sometimes it's pass "round" the stage as well as "over"; and that evidence is itself negated, I think, by the three or four examples that I have found of stage direction that read "Enter over the stage and exit at the other door," which gives the whole game away, it seems to me.

Standings: the Yard and the Gallery; the Pitch of the Roof

Q. *Hodges:* May I take up this question of the audience standing in the lower gallery? I think that it has to be considered pretty seriously, certainly for some playhouses. Let us take the case of the Hope, for example. We know for a fact that the Hope was a bear-baiting arena with a stage moved into it and later taken out. We know, also, that in October, 1614, Ben Jonson's *Bartholomew Fair* was presented in that arena, with groundlings standing around—we know this because the stagekeeper refers to them. So there they were on the 31st of October, and a day or two later the stage had been moved out and they were having "the game of bulls and bears." Now, where then did the groundlings go? They weren't in the yard, were they? They must have gone into the bottom gallery; but were they seated? Is seated accommodation typical of bear-baiting and bull-baiting? One would have thought that a shifting crowd of people standing would be more like it, and that, in fact, the groundlings instead went and stood on degrees— that is, on three or four stepped levels in the bottom gallery. There is that possibility to be considered. There are several contemporary references to "galleries made for people to stand in." This is, of course, irrespective of the fact that we know there were seats in the *middle* gallery. But the bottom gallery, it seems to me, is to be considered as a possible standing place. And this, again, would help very much with our computation of the number of people that could be accomodated.

A. *Hosley:* I'm not sure that we have any problem with the number of people that could be accommodated. When you use an unbiased method of computing the capacity of the playhouses, such as was conceived by Alfred Harbage in his book *Shakespeare's Audience* (1944), you find that a playhouse such as John Orrell is recommending, 100 feet in diameter, with 15½-foot galleries, will accommodate some 3,150 spectators. This corresponds to a capacity of 2,700 for the 96-foot-diameter Swan that I have computed. I haven't computed it for your 92-foot playhouse. For the Fortune, using the same methods, it comes out to about 2,500. The problem that you address at the Hope I have no answer to. It's a mysterious theatre and we just don't know what happened there. But the problem of accommodating the "understanding gentlemen" of the play day as the "understanding gentlemen" of the baiting day—when presumably they cannot be in the yard—can be solved most easily by making it a real bear garden, as in fact it was, according to Hollar's label. That would then give you what Professor Brownstein has called "groundstands" under there. That's the best solution, I think.

The question of references to standing in the galleries is a very vexing one. We have all *sat* in grandstands, have we not? When you have degrees to stand on, or to sit on, or to stand in or sit in, you don't have to do one thing or the other—you can do either or both. I think that the three or four references you have made in print to standing in the galleries can be explained in one or another of those ways.

Q. *Clifford Ashby:* I have two questions; why are the English roofs so steeply pitched, and what kind of flooring was provided for the groundlings in the yard?

A. *Hosley:* I don't really know the answer to the first question but I recommend a pitch of 48° for the second Globe, just as a gambit. Your other question about the flooring for the groundlings is a very difficult one, and one that will have to be faced if we're going to reconstruct the second Globe. As far as I know, there is no evidence, really, about the surface of the yard, if indeed there was one other than some kind of mixture of gravel and earth. Adams and Smith, of course, have supposed that Henslowe's purchase of bricks was for paving the yard. I doubt it very much; they must have gone into the foundation. Nevertheless, one would like to suppose that the yard was paved, because paving would help to keep the groundlings from getting mired in wet weather and would also permit the establishment of drains. There's been very little attention paid to that. But you would think that with this enclosed area and no place for the water to drain off to, it would be essential to have some elementary drains. The simplest way, of course, would be to slope back from the middle so that the drains could be placed around the perimeter of the yard and pass underneath the galleries and out into one of those bankside ditches; better than sloping it down toward the middle, because then you would have a much longer pipe. Mr. Rigold has some views on that.

Stuart Rigold: There is plenty of evidence about late medieval and submedieval flooring of courtyards. There is not much decent paving stone in the south of England. It wasn't much used in London until they could afford to bring it from Yorkshire, but there's a lot of cobbling either with unbroken flints or, more often, with broken flints, with the broken surface laid on top and the knob end of the flint driven in. And you can produce drainage channels, possibly lined with brick or bits of stone in them. There are plenty of examples of that. Of course you'd have to cover it with sand, but my feeling is that it was probably cobbled with broken flints, with the exposed end of them broken off on top.

Hodges: Two things about the drainage in the yard. The Boar's Head had drainage because it was originally a stable yard, so there certainly were drains and gulleys there. But what I want to bring up here is the Hope, on bear-baiting days; what about the blood and mess? This had to be cleared up. I think the sanding possibility here is very much to the point. But there must also have been some kind of drainage, because the blood and mess on the bear-baiting days had to be dealt with.

Features of the Tiring-house: Possible Variations

Q. *Marder:* Has any provision been made for a music room, which seems to have been lost sight of in the last two days?

A. *Wickham:* That is indeed a difficult question. Clearly, music became very much more important when the company moved into the Blackfriars, and we do know quite a lot about their handling of music there. Music, as it seems to me in Globe playhouse terms of reference—first or second—was rather ad hoc and occasional, and if there is room in the tiring-house at first gallery level that is probably where it was, though that does not preclude there having been music at ground level provided it could be heard, nor does it altogether eliminate the Cranford Adams idea of a third gallery up top, specially reserved for the musicians. One knows for certain in the Cockpit-in-Court that in Charles I's day the musicians occupied the upper room and that central opening, and they had to be moved when actresses were admitted after the Restoration, so that they could have a separate dressing room. But again I'm sorry I am forced back to saying that your guess is as good as mine.

Q. *John W. Velz:* I'm anxious, of course, as we all are, about your caveat about what happens if we build the stage wrong. I'd like to hear your comment, if you will, on making it flexible in some way. For example, suppose you could close off an inner stage so that it looks like a tiring-house wall, and this wall can be put in place or removed, depending on the production. Would you regard this as a prostitution of the art of certainty or would you welcome such flexibility in design?

A. *Wickham:* Yes, I would welcome such flexibility, in reasonable experimental terms. What I think is a bit frightening—and particularly in an academic institution, where the production is mounted with an aura of research behind it, as a demonstration of what actually occurred—is that it acquires a certain solidity of certainty which, in effect, is quite unwarranted.

Q. *Wilders:* What I should like to ask in general terms is, granted his very proper skepticism, what does Professor Wickham feel about the extreme detail and particularity of dimensions, sizes of stages, buildings, etc., that Professor Hosley so brilliantly argued this morning?

A. *Wickham:* Clearly, one must respect every fact that one can glean, especially when it comes to commissioning an architect who has the much more difficult task of not merely talking about the thing, but of actually translating it into an artifact. What worries me is what to do with those large areas where you have no facts at all. I think my dilemma is that which overtakes the curators of most art galleries when they have a seriously damaged Piero della Francesca or a Corot that some hooligan has savaged with a knife; what do you do? Do you restore it by repainting it in some way, so as to pretend that the repainting is the original; or do you simply repair it and leave the damaged patch clear so that those who come to see it know exactly what the situation is? You've got to come to terms with areas of the building which one knows to be or feels pretty confident are accurate to the last inch, and areas where one is making a rough guess in terms of what one knows went on in another theatre of approximately the same date.

Q. *Leonard Leone:* May I understand you correctly, Professor Wickham; would you recommend in our reconstruction that the back tiring-house wall or other parts of the building be so constructed that they could be removed and other experimental forms constructed in their place?

A. *Wickham:* That would be to me the ideal answer because it would get as near to making an equation of a recognizable kind between the known parts of the building and the unknown ones. Those that were fixed, stable, and unquestionable and those that, being subject to experiments, one expected to change.

Some Questions of Decoration

Q. *Leone:* May I ask a speculative question? Assuming that we have a third Globe and you were asked to decorate it, give us a gut feeling of what you think it should look like. Would it be close to the Teatro Olimpico in appearance, would it have a more wood-tone look, or what?

A. *John Ronayne:* The Teatro Olimpico is my personal temptation. It's such a good survival, of such a good date. It might be completely misleading, but when we've only got one thing, we've either got to reject it completely, because there aren't any others, or we've got to accept it.

Q. *George:* Following Professor Leone's question about the style, specifically in relation to the tiring-house. At McMaster University we have recently made a conjectural reconstruction of the decoration of the Fortune tiring-house (where we do have the advantage of some good, strong hints in the Fortune contract about the "carved proportions called satyrs" on the tops of the posts and so on). You can do a certain amount with that; but having done so, it seems to me that the big question we now have to decide is between two basic styles—either a wooden carved style, rather like the Middle Temple Hall screen, in London, which is a beautiful example, or, on the other hand, a possibility of producing fake stonework, that sort of thing. I wondered if you think that those are the two main ways we might go. Or are there other ways?

A. *Ronayne:* Assume that I'm a workman dressed in overalls, and you come to me and you want your playhouse decorated. I think I would tend to say, How long have I got and what do you want to spend? because all of the techniques are available.

Hodges: Might I give my own general feeling? Leaving aside all the additional painting or modeling of figures or any of the strapwork and other flourishes that one might put round the doors, I like the idea of the background being painted to represent stone, as one sees in the Stephen Harrison arches and in the Robert Fludd engraving and in the commedia dell'arte scenic props that were built to stand upon the stage. This seems to make a good and proper background, and goes very well with the idea of the tiring-house façade being used as a sort of castle. That's the way I tend to think, at the moment anyway.

Bradbrook: I wondered if, as the second Globe was built for the King's Men—after they *had* become the King's Men—we shouldn't have at least a royal emblem somewhere. Wouldn't they put the royal arms up, to show who they were? This is still as it's seen in some of the British theatres.

The Dutch *Rederijker* Theatre: Was There a Connection?

Q. *Bradbrook:* I'd like to ask you, sir, if there's any influence from the struggles in the Netherlands with the Spanish? Is there any connection between these religious plays and the Spanish religious plays? Or, on the other hand, taking the Reformed point of view, is there any connection between these and the small privileged religious morality plays that were acted by students of the colleges in England, little groups that were rather like your Chambers of Rhetoric? Do you feel influence from outside, either from the Spanish side or from the English side, or is it just a native tradition?

A. *W. M. H. Hummelen:* I think it is a native tradition. I never found any influence from the Spanish, though on the other hand one could suppose that the Spanish moralities were influenced by the Dutch, because they appear about the middle of the sixteenth century and could have been brought to Spain from the part of Brussels where Charles V had his court. I think there is a great difference between the English and the Dutch morality tradition. There are far more similarities between the French morality plays and the Dutch than there are between the English and the Dutch.

Q. *Marder:* I would like either Dr. Hummelen or the scholars here today to discuss the implications of the architectural evidence presented here, especially in relation to the inner stage, as all of this would apply to the reconstruciton of the Globe.

A. *Hummelen:* My line of thought is that when you are using an inner stage, as the Rhetoricians do, you get quite a different effect in the plays from what is shown, for example, in Beckerman's book *Shakespeare at the Globe.* If the English theatre really had inner stages, then they would have been something more like the Dutch than the evidence seems to show. You can see a difference between Holland and England—so much, I am afraid, that I don't *think* there was an inner stage in England. I think there was only a discovery-space—maybe behind the stage and maybe forward of the stage, but not an inner stage where you could have fifteen or twenty people, as could be done in Holland.

Q. *Hodges:* There was something that did strike me forcibly about these rather narrow discovery-spaces in doorways, Professor Hummelen, that you showed. Professor Hosley has often said that the discoveries on the Elizabethan stage could well have been displayed within doorways, such as either of those two doorways at the Swan Theatre.

A. *Hummelen:* Yes, I think that the stage of 1594 of the Brussels Chamber not only used the openings in the middle as inner stages but could also use the doorways, the two at the left and the two at the right; but I also think that they are larger than normal doorways would be because those *tableaux vivants* that are used in the *rederijker* plays are seldom very small. In many cases they use a lot of people, as many as four or five.

Q. *Wickham:* A question has been asked about collaboration, and a connection between the English and Dutch. I know of one, but only one, and on that occasion the Italians also collaborated. The occasion in question was the reception of James I into London in 1603, when the entire Dutch community resident in England and the entire Italian community resident in London were invited, and each accepted the invitation, to provide a scenic tableau for the entry. So we have one instance. Moreover, we do have pictures of it, in the Stephen Harrison engraving, so perhaps it's worth looking at that a little more closely. In any case, the Harrison engravings are so important in terms of all decorative features of tableau stages, and so near to those of the first Globe, that we ought not to overlook them in this context.

Q. *Bradbrook:* I think Professor Hummelen did say that the stage was used in many different plays, that the Rhetoricians had a continuous use of their mostly decorative settings, and that this might be taken in connection with what Professor Wickham has said about the great splendor of the arches for greeting James I when he came to London. But I would have thought that the influence was much more through books—the very strong typographical links between printing in England and Holland. A great many books were illegitimately printed in Holland that pretended to be printed in England. The connections of the learned groups provided a great deal for the drama. We had one Dutch dramatist of Dutch descent, Thomas Dekker, who might be worth looking at, especially in this respect. We should see if Dekker has anything in particular to tell us. But in any case I think Professor Hummelen has given us a stage background that should be followed up (since these were theatres for rhetoricians) in terms of its literary connections.

A. *Hummelen:* . . . In conclusion I should like to emphasize a point. I want to lay stress far more on the difference between the stages actually used and built by the Rhetoricians and those stages that were made by the city or by groups of foreign merchants. I think we have to start with those stages that can be attributed to the rederijkers chambers themselves. They are far simpler than the others—not nearly as elaborate as the ones that are erected by the city or by the merchants—simple stages, usually with three compartments on the stage level. I think there is no way to connect such a stage with the monumental arches of triumph you see in book title pages. If there was an influence from Holland on the English stage I think maybe it could have come from those people who went over with Leicester (there was a large group of English people who came to Holland with him) and saw the Rhetoricians play. They must have seen the plays; they were in places where there were Chambers of Rhetoric. I cannot but believe that, if they saw the use of the inner stage and how intensely it was used in Holland, and then didn't adopt it, it indicates that the two traditions kept themselves to themselves, and the Dutch tradition was not such an influence on the English as is sometimes supposed.

List of Discussants

Clifford Ashby, Texas Tech University
Bernard Beckerman, Columbia University
Arthur Beer, University of Detroit
Herbert Berry, University of Saskatchewan
M. C. Bradbrook, Girton College, University of Cambridge
John Russell Brown, University of Sussex
David George, McMaster University
Roger Gross, Bowling Green State University
C. Walter Hodges
Richard Hosley, University of Arizona
W. M. H. Hummelen, Catholic University of Nijmegen
Orville Larson, Kent State University
Leonard Leone, Wayne State University
Louis Marder, University of Illinois at Chicago Circle
Paul Mulholland, University of Guelph, Ontario
Stuart Rigold, Her Majesty's Department of the Environment
John Ronayne, Archetype Visual Studies
Margaret Smith, Women's Committee for the Theatre, Detroit
John W. Velz, University of Texas
Glynne Wickham, University of Bristol
John Wilders, Worcester College, University of Oxford

Appendix B. *Some Modern Requirements: An Architect's View*

(From the discussion with Mr. R. J. Thom, FRAIC, RCA)

Audience Capacity

Thom: . . . Yesterday somebody was talking about the audience count at the Globe. You were talking in figures of 3,000 people. Now I've done a rough calculation based on this in which, if I allow three square feet per person, or two when standing, I can account for 800 or 900 people—that's all.

One of the first disparities between the antiquarian reconstruction of what may have been and what we are practically able to do in modern terms is the space allowed for seating. The interval that they used, front to back, was horrendously low; 18 inches, 19 inches, and 20 inches. You would have to be sitting sideways. That's not practical for a modern theatre.

Richard Hosley: May I make a couple of comments? I think your perplexity about the capacity is a very real problem. I do think that you have given too generous, too modern an allowance for the space available to each spectator. If you were to assume 1.75 square feet for a stander and 2.25 square feet for a sitter, and if you were to use the overall playhouse diameter of 100 feet it would begin to serve the number 3,000, *if* we did the seating as they did it (which we will not do) and *if* we had them stand in the yard (as we presumably will not do). On that subject I can see one possible accommodation of the problem of the standing audience. If we hold with the 5½-foot height of the stage, which I think we certainly ought to do, it would be possible, I think, to leave the yard clear of seats for a standing audience when you wanted to experiment. Then you could bring in seats, for which you would have to provide a bit of rake, which could perhaps be installed. You couldn't seat people too close to the stage because the stage is awfully high.

APPENDIX B

Gallery Bays and Frame

Thom: The 16-sided configuration (of the building) plus the width of the bays are both such that they make a very easy wood frame. That's a very easy bay size to cope with, with the size of wood scaled to the drawing I have seen.

One of the things that came up in an interview with the Detroit city officials here was that the drawings show a middle gallery with an aisle that's 2 feet, 6 inches wide. The minimum fire precaution width is 46 inches; so that is going to have to be widened anyhow. But with a building of this dimension, if you make it a foot or two wider I really don't think anybody on earth—unless they have eyes like a calculating machine—will know the difference. To me, at least, that's not a thing worth arguing about, because the only alternative here would be to give up a row of seating.

Hosley: Relief is available on this, because the most recent research suggests the possibility that the 12½-foot depth of gallery that you've been working with is not enough, and it may be that the dimension is 15½ feet. Now you could have your 40-inch passage behind the seats easily in that case. . . .

I notice that you've brought in gallery posts. It's interesting that you've done that even with the 12½-foot depth. With 15½ feet we would certainly need those internal posts. I suppose with timber construction, whether we treat them as functional load-bearing posts or simply as studs doesn't matter. And the evidence shows that they had such posts.

Thom: The engineering department would tell you that with a live load you have to calculate for 100 pounds per foot.

Fire Laws. Air Conditioning

Thom: Now, going back to the changes that we have to make. There are fire precaution laws in the city which we can very well understand. It's a general law that wherever you're seated you've got to have two ways of escape. Now there are a number of means of solving this. The one I've chosen here is just a reverse stair going all the way up and all the way down. Along with that I've suggested something else, and this is another subject that has been put to me by the theatre people—and you've been discussing it here too—dressing room space: how much of that are you going to need? Somebody mentioned the matter of wardrobes being an endless buildup. Well they are, in every theatre. I'll give you my opinion.

238

I really don't think you can get people working for you from the actors' union if they're going to have to dress in the middle of an open space. In this day and age they've got to have some proper space, a make-up table, etc. So, if you have a stair going down like that, the stage is already up five and a half feet and you've suddenly got a huge volume of space under the stage and backstage, which can be used for properties or storage of costumes. There would be a very quick access for actors on and off the stage. Another change I made, which I did without being asked, but which the city authorities were very pleased was possible, was to suggest that the outside wall of the building be built of reinforced concrete. In most drawings of Elizabethan theatres that I've seen, the wood framing of the exterior has been completely plastered over, and I think if it was built here in reinforced concrete and plastered over, nobody would know the difference.

One thing I didn't agree with was what somebody was saying yesterday about storing properties up in the roof. First, it's a real drag to lift properties that far up, but second, you cannot forget that with wardrobes and properties you've got security problems, and I don't see where you can get security there.

A major consideration is that there is a sprinkler policy in the city. The city has asked if we could sprinkle the building, and I don't see why we can't. The size of piping is relatively small and I don't think it would be terribly conspicuous.

Q.: Are you assuming the building will be air conditioned?

Thom: I think I have to. I'm worried about heat gained from the glass roof. I really don't think I have a choice.

Q.: I assume the building will also be heated?

Thom: Yes, heating and cooling.

Q.: Is there room for those services within the framework?

Thom: Yes, that is one of the benefits of the excavation under the backstage area. There's enough space there for mechanical equipment, besides the fact that it's in the high side of the building, so that if we have to have vents or ducts they would be more easily hidden there than anywhere else.

Q.: Do you think that there should be an all-weather access to the theatre from the box office?

Thom: Yes. I think that in the long haul you are going to want this theatre to function as many days of the year as it can. Nobody has said it in so many words, but this theatre is a big investment. You are going to have to look after your audience. People are not going to want to put their coats on, just to go from here to there, and take them off again and put them on their laps in their two-foot seats.

Roof and Weather

Thom: Let us talk about the structure of the roof for a minute. Making no claim for myself as a historian, I simply point out that a truss of that depth—and I can't believe the old builders didn't know this—would span about twice that distance. If I had a truss to do today with those sizes of timbers I could go twice as far, easily.

Q.: You mean without those two supporting posts?

Thom: Yes, without posts.

Two more things on the roof. One of my delights with the Detroit Building Department is that they have a height limitation for wooden buildings which is the equivalent to our limit, so they're going to let us stick to that, the magic limit.

The next thing to do with the roof now—and this is something that kept getting thrown at me when people learned I was working on this—is that in a place like Detroit you can't have an open hole in the top of the building; it's just impossible. So working to an old principle of sticking to $22\frac{1}{2}°$ as a minimum pitch for a glazed roof, this works out all right for the roof pitch. What does happen, though, that you should be aware of, is that what you're creating with the roof is an endless valley that is going to need the wits of Solomon to solve, considering problems of freeze-thaw cycles, snow buildup, etc. That's going to be really tricky. We have got to consider mechanical systems. We probably have to be able to blow warm air on the glazed roof. This part of the country is a disaster story for weather. Sure, we can put in electric cables that are supposed to melt the snow—and I can tell you how many I've done that have leaked. It's tricky, and I just want you to be aware of that.

Q.: One of the major problems you will have with acoustics is that glass roof. How do you like that?

Thom: That's more of a problem than the concrete wall. I'm glad you raised that. I accept what you say, that that is going to cause a problem and it's going to have to be answered, but to be honest I'm not really worried about acoustics. I know that by putting in a glass roof we shall create a problem that didn't exist originally, but I also know that there are so many tricks that acoustical engineers can play that, one way or another, there will be an answer.

Notes

Note to Chapter I

1. The National Theatre building contains three separate individual theatres, each of a different size and character, called, respectively, the Olivier, the Lyttleton, and the Cottesloe.

Notes to Chapter II

1. See Braines, *Site of the Globe,* pp. 28–29; G. E. Bentley, *The Jacobean and Caroline Stage* (Oxford, 1968), 6:200; E. K. Chambers, *The Elizabethan Stage,* 4 vols. (Oxford: Clarendon Press, 1923), 2:374–75, 428, 431, 433; Sidney Fisher, *The Theatre, the Curtain and the Globe* (Montreal: McGill University Library, 1964), pp. 6–8, and a paper presented to the theatre history seminar at the meeting of the Shakespeare Association of America held in Toronto, 1978: "Shakespeare's London and Graphical Archaeology," pp. 6–9 (Mr. Fisher finds that maps support his view, but he uses only a few of them). The documents are C.5/448/137, the bill (1675); C.6/245/25, answer of Francis Brend (1682); C.7/616/26 (1703); C.9/320/16, the bill (1704); C.5/338/35 (1707). The dubious MS is now at the Folger (Phillipps 11613). (In referring to documents at the Public Record Office, I give only the call number; for all other documents I give first the archive in which the document is located.)

2. D&H, 9, 11–13, 16, 17, 24, 25, 29–31, 33, 35, 37–40, 42–45, 47, 50, 51b. Both exceptions are curious. One (D&H, 32) is evidently a copy taken from an unfinished plate, and the other (D&H, 51a) is one of six crude maps of English cities published ca. 1700 with many skillful engravings of English buildings (the maps of Canterbury and Colchester show nunneries as apparently still functioning). See also *The Survey of London,* vol. 22, *Bankside* (London: London County Council, 1950), p. 70.

3. D&H, 10, 14, 15, 21; 18–20, 26, 27 (the first four are those discussed in the text). No. 18 is drawn to a scale too small for the engraver to show a playhouse clearly, but a tiny blob on the south side of Maid Lane may be another attempt to show the Globe. No. 35 is attributed to Hollar but is almost certainly not his work.

4. D&H, 9–13, 15–17, 24, 25, 32, 37, 38, 50, 51a. No. 50 also shows a rectangular "Bare garden" east of Maid Lane, near St. Saviour's.

5. D&H, 14, 16 (2d and 3d eds.), 17 (2d ed.), 24, 26 (1st ed.), 40, 43, 51b.

6. C.54/450/m.50; /462/m.36, 38, 43(2); /468/#25; /499/#29; /500; /504/#32 (the site of the Globe); /505/m.18–20, 13; /516/m.34; /518/m.9; /522/m.36–37, 37–38; /527/m.46; /550/m.21; /559/m.22; /597/#39; /624/#29, 30; /646/#67; /652/#12; /665/#33; /680/#58; /703/#55; /812/m.27; /859/m.22; /1080/m.15; /1112/m.34; /1123/m.28; /1151/m.21–22; /1217/m.1; /1273/m.31; /1274/m.6; /1337/m.30; /1347/m.8; /1382/m.9; /1613/m.25.

7. St.Ch.5/L.27/19, interrogatories (second last list) nos. 5, 10; Ilderton nos. 1, 2 (where the allusion to Mr. Cawkett is) 3, 5, 7, 10.

8. Humphrey Collet, bowyer of Southwark, died in December, 1558, having vari-

ous unnamed married children and, presumably unmarried, Thomas (eldest son), Robert, and Nicholas. He owned property on both sides of the high street and, among other places, in Newington. Another Humphrey, also a bowyer of Southwark and son of Humphrey, bowyer, deceased, died childless in January, 1567, having brothers John, Thomas, Nicholas, and others (no Robert). See P.R.O. B.11/42A/f.122^v–23^v, /49/f.8^v–9. The Collets who had to do with the Brends must have been related to these, and perhaps the first Humphrey was their father (in her will, Thomas Brende's daughter, Judith, wrote that John Collet had a sister, Mercy Pattenson, who could have been his wife's sister rather than his own). Bodley explained his relationship with the Brends and hinted at Collet's: WARD 9/94/f.632. In their wills Thomas Brende called Bodley son-in-law and Judith called him brother. Thomas Brende called Collet cousin. The matter is fully explained in a visitation taken in 1623: *Visitations of Surrey in 1530, 1572, and 1623* (London: Harleian Society, 1899), p. 147.

9. P.R.O. B. 11/93/f.270^v–71^v. See also Nicholas' will, /98/f.325^v–26^v; Mercy Frobisher's deposition of Feb. 4, 1623 (where she gives her age as fifty): C.24/496/#114; and a lawsuit of her husband's: C.2/Jas.I/C.17/44.

10. C.54/1273/m.31.

11. St.Ch.5/L.27/19, interrogatories (second last list) no. 1; /L.43/11, Brende no. 1; C.54/1151/m.21–22. In the first document, John Whythorne described him as "one Brende of Toowe Lane in London Scryvenor" (no. 3–7). The signature reads, "per me Thomam Brende." Four other signatures survive, all dated July 18, 1562, and all spelled "Brende": C.54/450/m.50, /462/m.36, 43(2).

12. At about the same time, in 1582 and 1583, a William Brende bought a lease from the lord admiral: C.54/1141/m.43; /1194/m.10. This Brende's financier in 1572 was Thomas Cure, who two decades later financed the Swan: /892/m.25.

13. Much information about Brende and his family comes from this inscription. The rest of it reads: "Here lyeth bvried the body of Thomas Brende of Westmolsey Esqvire who had by his two wives eighteene children videlicit by Margerie his first wife foure sonnes & six davghters who dyed the second of Ivne 1564. by Mercie his last wife he had fovre sonnes and fower davghters she left her life the xiij of April 1597 and lyeth here bvried he . . . left one sonne and five davghters at his death." *Victoria Country History (V.C.H.), Surrey,* 3:455, mistakenly attributes his doings to a father and son. He did have a son and heir named Thomas in 1570 (C.66/1069/m.32), but by 1583 Nicholas was his son and heir (C.54/1151/m.21). He also had a brother named Thomas Brend, alive in 1599, whom he and his daughter, Judith, mentioned in their wills. That his doings belong to only one man is clear from (a) the five signatures, 1562(4), 1578, which were written by the same person, those of 1562 canceling loans made by Thomas Brende, citizen and scrivener of London, in 1547–48, and (b) the history of two properties, the manor of Gloverswick and the advowson of Walkern. A Thomas Brende, citizen and scrivener of London, bought each in the 1560s, and the purchaser sold each in 1587, the first as citizen and scrivener of London who had a wife named Mercy, the second as citizen and writer of the court letter of London who had a wife, Mercy, and lived in a house in St. Peter's Hill. See C.54/624/#30; /646/#67; /1274/m.6; /1273/m.31.

14. They were certainly married by May 20, 1595, when Lady Jane Townsend (who obviously knew of the marriage) described George Sayers as a brother-in-law to "my cousin Margaret Brend": Historical Manuscripts Commission (H.M.C.), *Salisbury,* 5:214. Moreover, Nicholas Brend's sister, Mercy, said on February 4, 1623, that she had known his wife for twenty-eight or twenty-nine years. She added that when Nicholas died his children were of the following ages: Jane five or six years, Mercy about four, Frances about three, and John a half or quarter year. See C.24/496/#114, nos. 1, 7.

15. The will is P.R.O. B. 11/93/f.270^v–71^v; the remark was made by a neighbor, Francis Drake, in May, 1607: C.24/333/pt.2/#36, interrogatory no. 5.

16. Who Margaret's parents were is a puzzle. Her senior Brend grandson said in 1662 that she was the daughter of Sir William Plummer, and a person of the name was knighted as of Surrey in 1616: *Visitation of Surrey, 1662–68* (London: Harleian Society, 1910), p.14; W. A. Shaw, *Knights of England* (London, 1906), 2:159. Her senior Zinzan grandson, however, said in 1665 that she was the daughter of Sir Philip Strelley of Strelley

in Notts., and a person of that name was knighted as of Leicester in 1603: *The Four Visitations of Berkshire* (London: Harleian Society, 1907), p. 320; Shaw *Knights of England,* 2:103. A Henry Strelley is described by others as her brother and Sir Sigismond's brother-in-law, and by himself as uncle to her children; and a Mary Strelley described herself as aunt to those children: S.P.16/256/#1/f.13, 19, 22; H.M.C., *Eleventh Report,* pt. 7, p. 159. Yet it must have been this Mary Strelley who, in testifying for Margaret and her second husband in January, 1623, gave herself as daughter of Humphrey Strelley of Strelley in Notts.: C.24/496/#114. Lord Stanhope and his sister, Lady Jane Townsend, were nephew and niece to an Anna Strelley: *Visitations of . . . Nottingham . . . 1569 and 1614* (London: Harleian Society, 1871), pp. 7–8, 19–22.

17. H.M.C., *Salisbury,* 5:214; Chambers, *Elizabethan Stage,* 1:63–65. An antagonist of hers asserted at the end of her life that her brother, Henry Strelley, had been more a servant to her next husband than an equal, an assertion which that husband vigorously denied: S.P.16/256/#1/f.22–23.

18. So Thomas Brende's inquisition post mortem reads and agrees with the funeral inscription that he died on Sept. 21, 1598: C.142/256/#68. His will is P.R.O. B.11/93/f.270ᵛ–71ᵛ.

19. C.54/1612/m.22(2).

20. Sir John Bodley made the remark in 1621–22: WARD 9/94/f.631ᵛ–32. The description of the property before the Globe was built is from the lease, recited in K.B.27/1454/m.692 (see Braines, *Site of the Globe,* p. 17, and Chambers, *Elizabethan Stage,* 2:416–17). Thomas Brende's inquisition post mortem reads that there were forty tenants in the property.

21. C.54/1682/m.11 and /1722/m.7 (both of 1601); /1947/#5 (of 1608); /2471/#15 (of 1622); /2594/#15 (of 1624). For Hendrik Sturman, see also /3063/#18.

22. P.R.O. B.11/93/f.270ᵛ–71ᵛ, 298ᵛ–99.

23. C.54/1674/m.26.

24. One of the two copies of Nicholas Brend's inquisition post mortem reads that Matthew was one year, eight months, and six days old when Nicholas died on Oct. 12, 1601, and Matthew himself said so in June, 1621, adding that he had come of age the previous February: C.142/271/#151; E.112/126/179, Matthew's reply. The other copy reads that he was one year old and the words following are perished: WARD 7/26/134. The decree in the Court of Wards, however, reads that he was only eight months and six days old—thereby perhaps qualifying the matter more obviously for that Court in the winter of 1621–22, since with that birthdate Matthew would have been a minor until February, 1622: WARD 9/94/f.632.

25. How Bodley (whose accounting this is) arrived at £2,150 is unclear. After Nicholas' death, he discovered additional debts of £237, and the repairs cost him nearly £300. Hence Nicholas' indebtedness should have been some £2,265. The heir, Matthew, eventually argued that his father's debts totaled only £1,865. See Nicholas' deathbed mortgages and allied documents: C.54/1722/m.7 (Oct. 7, containing a list of the debts Nicholas could remember, for £1,478), /1705/m.26 (Oct. 8), /1682/m.11 (Oct. 10); and a summary of Matthew's lawsuit against Bodley of 1621–22: WARD 9/94/f.631ᵛ–33. For the place of Nicholas' death, see C.24/496/#114, Archer no. 2, and for its date, the lawsuit, and inquisition post mortem (C.142/271/#151). His will is P.R.O. B.11/98/f.325ᵛ–26ᵛ, proved by his widow on Nov. 6, 1601.

26. Whatever was realized above the amount necessary for portions and maintenance was to be divided between the widow and John. This was the only provision made for him. Bodley was able to give his own second daughter, Jane (aged 7 in 1623), £3,000 when she married Robert Brocas in 1638: C.8/77/80 and *Visitations of Surrey in . . . 1623,* p. 147.

27. So John Brend eventually said, informed, perhaps (as Matthew Brend thought), by Bodley: C.2/Chas.I/B.153/39, bill and answer.

28. C.54/1947/#5 and some of Bodley's and Collet's remarks in the lawsuit of 1621–22: WARD 9/94/f.632ᵛ.

29. C.54/1721/m.21–22(3).

30. To stop these proceedings, Drake launched a lawsuit in Chancery of which I

have found only three orders together with some interrogatories and two depositions for Drake: C.33/109/f.535 and /113/f.153, 183; C.24/333/pt.2/#36. The Zinzans filed a demurrer in reply to Drakes's bill. In May, 1606, Drake got the court to stop the case at common law until they should answer directly, and when they did that in November, 1607, he got it stopped until Chancery should hear the case. His interrogatories belong to May, 1607, and his depositions to January and May, 1608. That there seem to be no more orders suggests either that the Zinzans abandoned the matter or that they settled it privately with Drake. Drake argued that the lord admiral had repaid the loan by giving Brende timber from the manor of Esher.

31. They were certainly married by May 21, 1606, when as her husband Zinzan acquired an interest in the estates of her father-in-law and previous husband: P.R.O. B.11/93/f.271ᵛ. Zinzan said on Feb. 14, 1625, that he had made a payment on behalf of his stepson, Matthew Brend, twenty years before: C.2/Chas.I/Z.1/17, the bill.

32. So Matthew Brend said on Jan. 12, 1625, in response to a lawsuit of his brother's that had nothing to do with Zinzan: C.2/Chas.I/B.153/39, the answer. Three weeks later, Zinzan said in another lawsuit that because his wife had no jointure with which she might support her children after Nicholas' death, the Court of Wards gave her control in her own right, rather than in trust for the heir, of the Brend properties (presumably those not committed to Bodley) during the heir's minority: /B.126/62, the answer. That she could then raise £1,000 from Brend lands to bestow on Zinzan suggests that she brought the family a portion when she married Nicholas and so was entitled eventually to a jointure or new portion from them. That Matthew Brend did not tax Zinzan with the portion money suggests that his mother received a reasonable jointure for it.

33. Once, at least, Sir Sigismond took an active interest in collecting his step-daughters' portions from Bodley, when in Lent, 1621, he discussed the matter with Bodley: C.24/496/#114, Fellowes, no. 2. His grandson, Henry, certified the list of children in March, 1665, together with the names of most of their wives or husbands: *The Four Visitations of Berkshire* (London: Harleian Society, 1907), p. 320. For the two Strelleys, see S.P.16/256/#1/f.13, 22–23, and Mary's deposition (which accompanies that of Fellowes) in which, on Jan. 31, 1623, she said she was thirty years old. Sir Sigismond's more remote descendants seem to have thought that he had an additional son: Charles Coates, *The History and Antiquities of Reading* (London, 1802), pp. 445–46. His uncle, Andrew Zinzan of Reading, mentioned several of the sons in his will (Mar. 14, 1622): P.R.O. B.11/148/f.196–96ᵛ.

34. Sir Sigismond's grandchildren called themselves Zinzano throughout one part of an extensive lawsuit but Zinzan before and after, and his uncle, Andrew, was buried as Zinzano in 1625 but had drawn his will as Zinzan: C.7/328/113; /392/23; C.8/341/208; /465/40; Coates, *Reading*, p. 229; and P.R.O. B.11/148/f.196–96ᵛ. See also Anthony Wood, *Athenae Oxoniensis* (London, 1721), 1: 625.

35. He gave himself as fifty years old on Jan. 24, 1598, and wrote on July 3, 1593, of his thirty-five "painful years of service" to the queen. Giving himself as of Walton, he declared his will orally on Sept. 21, 1607; his widow, Margaret, proved it on Jan. 27, 1608, and his son, Henry, succeeded to one of his offices on Dec. 21, 1607. See Req.2/183/62 (where there are three of his signatures); H.M.C., *Salisbury*, 13:268, 282 (and E.403/2559/f.225); Shaw, *Knights of England*, 2:116; P.R.O. B.11/111/f.5ᵛ; S.O.3/3/Dec. 1607. His royal gifts are recorded among the patent rolls and state papers (see esp. *Calendars of State Papers, Domestic, 1591–94*, pp.359, 483, and *1595–97*, p. 304), occasionally in lawsuits (see esp. St.Ch.5/Z.1/1, the bill, from which the quotation comes).

36. Zenzant owned a farm at Parkbury, near St. Albans, in 1547; Sir Robert and probably his brothers, Alexander and Andrew, were of St. Albans in 1588 and after, 1586, and 1607, respectively, though Andrew was of Reading when he died in 1625: Req.2/8/143 and /19/40; V.C.H., Herts., 3:92, 94; *Marriages Licences Issued by the Bishop of London* (London: Harleian Society, 1887), 1:148, 172; C.S.P., Dom., 1603–10, pp. 145, 157; C.54/1906/m.21.

37. A list of the horsemen who served the late King James includes Sir Sigismond, Henry, Andrew, and Robert Zinzan (a yeoman): H.M.C., *Sixth Report*, pp.324–26. It omits Alexander (whose place was filled by John Prichard in January, 1626) and Richard (who had

the reversion of Andrew's place). See *C.S.P., Dom., 1598–1601*, p. 216; *1611–18*, p. 28; *1623–25*, p. 295; *1625–26*, p. 558; *1635*, pp. 134, 492; C.54/2949/#21 and /3169/#26 (for Henry's two sons and wife, Elizabeth); and H.M.C., *Fifth Report*, pp. 57–58, 116 (for Joseph, who in 1643 wanted to locate his school in the stable and yard of Winchester House, not far from the deserted Globe). An Alexander Zinzan was the king's servant in 1553: *Calendar of Patent Rolls, 1569–72*, nos. 1108, 3328. For Evelyn (who was first cousin to Bodley's wife), see E. S. deBeer's edition of the *Diary* (Oxford, 1955), 1:10 and n. 54.

38. Charles Rogers, *Memorials of the Earl of Stirling and of the House of Alexander* (Edinburgh, 1877), 2:172–78, where, however, some details are wrong. Henry Alexander married Mary Vanlore in December, 1635, and became third earl in 1640; Henry Zinzan alias Alexander married Jacoba Vanlore before 1637 (his eldest son was twenty-eight years old in March, 1665): *C.S.P., Dom., 1635*, p. 566 and *1637–38*, p. 496; *Visitations of Berkshire*, p. 320. Sir Sigismond's youngest son, Charles, eventually settled in Leith: C.10/159/187.

39. On Feb. 4, 1623, Mercy Brend Frobisher said that she had known Sir Sigismond for twenty-five or twenty-six years: C.24/496/#114, no. 1. His brother, Henry, is regularly mentioned first in both their father's and uncle's wills, and in 1638 he described himself as heir: P.R.O. B.11/111/f.5^v; /148/f.196–96^v; C.54/3169/#26. Henry was born in 1563 or 1564, for on Feb. 22, 1656, he said that he was ninety-two years old: *C.S.P., Dom., 1655–56*, p.197. Sigismond's knighting is not recorded, but it took place between 1601, when he is mentioned as unknighted, and Mar. 24, 1605, from which time he is invariably mentioned as a knight: H.M.C., *Salisbury*, 11:540; 17:107.

40. A description of the tilt of 1581 (May 15–16) was printed as *The Tryumphe Shewed before the Quene and the Ffrenche Embassadors* and that of 1590 as *Polyhymnia*. See Chambers, *Elizabethan Stage*, 3:402; 4:63–64.

41. E.101/435/15; *The Letters of John Chamberlain*, ed. N. E. McClure (Philadelphia, 1939), 2: 298; H.M.C., *Rutland*, 4:494, 508.

42. See Appendix.

43. See Glynne Wickham, "Romance and Emblem: A Study in the Dramatic Structure of *The Winter's Tale*," in *Eliabethan Theatre 3*, ed. Dand Galloway (Toronto, 1973), pp. 87 ff.; and Jonson's *Works* (London, 1616) 1:995–1000.

44. H.M.C., *Cowper*, 1:195, 199.

45. John Nichols, *The Progresses . . . of King James the First* (London, 1828), 2:496–97.

46. At least fifteen signatures of Henry Zinzan survive because several of the issue books survive of the teller who paid his annuities: E.36/134/pp.53^v{sic}, 172 (where this one occurs); E.405/548–51. Sir Sigismond's signature is from his petition to the House of Lords (see below). Four others purport to be his, but none is genuine. Three are in the hands of the clerks who wrote the documents to which they belong and not Sir Sigismond: E.406/47/f.41, 47^v, 154. One is in the same hand as two others at the end of a petition; each of the three has been traced over by another hand holding another pen, possibly those of the purported signer who, when he came to sign the document, found that a scrivener had already signed for him: S.P.18/73/#34.

47. The quotation is from an undated note among the Lord Keeper Egerton's papers about a case in the Star Chamber: H.M.C., *Eleventh Report*, pt. 7, p. 159. For the fines, see E.159/440/Easter 9 Jas./m.256. In 1633 Strelley was a Brend tenant on seventy acres in Walton: C.54/2985/#6.

48. So Matthew Brend asserted in 1625, offering chapter and verse: C.2/Chas. I/ Z.1/17, the answer.

49. Shaw, *Knights of England*, 2:165.

50. WARD 9/94/f.631^v–33; C.54/2471/#15. Another result of Matthew's coming of age was that Sir Sigismond's brother, Henry, living as their father had done in Walton, sued Sir Matthew in the summer of 1621 about a house and some sixty-four acres near Walton Common. Henry argued that the properties belonged to him but that the Brends has appropriated them about three years before. Had he sued a few months earlier, of course, the defendant would have been Sir Sigismond. See E.112/126/179.

51. Shaw, *Knights of England,* 2:178.

52. The lawsuit survives as a replication dated merely Easter (C.2/Chas.I/Z.1/6), interrogatories and depositions (taken between Jan. 24 and Feb. 4, 1623) for the Brends (C.24/496/#114), and various decrees and orders (see below).

53. When Sir Matthew and Sir Sigismond came to sue one another about Dame Margaret's dower rights and their ramifications (C.2/Chas.I/B.126/62 and /Z.1/17), it was not in Sir Matthew's interest to admit that the first arrangement existed, nor was that arrangement of first importance to Sir Sigismond. So what one knows about it derives from allusions, sometimes confused, in Sir Sigismond's parts of the lawsuits. He and Sir Matthew both described the new arrangement and the trouble it caused. See Sir Matthew's bill of Dec. 3[?], 1624 (the day begins "tr" and is then illegible); Sir Sigismond's answer of Feb. 4, 1625, and his bill of Feb. 14, 1625; Sir Matthew's undated answer. Sir Matthew also alluded to the matter in his answer of Jan. 12, 1625, to his brother's lawsuit about something else: C.2/Chas.I/B.153/39.

54. C.54/2594/#15. I quote the description of the property above. The rent for the land on which the Globe stood was still £14.10s.0d. a year (it would eventually be £40.) At twelve years purchase that land alone should have been worth £174.

55. Sir John Shelley was one of the original baronets in 1611. Two of his uncles were implicated in Catholic plots, one of whom was attainted though not hanged. two of his great uncles were knights of St. John (one the last grand prior in England). See *The Complete Baronetage, D.N.B.* ("Sir Wm. Shelley" and "Sir Richard Shelley"), and the pedigree in the visitations of Sussex: *1530 . . . 1633–34* and *1662* (London: Harleian Society, 1905 and 1937), pp. 36–37 in the first and p. 99 in the second visitation.

56. S.P.16/256/#1, a brochure of forty-four leaves in which the Zinzans' case was summarized in the early 1630s from what must have been massive documentation in the Star Chamber. The whole brochure is relevant, but see esp. f.1–4, 6–9, 14, 17, 19–20, 33, 36–38, 44. Because her parents were married in 1605 or a little after, the bride cannot have been more than eighteen years old and may have been a good deal less. One witness said that Sir Sigismond could have given between £600 and £700 with his daughter and another said a thousand marks (£666).

57. S.P.16/256/#1, f.15–16.

58. For Sir Sigismond, see S.P.14/168/#27, 28; S.P.84/118/f.172, 174, 176; /119/f.152ᵛ. For Sigismond the son, see *C.S.P., Ireland, 1647–60 and Addenda, 1625–60,* pp.47–48, where in February, 1625, he is said to have served as a lieutenant in the Palatinate. For Henry Strelley (who served under the earl of Lincoln), see S.P.16/256/#1, f.23. One of Sir Sigismond's men was apparently Shackerley Marmion, author of *Holland's Leaguer,* who found advancement under him slow and soon returned to England: Wood, *Athenae Oxoniensis,* 1:625.

59. See Sir John Coke's notes of Sir Matthew's and Sir Sigismond's lawsuits: H.M.C., *Cowper,* 1: 185.

60. Brend's figure is my extrapolation drawn from an exchange between him and Bodley in their lawsuit of 1621–22. Bodley said that the properties were worth £90 a year and those in Bread Street and Southwark together £160. Brend argued that the two groups of properties were worth £400. Though Brend won the case, the court seems to have sided with Bodley in such matters, as Brend thought. See WARD 9/94/f.631ᵛ–32. In two contracts of October, 1601, Brend's dying father agreed with Bodley that the Southwark properties were worth £90 a year: C.54/1682/m.11 and /1722/m.7.

61. *C.S.P., Dom., 1623–25,* p. 490; S.P.16/256/#1, f.19, 20, 30, 42; E.159/466/Hil.3Chas.I/32/ 62–64. See also House of Lords, Papers, Feb. 27–Mar. 10, 1641, f.113.

62. The decrees and orders for Sir Matthew's case are (in the A books) C.33/147/f.932ᵛ; /149/f.537, 936–36ᵛ; /151/f.485ᵛ, 528. Bodley said on Feb. 8, 1625, that Sir Matthew had made him defend three lawsuits in Chancery about the matter, one of which was probably John Brend's. The court ordered that if Lady Zinzan had consented to the lawsuit Sir Sigismond should pay part of the costs. Sir Matthew asserted that she had, and he suggested that all five plaintiffs should pay £2 each (John Brend had dissociated himself from the case).

63. The case survives as a bill and answer: C.2/Chas.I/B.153/39; and decrees and orders (in the A books): C.33/147/f.183ᵛ, 508, 552, 665, 949; /149/f.391, 476, 537, 818; /151/f.31, 337, 1097, 1320; /153/f.52ᵛ. It becames a question of how the interest should be calculated on money that Bodley got for the properties sold to raise portions. Should his disbursements and expenses come first from the principal (so reducing the interest) or first from the interest (so that the principal continued to produce interest)? The court decided the latter on June 10, 1625, but two years later ordered a judge and master of the court to review the question while negotiating a final settlement with John Brend and Bodley. The gross sum at stake was £230.2s.0d. Eventually Bodley seems to have had to pay £30 each to Brend and to his mother's estate, which is to say, to Sir Sigismond, whom the court excluded from collecting his part, presumably because he was still an outlaw.

64. C.54/2690/#84, a performance bond for £1,200, dated Dec. 11, 1626. Usually such bonds were for twice the amount borrowed. The lender was Hilary Mempris, to whom Sir Matthew's brother, John, had been apprenticed.

65. She was mentioned on Jan. 29, 1627, as alive: C.33/151/f.528. She left no will, and the administration of her goods was granted to her husband on June 20, 1627: P.R.O. B.6/12/f.151ᵛ.

66. C.54/2985/#6 (June 20).

67. S.P.16/135/#39; E.403/2565/f.152. It is not known whether he served with military enterprises abroad after September, 1626. The four regiments were to be withdrawn in November, 1626. He was one of the commanders proposed in February, 1625, for service in Ireland (*C.S.P., Ireland, 1647–60, and Addenda, 1625–60,* p. 47), where evidently he did not go. He does not appear in Henry Hexham's books about the siege of Bois-le-duc in 1629, the campaigns of 1632, or the siege of Breda in 1637, though many Englishmen do: *A Historicall Relation of the Famous Siege of the Busse* (Delft, 1630), *A Journal of the taking in of Venlo, . . .* (The Hague, 1633), and *A True and Brief Relation of the Famous Siege of Breda* (Delft, 1637).

68. E.403/2567/f.7ᵛ–8 (dated Dec. 14, 1632). Two of his assignments are recorded: E.406/47/f.41, 154 (July 18, 1633, and Feb. 9, 1636).

69. S.P.15/43/f.295 (undated). In 1654 Sir Sigismond claimed that he had received from Charles I not only his pension of £100 a year but a salary as equerry of almost as much (S.P.18/74/f.82). He certainly received his pension then (see, for example, E.403/1753/14 June, 1639, and Jan. 10, 1640), but his salary then and earlier, unlike his brother's, must have been paid out of the royal household rather than the Exchequer directly. Henry had a patent in 1603 for £100 a year as equerry and another in 1607 for £10 a year as keeper of armor in the Tower (C.66/1624/m.3; /1737/m.4), and his payments are regularly recorded.

70. S.P.16/256/#1, f.30–38, 42–44.

71. *C.S.P., Dom., 1635–36,* p. 250; *1636–37,* p. 105; E.405/548/f.102, etc.; House of Lords, Papers, Feb. 27–Mar. 10, 1641, f.113; Shaw, *Knights of England,* 2: 204. The marriage took place between Feb. 23 and Aug. 28, 1636. The lady was apparently the daughter of the queen's nurse.

72. P.R.O. B.6/17/f.79 (Sir Wm. Shelley's admon. act, Nov. 22, 1639); P.R.O. B.11/182/f.44ᵛ–45 (Lady Shelley's will, dated at Paris Jan. 2/12, 1640, and proved at London on Jan. 28 by her executor in England, Sir James Vantelet, her father, not one of the Shelleys); E.405/550/Easter/f.9 (her father collected the last payment of her pension).

73. House of Lords, Papers, Feb. 27–Mar. 10, 1641, f.113.

74. S.P.18/74/f.82 and attachment; E.403/2523/p. 63 (July 19, 1655); *C.S.P., Dom., 1659–60,* pp.228, 587, 590; *Commons Journal,* 4:179. Four Strelleys also joined Essex's army, including a Henry as lieutenant in John Gunter's troop of horse: *The List of the Army Raised under the Command of his Excellency, Robert Earle of Essex* (London, 1642).

75. S.P.18/124/#91; E.403/2608/p.40 (Mar. 31, 1656).

76. E.403/2569/f.107ᵛ; /1761/f.39. A Mrs. Zinzan of Reading had a picture of him in 1809: Charles Coates, *A Supplement to the History and Antiquities of Reading* (Reading, 1809), sig. F4.

'77. Req.1/63/6 Feb.; /64/3 Nov.; /76/p.232; /137/6 June; /156/f.91ᵛ, 97ᵛ, 147ᵛ, 171, 171ᵛ; /157/f.37, 64, 65ᵛ; /160/f.101ᵛ, 181; /185/f.14ᵛ; IND.9033/20, Nov. 21,

1637. I found these documents several months after the symposium in Detroit; hence, I am able only to summarize them briefly here.

78. See his testimony for the Brends on Feb. 1, 1623 (where his signature appears): C.24/496/#114. He gave his age as sixty and his address as Maid Lane. He said that he had known Sir Sigismond twenty-and-a-half years, Dame Margaret twenty, and Bodley well for ten but by sight much longer. He also said that he had delivered to the Zinzans, and got acquittances for, the quarterly sums that Bodley had contributed to the maintenance of the Brend children while Matthew was still a minor. Curiously, this remark and others of his pointedly did not make the case against Bodley that the Brends wanted him to make. Sir Sigismond said on Feb. 14, 1625, that Archer was Sir Matthew's rent-gatherer and had delivered the two payments (at Midsummer and Michaelmas, 1624) meant as rent for the properties in Southwark: C.2/Chas.I/Z.1/17, the bill (see above). For Archer's house see Braines, *Site of the Globe*, p. 72n., and a contract by which Sir Matthew sold it and six others on Jan. 13, 1636: C.54/3063/#19.

Notes to Chapter IV

1. "The First Globe Playhouse," in Clifford Leech and T. W. Craig, gen. eds., *The Revels History of Drama in English*, vol. 3, *1576–1613* (London: Methuen, 1975), p. 176.

2. This is clear from a draft for a return of new and divided houses made for the Earl Marshall in 1634: "The Globe Playhouse near Maid Lane, built by the company of players, with the dwelling-house thereto adjoining, built with timber, about twenty years past, upon an old foundation." Quoted (with modernized spelling and punctuation) from E. K. Chambers, *The Elizabethan Stage*, 4 vols. (Oxford: Clarendon Press, 1923), 2:426.

3. Richard Hosley, "The Theatre and the Tradition of Playhouse Design," in *The First Public Playhouse: The Theatre in Shoreditch, 1576–1598*, ed. Herbert Berry (Montreal: McGill–Queen's University Press, 1979), pp. 57–60.

4. See Chapter V, p. 116 and n. 9.

5. "The Plans of the Fortune and the Globe," *Shakespeare Survey* 33 (1980).

6. *Shakespeare's Second Globe: The Missing Monument* (London: Oxford University Press, 1973), p.39.

7. Hosley, "The Theatre and the Tradition of Playhouse Design," pp.73–74.

8. Hosley, "The Swan Playhouse," in *Revels History of Drama*, 3:144–48. A more detailed statement of the hypothesis that the Swan was a 24-sided building, presented in my Globe Symposium paper, has been omitted from the present essay.

9. *Philip Henslowe's Diary*, ed. R. A. Foakes and R. T. Rickert (Cambridge: University Press, 1961), p. 308.

10. Reproductions in Orrell, "Inigo Jones at the Cockpit," *Shakespeare Survey* 30 (1977): 157–68. I accept Orrell's identification of the depicted playhouse as the Phoenix or Cockpit in Drury Lane.

11. *Malone Society Collections*, vol. 10, ed. F. P. Wilson and R. F. Hill (Oxford: Malone Society, 1977), p. 32.

12. As in the stage proposed by Hodges in *Shakespeare's Second Globe*, p. 63.

13. My interpretation here runs counter to John Orrell's suggestion, in "The Plans of the Fortune and the Globe," that the Globe stage measured 49 feet 6 inches in width. Such a stage, in theory measuring 24 feet 9 inches in depth, would have had width-to-depth proportions of 2:1 or 2.000; and although 6 bays of a 24-sided frame would have chorded the necessary central angle (90°), such a stage could not have run between inner corners of such a frame since the major axes of the second Globe appear to have run not through bay junctures but through bay middles.

14. It remains to comment on the 18- and 20-sided shapes. That the second Globe was an 18-sided building, a form for which there seems to have been no known architectural precedent, is improbable in part because an 18-sided ground plan, like its parent the 9-sided polygon, cannot be constructed by Euclidean methods. The 18-sided shape also fails to harmonize in general with Hollar's pictorial evidence, and it would presumably have enforced a stage with untraditional proportions of width to depth (arithmetical ratio 1.679). Moreover,

that the Globe was a 20-sided building, a form for which there again appears to have been no architectural precedent (other than 10-sided chapter houses), is ruled out by Hollar's pictorial evidence: Hollar depicts twelve windows in a 90° arc of the outer face of the building, but that arc, since it would have corresponded to 5 bays of the frame, would have exhibited either 10 windows in the case of 2-window bays or 15 windows in the case of 3-window bays.

15. It is only a pleasant coincidence that the face-to-face diameter of the building turns out to be the same as the diameter taken on post centers.

16. Six feet is the internal width of the winding staircase given as a model by Joseph Moxon in *Mechanick Exercises, or the Doctrine of Handiworks Applied to the Art of House Carpentry* (London, 1679), pl. 10.

17. I am indebted to Walter Hodges, John Orrell, and T. J. King for helpful criticism of the original draft of this essay; and to Richard Johnson for making the axonometric projection reproduced as figure IV-17.

Notes to Chapter V

1. C. Walter Hodges, *Shakespeare's Second Globe: The Missing Monument* (London: Oxford University Press, 1973), p. 47. Compare the review by Richard Hosley, "The Second Globe," *Theatre Notebook* 29 (1975): 142.

2. Leon Battista Alberti, *On Painting and Sculpture,* ed. and trans. Cecil Grayson (London: Phaidon, 1972), pp. 66–69. See also Irma A. Richter, ed., *Selections from the Notebooks of Leonardo da Vinci* (London: Oxford University Press, 1952), pp. 119, 121–22.

3. The possibility of taking scaled measurements from drawing frame compositions is explored by Arthur Hopton, *Speculum Topographicum; or, the Topographicall Glasse* (1611), pp. 179–80. By the early seventeenth century the drawing frame had become a commonplace of the perspective handbooks. Very full accounts are given in Jean Dubreuil's *La Perspective Pratique* (Paris, 1641–49), where frames of glass, reticulated strings, and fine linen are all described. The English translation, by Robert Pricke, was published in London in 1672 as *Perspective Practical*.

4. British Library, Print Room B.C.M. 3 1882–8–12–489.

5. This evidence consists of a close analysis of the three panoramas too long to include here. The bearings of the "takes" in Norden and Visscher are sufficiently close to each other to suggest a common source; Hollar's are quite different.

6. In *The Revels History Of Drama in English,* Clifford Leech and T. W. Craig, gen. eds., vol. 3, *1576–1613* (London: Methuen, 1975), pl. 12a. The positions of the landmarks have been fixed as follows. St. Paul's east gable was close to the present east end of the cathedral; see W. R. Matthews and W. M. Atkins, *History of St. Paul's Cathedral* (London: Phoenix House, 1957), plan on p. 344. Bulmer's water tower was rebuilt on its original foundations after the fire; B.B. Add. MS 5095, fols. 209b–10b. St. Martin's Ludgate extended farther south and west than the present church, being built hard up against Ludgate itself. Ludgate Hill was widened from some 17 feet to 45 feet after 1666; see T. F. Reddaway, *The Rebuilding of London after the Great Fire* (London: Cape, 1940), p. 299. Wren's church is therefore somewhat more to the north than the old one, but not so far as to prevent parts of the old fabric from being incorporated into it. For the west tower of St. Bride's and its relation to the post-1666 church, see Walter H. Godfrey, *The Church of St. Bride, Fleet St.,* London Survey Committee, Fifteenth Monograph (London, 1944), pp. 8–9. The Savoy Hospital is shown on a reconstructed plan in *The History of the King's Works,* H. M. Colvin, gen. ed., vol. 3, *1485–1660* (pt. 1) (London: H.M.S.O., 1975), p. 197. See also Walter H. Godfrey, "The Strand in the Seventeenth Century: Its River Front," *Transactions of the London and Middlesex Archaeological Society,* n.s. 4 (1918–22): 211–27.

7. *Survey of London,* vol. 22, *Bankside* (London: London County Council, 1950), p. 52.

8. *The Site of the Globe Playhouse* (London: London County Council, 1923).

9. The calculations are as follows. The Hope: plane distance from observer 1,513 ft.; width measured on Hollar's sketch 14.75 mm. Anamorphosis is very slight, the drawing overstating the true reading by 0.21 percent. The width of the Hope is therefore:

$$\frac{14.75}{306} \times 1513 \times 2 \tan 34.3 \times \frac{100}{100.21} = 99.29 \text{ ft.}$$

The Globe: plane distance from observer 1,144 ft.; width measured on Hollar's sketch 21 mm. Anamorphosis is 3.64 percent. The width of the Globe is therefore:

$$\frac{21}{306} \times 1144 \times 2 \tan 34.3 \times \frac{100}{103.64} = 103.35 \text{ ft.}$$

Notes to Chapter VI

1. The fundamental drawing in the Mellon collection, reproduced in C. Walter Hodges, *Shakespeare's Second Globe: The Missing Monument* (London: Oxford University Press, 1973), figs. 12, 16, 17.

2. E.g., *Old London Bridge,* 1630, Kenwood, Hampstead, Greater London Council, Iveagh Bequest, and a *View of Westminster Palace,* New Haven, Conn., Yale Center for British Art.

3. C.f., for instance, C. A. Hewett, *English Cathedral Carpentry* (London: Wayland: 1974), figs. 2–20, 40, 42, 62, 64.

4. See below, p. 133 and n. 35.

5. A convenient study, reproducing early drawings of continental European precedents, is M. C. Donnelly, *The New England Meeting Houses of the Seventeenth Century* (Middletown, Conn.: Wesleyan University Press, 1968).

6. The original Elizabethan Royal Exchange, in the City of London, and, early in the seventeenth century the New Exchange, in the Strand.

7. The famous *beffroi* physically dominates the relatively restricted, galleried *halles.*

8. The palace of Nonesuch, late in Henry VIII's reign, was a trend-setter in heavy nogging, including carven slabs, of a framed building; from this date nogging with brick and occasionally, as at Nether Hale in northeast Kent, flint became increasingly common. Late framed buildings, as in the salt-producing region of Cheshire, sometimes amounted to brick buildings, timber-laced for stability.

9. This fashion, found in the earliest, excavated structures of Antwerp, suggests an "endoskeletal" view of a primitive frame, later to give way to the normal, "exoskeletal" concept of the frame as the main substance of the wall, this in turn to revert to a largely concealed, but integral, reinforcement.

10. See n. 9.

11. The porch of Boxford Church, Suffolk, is perhaps the chef d'oeuvre of this timber counterfeit of masonry, so marked in fourteenth-century England, but timber vaults, as at York Minster and Selby Abbey (both now renewed), and the commoner web of boarding set in rebates, flush with the frame on plane faces, are in the same mode.

12. As in the long window frames, in advance of the main frame and independant of its bay-division, widely distributed in urban houses of the early seventeenth century (as at Gloucester, Chester, Newcastle-on-Tyne).

13. Both straight and curved bracing occur together in the same building at the Queen's House, Tower of London (late Henry VIII), and the straight may still occur in the early seventeenth century.

14. J. T. Smith, "Timber-Framed Building in England," *Archaeological Journal* 122 (1966 [for 1965]): 133–58, passim.

15. A. Vallance, *Old Crosses and Lych-Gates* (London, 1920), figs. 180–81.

16. At a conference of the Vernacular Architecture Group, London, December, 1978.

17. No full description published, but cf. *Victoria County History, Hampshire* (1921), 5:7, 34.

18. Quite exceptionally for southeast England, the very 'mixed' but largely contemporaneous frame of the Queen's House, Tower of London (cf. n. 13), has one roof with king posts rising to the juncture of the principal rafters, but this still has no ridge piece.

19. Both known contracts for theatres are given *in extenso* in C. Walter Hodges, *The Globe Restored*, 3rd ed. (New York: Norton, 1973), appendixes F and G (pp. 163–69).

20. Ibid., appendix G.

21. The great barn at Harmondsworth, Middlesex (between London and Heathrow airport), where a combination of dendrochronology and limited documentation points to a mid-fifteenth-century date, has a precocious use of relatively short, butted timbers.

22. This form of overhang, as in A. L. Cummings, *The Framed Houses of Massachusetts Bay, 1625–1725* (Cambridge, Mass.: Harvard University Press, 1979), figs. 74–75, 81–83, 166, 169, does not flourish until the last quarter of the seventeenth century, when *any* form of overhang was, at least, obsolescent in England.

23. Stair turrets, either with a vise or more often with parallel rises, are common in early seventeenth-century houses, framed as well as brick-shelled, in most parts of England (but very unusual in New England).

24. Hodges, *Globe Restored*, appendix F.

25. As can be seen in many contracts printed in L. F. Salzman, *Building in England down to 1540* (Oxford: Oxford University Press, 1952), appendix B (pp. 413–584).

26. According to Ben Jonson, cited in Hodges, *Globe Restored*.

27. S. E. Rigold, "Structural Aspects of Medieval Timber Bridges," *Medieval Archaeology* 19 (1975): 48–91.

28. The quasi-architectural designs, with their niches for postured figures and semblance of a polychrome effect, used for certain engraved title pages, and in particular for John Speed's *Theatre of . . . Great Britaine* (1614) (Hodges, *The Globe Restored*, pl. 47), are clearly in the idiom of architectural "frontispieces"—portal-façades, the surrounds and reredoses of monuments and the apparatus of pageantry and, almost inevitably, and with some classical precedent in places such as Orange, the static reredos of theatres.

29. This, the precise arc where grace and *gravitas* overlapped, where not only mannerism but also a *unanime* with courtly French taste was accepted, extended to a limited range of prestigious cabinetwork; compare the selection presented in E. Mercer, *Furniture, 700–1700* (London, 1969), pp. 112–41 and pls. 124–46, where the design on pl. 124 is actually ascribed to Inigo Jones.

30. Hodges, *Globe Restored*, pls. 34–39.

31. The façade, essentially a screen and relatively independent of the frame, is in the Victoria and Albert Museum, London; for views of the interior by the great recorder, J. T. Smith (ca. 1800), see W. H. Godfrey, *The Story of Architecture in England* (London, 1931), fig. 77 (term figures, etc.)

32. A subject much recorded but nowhere fully discussed, except possibly in the several works of Mrs. Arundell Esdaile.

33. Donnelly, *New England Meeting Houses*, figs. 3–5, pp. 25–27.

34. Ibid., fig. 6.

35. Although the meetinghouses and the Sheldonian, were roofed overall, and the theatres were not, the cupola (signalpost, and often also the light-well) was common to all.

Notes to Chapter VII

1. A ground plan of a stage purporting to be that of the Globe itself appeared in an article in *Theatre Notebook* (vol. 23, no. 2 [1978]:63-67) by Mr. David George, but I regret that I have not had the opportunity to read it.

Notes to Chapter VIII

1. *Philip Henslowe's Diary*, ed. R. A. Foakes and R. T. Rickert (Cambridge: University Press, 1961), p. 319.

2. Ibid., p. 7.

3. Bernard Beckerman, *Shakespeare at the Globe, 1599–1609* (New York: Macmillan, 1962), p. 8.

4. *Henslowe's Diary*, p. 217.

5. Ibid., pp. 72–74, 86–107, 121–26.

6. Ibid., p. 107.

7. Thomas Platter as quoted in E. K. Chambers, *The Elizabethan Stage,* 4 vols. (Oxford: Clarendon Press, 1923), 2:365.

8. Richard Hosley, "The Playhouses," in *The Revels History of Drama in English,* Clifford Leech and T. W. Craig, gen. eds., vol. 3, *1576–1613* (London: Methuen, 1975), p. 195. Hosley does not accept the possibility that there may have been three tiring-house doors.

Notes to Chapter IX

1. George R. Kernodle, *From Art to Theatre: Form and Convention in the Renaissance* (Chicago: University of Chicago Press, 1944), pp. 111 ff.

2. W. M. H. Hummelen, "Het speeltoneel van Het Wit Lavendel," in *Handelingen v.h. dertigste Nederlands Filologencongres . . . te Leiden . . . 1968* (Groningen: Wolters, 1968), pp. 78 ff.; idem, "Typen van toneelinrichting bij de rederijkers. De opvattingen van Endepols en Kernodle kritisch onderzocht, en geconfronteerd met conclusies op grond van werken van Jacob Duym en Willem van Haecht," *Studia Neerlandica* 2 (1970): 65 ff.; idem, "Illustrations of Stage Performances in the Work by Crispijn de Passe the Elder (ca. 1560–1637)," in *Essays on Drama and Theatre. Liber Amicorum Benjamin Hunningher* (Amsterdam: Moussault, 1973), pp. 67 ff.; idem, "Der Bühenwettstreit in Gent (1539): Zusammenhang zwischen Bühne und Spielen," in *Akten des V. Internationalen Germanisten-Kongresses, Cambridge 1975,* no. 3 (*Jahrbuch für Internationale Germanistik,* ser. A, vols. 2-3), pp. 47 ff.; idem, "Inrichting en gebruik van het toneel bij Job Gommersz (1565)," in *Jaarboek van de Koninklijke Soevereine Hoofdkamer van Retorica 'De Fonteine' te Gent,* 1975, vol. 1, no. 25 (Ghent, 1976), pp. 7 ff.; idem, "Sporen van gebruik in handschriften van rederijkersspelen," in *Opstellen door vrienden en vakgenoten aangeboden aan Dr. C. H. A. Kruyskamp* ('s-Gravenhage: Nijhoff, 1977), pp. 108 ff.

3. Cf. W. M. H. Hummelen, *Repertorium ven het Rederijkersdrama 1500–ca. 1620* (Assen: Van Gorcum, 1968). In his bibliography Kernodle names 136 plays in old editions (of which 121 are competition plays) and 41 recently published from manuscripts (of which, by chance, again at least 10 are competition plays).

4. George R. Kernodle, "The Open Stage: Elizabethan or Existentialist?" *Shakespeare Survey* 12 (1959): 5.

5. One of the most important contests, and also the earliest to have produced printed plays (Ghent, 1539), required the answers to be given not only *schriftuerlijckst,* i.e., with the aid of the Bible, but also *figuerlijckst,* i.e., using the *tableaux vivant* as a medium of explication and demonstration. The result is that among the nineteen plays performed at the contest there are as many containing four or more *tableaux vivants* as there are among all other surviving rhetoricians' plays together.

6. *From Art to Theatre,* p. 122. The only example of an exterior scene ("Bacchus sitting before his vineyard," etc.) is taken from a *factie,* viz, that of Zout Leeuw (not Louvain). *Facties* were performed *achter straten,* i.e., at the wayside, and not on the same staging as *spelen van sinne.* The conclusion that an inner stage was used here, too, is therefore not justified.

7. *From Art to Theatre,* p. 116.

8. Two Pyramus and Thisbe plays have survived; cf. my *Repertorium,* nos. 1 OB 11 and 4.05.

9. As regards the positioning and gestures of the main characters and the physical appearance of the fountain, de Passe has followed earlier models that essentially have nothing to do with the theatre. This does not apply, however, to the *mise en scène:* the position of Pyramus and Thisbe and of the fountain on the stage, and the open curtains.

10. C. Walter Hodges, "Unworthy Scaffolds: A Theory for the Reconstruction of Elizabethan Playhouses," *Shakespeare Survey* 3 (1950): 86.

11. I have disregarded the contribution made by the colonies of foreign merchants in the city (in 1582, in fact, there were none). The chambers were reimbursed the costs of

decorating the façade with silk drapes and murals, most of which could naturally be used for only one occasion. They also received a subsidy of £150

12. From a play by one of the Marigold's sister chambers, which I shall discuss later, it is clear that the chamber producing it already had such a screen in 1563, so they could show prisoners in their cell and the guard asleep in front of the cell door at one and the same time. Perhaps this is the screen that was used for the theatre erected by the city next to the monastery of St. Michael.

13. Hodges, "Unworthy Scaffolds," p. 88.

14. It is probable that there are also three compartments on the upper level. The use of the spaces at either end of the top of the set for lighthouse keepers, and the fact that two years earlier the Gillyflowers had made use of a stage façade with three upper compartments, would seem to support this view.

15. It is impossible to date this play more exactly. It is part of a collection that was owned by the Gillyflowers, a chamber of rhetoric in 's-Gravenpolder, a very small village in Zeeland. As late as the first decades of the eighteenth century, sixteenth-century plays were being copied, bought (from other chambers), and performed there.

16. Kernodle, *From Art to Theatre,* p. 86.

17. Richard Southern, "On Reconstructing a Practicable Elizabethan Public Playhouse," *Shakespeare Survey* 12 (1959): 32; Bernard Beckerman, *Shakespeare at the Globe, 1599–1609* (New York: Macmillan, 1962), p. 100, n. 1.

18. As when Eutychus, seated in one of the openings on the upper floor, falls behind the façade to the floor of the inner stage at ground level. At that moment, moreover, the forestage where Paul is giving his sermon is an interior and the space behind the façade an exterior.

19. "The Open Stage," p. 5. Kernodle contradicts himself, it seems to me, when he attributes the advancing simplification of the façade to the character of the plays performed before it; furthermore, he gives an extremely one-sided picture of their character in the first place.

20. Kernodle, *From Art to Theatre,* p. 103.

21. W. M. H. Hummelen, *Inrichting en gebruik van het toneel in de Amsterdamse Schouwburg van 1637* (Amsterdam: Noord-Hollandse Uitgevers Maatschappij, 1967), pp. 7 ff.

22. Beckerman (*Shakespeare at the Globe,* p. 88) theorizes that the use of the space behind the curtains as a "discovery-space" is connected with the fact that the façade of the booth stage became a permanent fixture. It is not clear how this is to be understood.

23. Ibid., p. 108.

24. Richard Southern, *The Seven Ages of the Theatre* (1962; reprint ed., London: Faber & Faber, 1973), pp. 159 ff.

25. A character can "exit" by the curtains being closed, just as a character can "enter" by means of their being opened. This contrasts with what happens in the Globe plays; cf. Richard Hosley, "The Discovery-Space in Shakespeare's Globe," *Shakespeare Survey* 12 (1959): 45.

26. In de Koning's *Simson* (1618), for example, two inner stages, one above the other, act as the temple roof, where the Philistine princes were feasting, and as the interior of the temple, where Samson is displayed to visitors.

27. In 1632 the city authorities ordered the amalgamation of the White Lavender and the Eglantine, and the Academie Theatre was thereafter used by this new organization. In 1637 the wooden building was due for replacement, and the city orphanage and old people's home paid for the architect Jacob van Campen to build the Schouwburg.

28. This does not mean, any more than it did in the rhetoricians' plays of the sixteenth century, that all localization is specific or even general. Much of it stays neutral.

Notes to Chapter X

1. See the article by John Harris in *Country Life,* December 1, 1977, p. 1576.

2. The mid-sixteenth-century German auto-da-fé scaffold, illustrated in *The Horizon*

Book of the Elizabethan World (London: Paul Hamlyn, 1967), p. 217, is an example of vertical boarding; for an example of horizontal boarding, see Robert Fludd (1574-1637), *The Art of Memory*, 2 vols. (Oppenheim, 1617, 1619).

3. Public Records Office (hereafter P.R.O.) E351/3271, Appendix E in Glynne Wickham's *Early English Stages*, 3 vols. (London: Routledge & Kegan Paul, 1963–72).

4. Nicola Sabbattini, *Practica di fabricar scene e machine ne'teatri* (Ravenna, 1638; facsimile edition, Rome: Carlo Bestetti, 1955), bk. 1, chap. 12. *Practica* is available in modern translation in *The Renaissance Stage: Documents of Serlio, Sabbattini, and Furttenbach*, ed. Barnard Hewitt and trans. Allardyce Nicoll, John D. McDowell, and George R. Kernodle (Coral Gables: University of Miami Press, 1958). Subsequent references, to book and chapter of *Practica* appear within parentheses in the text.

5. Joseph Furttenbach the Elder, *Architectura Civilis* (Ulm, 1628); *Architectura Recreationis* (Augsburg, 1640); *Mannhafter Künstspiegel* (Augsburg, 1663). Modern translations are found in Hewitt, *Renaissance Stage;* see pp. 209, 195.

6. See pl. 167 in Margarete Baur-Heinhold, *Baroque Theatre* (London: Thames & Hudson, 1967). Flat-sawn balusters of 1624 can be seen in the chapel of Haddon Hall, Derbyshire. Those on the staircase at the rear of the auditorium of the Olimpico, Vicenza, are modern replacements.

7. Sabastiano Serlio, *Le Deuxième livre d'architecture* (Paris, 1545). A modern translation is found in Hewitt, *Renaissance Stage;* see p. 30.

8. Dulwich College ms. 49, appendix G in C. Walter Hodges, *The Globe Restored* (London; Ernest Benn, 1953; rev. ed. New York: Coward, McCann & Geoghegan, 1968).

9. Joseph Moxon, *Mechanick Exercises; or the doctrine of handy-works, etc.*, 2 vols. (London, 1683).

10. The Fortune contract of 1599 is appendix F in Hodges, *Globe Restored*.

11. Statement in House of Commons in support of a bill brought in by the Painter-Stainers; printed in *Tudor Economic Documents*, ed. R. M. Tawney and E. E. Power (London: Longman Green & Co., 1924), 1:136. Quoted by Oliver Baker, *Shakespeare's Warwickshire* (London: Simpkin Marshall & Sons, 1937), pp. 139-40.

12. *Vasari on Technique* (reprint ed., New York: Dover, 1960), p. 170.

13. The accounts are appendix B in vol. 2, pt. 2, of Wickham's *Early English Stages*.

14. John Smith, *The Art of Painting, wherein is included the whole Art of Vulgar Painting according to the best rules for preparing and laying on of Oyl Colours* (London, 1676).

15. P.R.O. E351/3263; quoted in Wickham, *Early English Stages*, vol. 2, pt. 2, p. 236, n. 28.

16. P.R.O. E351/3271; quoted in ibid., appendix E.

17. Illustrated in the magazine *L'Oeil*, no. 172 (April, 1969), p. 29.

18. Richard Tothill, *A very proper treatise, wherein is briefly sett forthe the arte of Limming . . .* (London, 1573).

19. Quoted in Hodges, *Globe Restored*, p. 69.

20. Pier Francesco Macci, *Relazione d'apparati fatti in Pesaro nella ventura della Serenissima Principessa Claudia de' Medici* (Pesaro, 1621), printed in Bestetti's facsimile edition of Sabbattini's *Practica*.

21. *Vasari on Technique*, p. 240.

22. *A short Introduction to the Art of Painting and Varnishing* (London, 1685), thought by the British Library catalog to be by Smith, but in a coarser and more obscure style of writing.

23. Wickham, *Early English Stages*, vol. 1, pp. 100–101.

24. Raphael Holinshed, *The Chronicles of England, Scotland, and Ireland*, 3 vols. (London, 1577), 3:1315; quoted by Wickham, *Early English Stages*, vol. 2, pt. 1, p. 283.

25. Illustrated respectively in Roy Strong, *Splendour at Court* (Boston: Houghton Mifflin, 1973), p. 247, and in Baur-Heinhold, *Baroque Theatre*, p. 237.

26. Illustrated in color in *Horizon Book of the Elizabethan World*, pp. 98–99.

27. Illustrated in Frances A. Yates' *Theatre of the World* (London: Routledge & Kegan Paul, 1969).

28. Hewitt, *Renaissance Stage*, p. 217.

29. Kernodle, in ibid., p. 5.

30. Illustrated in Hodges, *Globe Restored,* p. 71.

31. Quoted in E. K. Chambers, *The Elizabethan Stage,* 4 vols. (Oxford: Clarendon Press, 1923), 3:72.

32. Hodges, *Globe Restored,* p. 56.

33. Strong, *Splendour at Court,* fig. 64, and Irwin Smith, *Shakespeare's Globe Playhouse* (New York: Charles Scribner's Sons, 1956).

34. Except for the Royal Arms, which would be afforded true gilding. See Björn Landstrom, *The Ship* (London: Allen & Unwin, 1961), p. 161.

35. Quoted in L. G. Carr Laughton, *Old Ship Figure-Heads and Sterns (and Other Parts) of Old Sailing Ships* (London, 1925).

36. Prologue added to *Every Man in His Humour* in 1616; quoted in full by Wickham, *Early English Stages,* vol. 2, pt. 1, p. ix.

37. Quoted by John Cranford Adams, *The Globe Playhouse: Its Design and Equipment,* 2d ed. (London: Constable & Co., 1961); see p. 123.

38. Illustrated and discussed in J. Kenneth Major, *Animal-Powered Engines* (London: Batsford, 1978); see pl. 25 and p. 106.

39. Illustrated in K. Ellis, *Man and Measurement* (London: Priory Press, 1973).

40. Biblioteca Palatina; illustrated in Hodges, *Globe Restored,* pl. 55; Strong, *Splendour at Court,* p. 186.

41. See Hewitt, *Renaissance Stage,* p. 196.

42. *De re metallica* (Basel, 1556).

43. *Le Diverse et Artificiose Machine* (Paris, 1588).

44. Heinrich Zeising, *Theatrum Machinarum* (Leipzig, 1708). This was a posthumous publication—the illustrations were prepared before 1613.

45. John Pory to Sir Robert Cotton, January 7, 1606 (BM Cotton MS Julius C iii 301); quoted by Chambers, *Elizabethan Stage,* 3: 379.

46. Drawing by H. Grosse of mines at Sainte-Marie-aux-Mines, reproduced in Bertrand Gille, *Les Ingenieurs de la Renaissance* (Paris: Hermann, 1964), and in a translated edition, *The Renaissance Engineers* (London: Lund Humphries, 1966).

47. Based on figures in S. Svensson's *Handbook of Seaman's Ropework* (New York: Dodd, Mead & Co., 1971), a translation of the 1940 Swedish edition.

48. I am grateful to Edward A. Craig for explaining this to me as the traditional method in the theatre.

49. Hewitt, *Renaissance Stage,* pp. 220, 222.

50. As suggested by Wickham, *Early English Stages,* vol 2, pt. 1, p. 314.

51. P.R.O. E351/3465. of 1631–32; quoted in ibid., pt. 2, p. 235, n. 23, and discussed on p. 120.

52. See John Orrell's article "The Agent of Savoy at 'The Somerset Masque,' " *Review of English Studies,* n.s. 28 (August, 1977): 301–9.

53. *Shakespeare's Second Globe: The Missing Monument* (London: Oxford University Press, 1973), p. 49.

54. In News from Hell (1606); quoted in *The Non-Dramatic Works of Thomas Dekker,* etc., 5 vols., 2:92, part of *The Huth Library,* ed. Alexander Balloch Grosart, 29 vols. (London and Aylesbury: privately circulated limited edition, 1881–86).

55. Line 902, quoted in Adams, *Globe Playhouse,* p. 115.

56. Sig. E8 verso, quoted in ibid., p. 120. A trap is illustrated in the title page vignette of *Messalina* (1640).

57. *Early English Stages,* vol. 2, pt. 1, p. 176.

BERNARD BECKERMAN, Brander Matthews Professor of Dramatic Literature, Columbia University, and Chairman, Theatre Arts Division. His directing credits include many Shakespeare productions for the Hofstra Shakespeare Festival in New York, which he organized. Among his publications are *Shakespeare at the Globe, 1599–1609; Dynamics of Drama;* "Shakespeare's Theatre" in the Pelican *Complete Works of William Shakespeare;* and articles on the theatre in the *Encyclopedia Americana, Encyclopaedia Britannica,* and the *Shakespeare Quarterly.*

HERBERT BERRY, Professor of English and Lecturer in Drama, the University of Saskatchewan; specialist in British documents of the sixteenth and seventeenth centuries; member of the Editorial Advisory Board of REED *(Records of Early English Drama).* He is the author of numerous articles, papers, reviews, and books, many on the subject of Elizabethan theatres, including *The First Public Playhouse,* a collection of essays from the second World Shakespeare Congress which he edited and to which he contributed two essays.

JOHN RUSSELL BROWN, Professor of English, the University of Sussex, and Associate Director of the National Theatre, London. In 1979 he was a Visiting Fellow at the Folger Library, where he gave the annual Birthday Lecture in April. His publications include *Shakespeare and His Comedies, Shakespeare's Plays in Performance, Shakespeare's Dramatic Style,* and *Theatre Language.* He has been General Editor of *Stratford-upon-Avon Studies* and has edited plays in several series. He has also directed many plays for student and professional theatres, including the National Theatre.

C. WALTER HODGES, author, illustrator, designer, artist, and authority on the structure of Elizabethan playhouses. His design work includes scenery and costumes for the Everyman and Mermaid theatres in London. He is the writer and illustrator of many children's books, including his self-illustrated *Shakespeare's Theatre,* winner of the Kate Greenaway Medal of the Library Association of England. His works for adults, in addition to numerous articles on Shakespearean theatre, include *The Globe Restored* and *Shakespeare's Second Globe,* the latter the result of his preliminary studies for a reconstruction of Shakespeare's last theatre.

RICHARD HOSLEY, Professor of English, the University of Arizona; specialist in Shakespeare and in Elizabethan drama. His research has centered on the Elizabethan stage, Elizabethan dramatic texts, and Renaissance Italian comedy. His publications comprise many books, articles, and papers, including more than thirty on the Elizabethan stage and its methods of staging; and editions of plays, including several by Shakespeare. He has also edited two collections of essays on Shakespeare.

W. M. H. HUMMELEN, Professor of Dutch Literature, Catholic University of Nijmegen, The Netherlands. His special interests are history and theory of the drama and history of the theatre, including the stages of the Flemish rederijker (rhetoricians') societies of the sixteenth century. His major publications are *De sinnekens in het rederijkersdrama, Inrichting en gebruik van het toneel in de Amsterdamse schouwburg van 1637,* and *Repertorium van het rederijkersdrama, 1500–ca. 1620.*

LEONARD LEONE (Symposium Director), Distinguished Professor of Theatre Arts and Director of the Theatre, Wayne State University; specialist in the Italian Renaissance theatre. Under his direction, the University Theatre renovated and reopened Detroit's historic Bonstelle Theatre, created the Hilberry Theatre and its graduate repertory company, began a Black Theatre program, and established a nationwide playwriting competition. He was one of the founding members of the American College Theatre Festival.

JOHN ORRELL, Professor of English, the University of Alberta; specialist in Elizabethan and Jacobean drama, seventeenth-century theatre history, and Canadian theatre history. His publications include *Studies of Major Works in English* (editor), articles on the Elizabethan and Restoration theatre, and documentary television and film scripts for the Canadian Broadcasting Corporation and educational television.

257

STUART EBORALL RIGOLD was, until his sudden death in the summer of 1980, Principal Inspector of Ancient Monuments for England. In addition to holding this position with the Department of the Environment (formerly the Ministry of Works) in London, he made a lifelong study of timber-framed buildings, including the "late" Elizabethan and Jacobean kind in England, and was therefore especially well-qualified to talk about structural possibilities.

JOHN RONAYNE, designer and theatre researcher, London; visiting lecturer at the London Architectural Association and many design colleges; a principal of the design and research organization Archetype Visual Studies, London. For several years he was on the teaching panel of the Victoria and Albert Museum's Education Department. His design work includes reconstruction models of stage scenes, machines, and theatres, including the Curtain Theatre of 1577; Inigo Jones' theatre of 1616; and, for the Harvard College Theatre Collection, the Globe Theatre of 1599.

S. SCHOENBAUM (Chairman), Distinguished Professor of Renaissance Studies, the University of Maryland; lecturer and writer on various Renaissance subjects, including theatrical history. Among his many published works are *Shakespeare's Lives, William Shakespeare: A Documentary Life,* and *Shakespeare: The Globe and The World.* He is founder and past editor of the journal *Renaissance Drama* and has reviewed films for *Times Literary Supplement.* He will co-edit with Stanley Wells the Oxford Standard Authors edition of *The Complete Works of Shakespeare.*

GLYNNE WICKHAM, Professor of Drama, the University of Bristol; a Governor of the Bristol Old Vic; member of the Executive Committee of the Bankside Globe Theatre Trust; and Chairman of the National Drama Conference for the National Council of Social Services. His publications include the three-volume *Early English Stages, Shakespeare's Dramatic Heritage,* and *The Medieval Theatre.* He has also directed many plays, at the Bristol Old Vic as well as elsewhere in England and the United States.

Index

The manuscript was prepared for publication by Barbara L. Kraft and Jean Owen. The book was designed by Richard Kinney. The typeface for the text and display is Mergenthaler's VIP Garamond, based upon an original design by Claude Garamond about 1530.

The text is printed on 80 lb. Mead's Moistrite Matte paper, and the book is bound in Holliston Mills' Kingston Linen Finish cloth over binder's boards. Manufactured in the United States of America.

Somerset h.   Arundel house   Essex house   Temple stayres   Tem

Beere bayting h.

Arundel house   Essex house   Tem